Accounting and Financial Analysis in the Hospitality Industry

Accounting and Financial Analysis in the Hospitality Industry

Dr. Anoop Pant

RANDOM
RANDOM PUBLICATIONS
NEW DELHI (INDIA)

Accounting and Financial Analysis in the Hospitality Industry

ISBN 978-93-5111-333-1

Published in 2014 in India by

RANDOM PUBLICATIONS

4376-A/4B, Gali Murari Lal, Ansari Road
New Delhi-110 002
Phone : +91-11-43580356, +91-11-23289044
e-mail: randomexports@gmail.com, sales@randompublications.com, info@randompublications.com

Reprinted 2025

Type Setting by : Keystoneprintads, Delhi-110051
Digitally Printed at: Replika Press Pvt. Ltd.

Preface

A financial system supports the financial functions required to track financial events, provide financial information significant to the financial management of the agency, and/or required for the preparation of financial statements. A financial system encompasses automated and manual processes, procedures, controls, data, hardware, software, and support personnel dedicated to the operation and maintenance of system functions.

A financial system may include multiple applications that are integrated through a common database or are electronically interfaced, as necessary, to meet defined data and processing requirements.

In accountancy, an account is a label used for recording and reporting a quantity of almost anything. Most often it is a record of an amount of money owned or owed by or to a particular person or entity, or allocated to a particular purpose. It may represent amounts of money that have actually changed hands, or it may represent an estimate of the values of assets, or it may be a combination of these.

Accounting reform is an expansion to accounting rules that goes beyond the realm of financial measures for both individual economic entities and national economies.

It is advocated by those who consider the focus of the present standards and practices wholly inadequate to the task of measuring and reporting the activity, success, and failure of modern enterprise, including government. The basic bookkeeping concepts underlying contemporary accounting date back about 500 years to Renaissance Italian practices.

Obviously, the vast majority of articulations by modern standard setters have little in common with the accounting practices then used. Real debate concerns concepts such as whether to report transactions, such as asset acquisitions, at their cost or to report them at their current market values.

The book explains the concepts and procedure and unfolds the complexities of the subject matter in a simple and lucid style to provide conceptual clarity.

I would like to thank my team for standing beside me throughout my career and writing this book. My special thanks go to "Random Publications" who have published the book.

– Dr. Anoop Pant

Contents

1

Management Accounting

INTRODUCTION

Management accounting is concerned with the provisions and use of accounting information to managers within organizations, to provide them with the basis in making informed business decisions that would allow them to be better equipped in their management and control functions. Unlike financial accountancy information (which, for the most part, is public information), management accounting information is used within an organization (typically for decision-making) and is usually confidential and access to which is only available to a select few. According to CIMA, The Chartered Institute of Management Accountants, Management Accounting is "the process of identification, measurement, accumulation, analysis, preparation, interpretation and communication of information used by management to plan, evaluate and control within an entity and to assure appropriate use of and accountability for its resources.

Management accounting also comprises the preparation of financial reports for non management groups such as shareholders, creditors, regulatory agencies and tax authorities" (CIMA Official Terminology)

TRADITIONAL VS. INNOVATIVE MANAGEMENT ACCOUNTING

In the late 1980s, accounting practitioners and educators were heavily criticized on the grounds that management accounting practices (and, even more so, the curriculum taught to accounting students) had changed little over the preceding 60 years, despite radical changes in the business environment. Professional accounting institutes, perhaps fearing that management accountants would increasingly be seen as superfluous in business organizations, subsequently devoted considerable resources to the development of a more innovative skills set for management accountants.

The distinction between 'traditional' and 'innovative' management accounting practices can be illustrated by reference to cost control techniques. Traditionally, management accountants' principal technique was variance analysis, which is a systematic approach to the comparison of the actual and budgeted costs of the raw materials and labour used during a production period. While some form of variance analysis is still used by most manufacturing firms, it nowadays tends to be used in conjunction with innovative techniques such as life cycle cost analysis and activity-based costing, which are designed with specific aspects of the modern business environment in mind.

Lifecycle costing recognizes that managers' ability to influence the cost of manufacturing a product is at its greatest when the product is still at the design stage of its product lifecycle (i.e., before the design has been finalised and production commenced), since small changes to the product design may lead to significant savings in the cost of manufacturing the product. Activity-based costing (ABC) recognizes that, in modern factories, most manufacturing costs are determined by the amount of 'activities' (e.g., the number of production runs per month, and the amount of production equipment idle time) and that the key to effective cost control is therefore optimizing the efficiency of these activities. Activity-based accounting is also known as Cause and Effect accounting. Both lifecycle costing and activity-based costing recognize that, in the typical modern factory, the avoidance of disruptive events (such as machine breakdowns and quality control failures) is of far greater importance than (for example) reducing the costs of raw materials.

Activity-based costing also deemphasizes direct labour as a cost driver and concentrates instead on activities that drive costs, such as the provision of a service or the production of a product component.

Development of Throughput Accounting

The most significant recent direction in managerial accounting is throughput accounting, which recognizes the interdependencies of modern production processes and provide managers with a tool that will allow them to measure the contribution per unit of constrained resource for any given product, customer or supplier.

An Alternative View

A seldom expressed alternative view of management accounting is that it is neither a neutral or benign influence in organizations, rather a mechanism for management control through surveillance. This view locates management accounting specifically in the context of management control theory.

In throughput accounting, the cost accounting aspect of Theory of Constraints (TOC), operating expense is the money spent turning inventory into throughput. In TOC, operating expense is limited to costs that vary strictly with the quantity produced, like raw materials and purchased components. Everything else is a fixed cost, including labour unless there is a regular and significant chance that workers will not work a full-time week when they report on its first day.

OPERATING THE MANAGEMENT CONTROL SYSTEM

A financial system supports the financial functions required to track financial events, provide financial information significant to the financial management of the agency, and/or required for the preparation of financial statements. A financial system encompasses automated and manual processes, procedures, controls, data, hardware, software, and support personnel dedicated to the operation and maintenance of system functions. A financial system may include multiple applications that are integrated through a common database or are electronically interfaced, as necessary, to meet defined data and processing requirements.

The term "non-financial system" means an information system that supports non-financial functions of the Federal government or components thereof and any financial data included in the system are insignificant to agency financial management and/or not required for the preparation of financial statements. The term "mixed system" means an information system that supports both financial and non-financial functions of the Federal government or components thereof.

The term "financial management systems" means the financial systems and the financial portions of mixed systems necessary to support financial management. The term "single, integrated financial management system" means a unified set of financial systems and the financial portions of mixed systems encompassing the software, hardware, personnel, processes (manual and automated), procedures, controls and data necessary to carry out financial management functions, manage financial operations of the agency and report on the agency's financial status to central agencies, Congress and the public. Unified means that the systems are planned for and managed together, operated in an integrated fashion, and linked together electronically in an efficient and effective manner to provide agency-wide financial system support necessary to carry out the agency's mission and support the agency's financial management needs.

MANAGEMENT CONTROL AND STAFFING

Although there is a tendency to want a "bright line" to define businesses as small, medium-size or large, this guidance does not provide such definitions. It uses the term "smaller" rather than "small" business, suggesting there is a wide range of companies to which the guidance is directed. The focus is on businesses that have many of the following characteristics:

- Fewer lines of business and fewer products within lines
- Concentration of marketing focus, by channel or geography
- Leadership by management with significant ownership interest or rights
- Fewer levels of management, with wider spans of control
- Less complex transaction processing systems and protocols

- Fewer personnel, many having a wider range of duties
- Limited ability to maintain deep resources in line as well as support staff positions such as legal, human resources, accounting and internal auditing.

None of these characteristics by themselves is definitive. Certainly, size by whatever measure - revenue, personnel, assets, or other - affects and is affected by these characteristics, and shapes our thinking about what constitutes "smaller."

COSTS AND BENEFITS

Management and other stakeholders of public companies, particularly smaller ones, have focused great attention on the cost of complying with Section 404, with less attention given to the associated benefits. Although it may be difficult to measure impacts associated with inaccurate financial reporting, market reactions to corporate misstatements clearly signal that the investment community does not readily tolerate inaccurate reporting, regardless of company size. In that respect and with other benefits described below, effective internal control adds significant value.

Among the most significant benefits is the strengthened ability of companies to access the capital markets, providing capital which drives innovation and economic growth. Other benefits include reliable and timely information supporting management's decision-making, consistent mechanisms for processing transactions across an organization enhancing speed and reliability, and ability to accurately communicate business performance with partners and customers.

Meeting Challenges in Attaining Cost-Effective Internal Control

The characteristics of smaller companies provide significant challenges for cost-effective internal control. This particularly is the case where managers view control as an administrative burden to be added onto existing business systems, rather than recognizing the business need and benefit for effective internal control that is integrated with core processes.

Among the challenges are:

- Obtaining sufficient resources to achieve adequate segregation of duties
- Management's ability to dominate activities, with significant opportunities for management override of control
- Recruiting individuals with requisite financial reporting and other expertise to serve effectively on the board of directors and audit committee
- Recruiting and retaining personnel with sufficient experience and skill in accounting and financial reporting
- Taking management attention from running the business in order to provide sufficient focus on accounting and financial reporting

- Maintaining appropriate control over computer information systems with limited technical resources.

While all companies incur incremental costs to design and report on internal control over financial reporting, costs can be proportionally higher for smaller companies. Yet despite resource constraints, smaller businesses usually can meet this challenge and succeed in attaining effective internal control in a reasonably cost-effective manner. This is accomplished in a variety of ways, outlined in this guidance, many of which already exist today in smaller companies and for which management can "take credit" in considering internal control effectiveness.

Wide and Direct Control from the Top

Many smaller businesses are dominated by the company's founder or other leader who exercises a great deal of discretion and provides personal direction to other personnel. While key to enabling the company to meet its growth and other objectives, this positioning also can contribute significantly to effective internal control over financial reporting. In-depth knowledge of different facets of the business - its operations, processes, array of contractual commitments and business risks - enables its leader to know what to expect in reports generated by the financial reporting system and to follow up as needed when unanticipated variances surface. A related downside in terms of ability to override established control procedures can be addressed with specified protocols.

Effective Boards of Directors

Smaller hotels typically have relatively straightforward business operations with less complex business structures, enabling directors to gain more in-depth knowledge of business activities. Directors may have been closely involved with the company during its evolution and have a strong historical perspective. Coupled with what often is exposure to and frequent communication with a wide range of managers, this assists the board and its audit committee in performing oversight responsibilities for financial reporting in a highly effective manner.

Compensating for Limited Segregation of Duties

Resource constraints may limit the number of employees, sometimes resulting in concerns regarding segregation of duties. There are, however, actions management can take in order to compensate for potential inadequacy. These include managers reviewing system reports of detailed transactions; selecting transactions for review of supporting documents; overseeing periodic counts of physical inventory, equipment or other assets and comparing them with accounting records; and reviewing reconciliations of account balances or performing them independently. In many small companies managers already are performing these and other procedures supporting reliable reporting, and credit should be taken for their contribution to effective internal control.

Information Technology

The reality of limited internal information technology resources often can be dealt with through use of software developed and maintained by others. These packages still require controlled implementation and operation, but many of the risks associated with in-house developed systems are avoided. Typically there is a limited need for Programme change controls, inasmuch as changes are done exclusively by the developer company, and generally a smaller company's personnel lack technical expertise to make unauthorized modifications.

Such commercially available packages also bring advantages in the form of embedded facilities for controlling which employees can access or modify specified data, performing checks on data processing completeness and accuracy, and maintaining related documentation. Further advantage can be gained by utilizing software that comes with a variety of built-in application controls that can improve consistency of operation, automate reconciliations, facilitate reporting of exceptions for management review, and support proper segregation of duties. Smaller companies can take advantage of these capabilities, ensuring "flags" or "switches" are properly set to take advantage of the software's capabilities.

Monitoring Activities

The monitoring component is an important part of the Framework, where a wide range of activities routinely performed by managers in running a business can provide feedback on the functioning of other components of the internal control system. Management of many smaller businesses regularly perform such procedures, but have not always taken sufficient "credit" for their contribution to internal control effectiveness. These activities, usually performed manually and sometimes supported by computer software, should be fully considered in designing and assessing internal control. From a different perspective, there is another way monitoring activities can promote efficiency.

After the first year of assessing and reporting on internal control, many companies repeated the assessment process in year two with little if any cost savings. A different approach, however, can be taken to promote efficiency. By focusing on monitoring activities already in place or that might be added with little additional effort, management can identify significant changes to the financial reporting system since the prior year, thereby gaining insight into where to target more detailed testing. While for effective internal control all five components must be in place and operating effectively and some testing of each component is necessary, highly effective monitoring activities can both offset certain shortcomings in other components and sharpen targeting of assessment work with resulting overall efficiency.

Achieving Further Efficiencies

In addition to considering the above, companies can gain additional efficiencies in designing and implementing or assessing internal control by focusing on only those financial reporting objectives directly applicable to the company's activities and circumstances, taking a risk based approach to internal control, right sizing documentation, viewing internal control as an integrated process, and considering the totality of internal control. The COSO Framework recognizes that an entity must first have in place an appropriate set of financial reporting objectives.

At a high level, the objective of financial reporting is to prepare reliable financial statements, which involves attaining reasonable assurance that the financial statements are free from material misstatement. Flowing from this high level objective, management establishes supporting objectives related to the company's business activities and circumstances and their proper reflection in the company's financial statement accounts and related disclosures. These objectives may be influenced by regulatory requirements or by other factors that management may choose to incorporate when setting its objectives. Efficiencies are gained by focusing on only those objectives directly applicable to the business and related to its activities and circumstances that are material to the financial statements.

Experience shows that this can be most efficiently accomplished by beginning with a company's financial statements and identifying supporting objectives for those business activities, processes and events that can materially affect the financial statements. In this way, a basis is formed for giving attention only to what is truly relevant to the reliability of financial reporting for that company.

Focusing on Risk

While management considers risks in several respects, its overarching consideration is the risks to key objectives, including the risks to reliable financial reporting. Risk-based means focusing on quantitative and qualitative factors that potentially affect the reliability of financial reporting, and identifying where in transaction processing or other activities related to financial statement preparation something could go wrong. By focusing on key objectives management can tailor the scope and depth of risk assessments needed. Often risk is considered in the context of initially designing and implementing internal control, where risks to objectives are identified and analyzed to form a basis for determining how the risks should be managed. Another is in the context of assessing whether internal control is effective in mitigating risks to objectives.

In the context of assessing internal control effectiveness, there sometimes is a tendency to consider internal control using generic lists of controls appropriate to a "typical" organization. While these tools in questionnaire or other form may be useful, an unintended result is that management sometimes focuses on "standard" or "typical" controls that simply are not relevant to the company's financial reporting objectives or risks associated with those objectives. A related problem encountered is starting assessments with the details of accounting systems and documenting them in extreme depth without recognizing whether the entirety of processes are truly relevant to achieving reliable financial reporting. This is not to say that such approaches cannot be useful, as they can be. However, whatever approach is followed, efficiencies are gained when attention is directed to the objectives management has established specific to the company's business activities and circumstances.

Right-Sizing Documentation

Documentation of business processes and procedures and other elements of internal control systems is developed and maintained by companies for a number of reasons. One is to promote consistency in adhering to desired practices in running the business. Effective documentation assists in communicating what is to be done, and how, and creates expectations of performance. Another purpose of documentation is to assist in training new personnel and as a refresher or reference tool for other employees. Documentation also provides evidence to support reporting on internal control effectiveness. The level and nature of documentation varies widely by company. Certainly, large companies usually have more operations to document, or greater complexity in financial reporting processes, and therefore find it necessary to have more extensive documentation than smaller ones.

Smaller companies often find less need for formal documentation, such as in-depth policy manuals, systems flowcharts of processes, organization charts, job descriptions, and the like. In smaller companies, typically there are fewer people and levels of management, closer working relationships and more frequent interaction, all of which promotes communication of what is expected and what is being done. A smaller business, for example, might document human resources, procurement or customer credit policies with memoranda and supplement the memoranda with guidance provided by management in meetings. A larger company will more likely have more detailed policies (or policy manuals) to guide their people in better implementing controls.

Questions arise as to the extent of documentation needed to deem internal control over financial reporting as effective. The answer is, of course, it depends on circumstances and needs. Some level of documentation is always necessary to assure management that its control processes are working, such as documentation to help assure management that all shipments are billed, or periodic reconciliations are performed. In a smaller business, however, management is often directly involved in performing control procedures and for those procedures there may be only minimal documentation because management can determine that controls are functioning effectively through direct observation. However, there must be information available to management that the accounting systems and related procedures, including actions taken in connection with preparation of reliable financial statements, are well designed, well understood, and carried out properly.

When management asserts to regulators, shareholders or other third parties on the design and operating effectiveness of internal control over financial reporting, management accepts a higher level of personal risk and typically will require documentation of major processes within the accounting systems and important control activities to support its assertions. Accordingly, management will review to determine whether its documentation is appropriate to support its assertion. In considering the amount of documentation needed, the nature and extent of the documentation may be influenced by the company's regulatory requirements. This does not necessarily mean that documentation will or should be more formal, but it does mean that there needs to be evidence that the controls are designed and working properly.

In addition, when an external auditor will be attesting to the effectiveness of internal control, management will likely be expected to provide the auditor with support for its assertion. That support would include evidence that the controls are properly designed and are working effectively. In considering the nature and extent of documentation needed by the company, management should also consider that the documentation to support the assertion that controls are working properly will likely be used by the external auditor as part of his or her audit evidence.

There may still be instances where policies and procedures are informal and undocumented. This may be appropriate where management is able to obtain evidence captured through the normal conduct of the business that indicates personnel regularly performed those controls. However, it is important to keep in mind that control processes, such as risk assessment, cannot be performed entirely in the mind of the CEO or CFO without some documentation of the thought process and management's analysis. Many of the examples contained later in this guidance illustrate how management can capture evidence through the normal course of business. Documentation of internal control should meet business needs and be commensurate with circumstances. The extent of documentation supporting design and operating effectiveness of the five internal control components is a matter of judgment, and should be done with costeffectiveness in mind. Where practical, the creation and retention of evidence should be embedded with the various financial reporting processes.

Viewing Internal Control as an Integrated Process

It is useful to view the Framework's five internal control components as comprising an integrated process, which indeed internal control is. A process perspective highlights the interrelationship of the components, and recognizes that management has flexibility in choosing controls to achieve its objectives and that an organization can adjust and improve its internal control over time. As noted, the internal control process begins with management setting financial reporting objectives relevant to the company's particular business activities and circumstances.

Once set, management identifies and assesses a variety of risks to those objectives, determines which risks could result in a material misstatement in financial reporting, and determines how the risks should be managed through a range of control activities. Management implements approaches to capture, process and communicate information needed for financial reporting and other components of the internal control system. All this is done in context of the company's control environment, which is shaped and refined as necessary to provide the appropriate tone at the top of the organization and related attributes. These components all are monitored to help ensure that controls continue to operate properly over time.

The Totality of Internal Control

Each of the five components of internal control set forth in the Framework is important to achieving the objective of reliable financial reporting. Determining whether a company's internal control over financial reporting is effective involves a judgment. Internal control has five components that work together to prevent or detect and correct material misstatements of financial reports.

When the five components are present and functioning, to the extent that management has reasonable assurance that financial statements are being prepared reliably, internal control can be deemed effective. While each component must be present and functioning, this does not mean, however, that each component should function identically or even at the same level in every company. Some trade-offs may exist between components. Accordingly, effective internal control does not necessarily mean a "gold standard" of control is built into every process. A deficiency in one component might be mitigated by other controls in that component or by controls in another component strong enough such that the totality of control is sufficient to reduce the risk of misstatement to an acceptable level.

EXPENSE ACCOUNTING IN HOSPITALITY INDUSTRY

In the accounting terminology, expense is an income statement account representing the cost of items consumed in the process of generating revenue (ex. Cost of Goods Sold) or that expires due to the passage of time (ex. Depreciation Expense). Expense cannot be mixed with expenditure. For, Expenditure represents the purchase amount (whether paid in cash or credited with the Accounts Payable) of a certain asset. To illustrate, suppose, on January 1st, 2001, XYZ Company paid $ 10,000 cash in order to purchase some equipment this is called expenditure and is journalized as follows:

Cash	$ 10,000
Equipment	$ 10,000

However, on December 31st, 2001, XYZ shall allocate a certain value of the initial investment of equipment to be placed as an expense to show that a certain portion of the equipment has been already used to contribute to Company's revenue. Suppose that this amount was determined to be $ 650. This very amount is called an expense and is journalized as follows:

Depreciation Expense-Equipment	$ 650
Accumulated Depreciation-Equipment	$ 650

According to the matching principle, all expenses must be recorded in the same accounting period as the revenue that they helped to generate.

In the hotel industry, expenses are divided into two main categories:

- Direct Expenses: These are the expenses that vary with the level of production. For example, in the Food and Beverage department, the Cost of Food Sales is a direct expense. For, the more dishes we serve, the more cost of Food Sales the Hotel incurs. Moreover, in the Telephone Department, the Cost of Calls is a direct expense. For, the more we connect guests to whatever destination wanted, the more cost of calls the hotel incurs.

At this very stage a bracket would be opened to explain that there is a primordial difference between revenue generator departments. In fact, revenue generator departments are classified into two: *Service Type* departments versus *merchandising* departments. Service type departments are revenue generators making money from solely providing services (Ex. Rooms Division department). On the other hand, merchandising departments ensure revenue by getting use of certain raw material, processing it, and than sell the final product (Ex. F&B department, Telephone department...). Therefore, only merchandising departments have a direct expense called Cost of Sales.

- Indirect Expenses: These are the expenses that do not vary with the level of production, or variable costs that can not be feasibly distributed to various Financial Reporting Centers. In the hotel industry, indirect expenses are, hence, divided into two different categories:
  1. Fixed Charges: Examples might include rent, insurance, property taxes, and interest expense. For, these very expenses are incurred for the benefit of the hotel as a whole not for the benefit of each single department. To illustrate, if a hotel insures itself against fire, theft and burglary, and one day some valuable equipment has been stolen, from any department whatsoever, the insurance company will indemnify the hotel.
  2. Undistributed Expenses: Examples might include electricity, energy, and water expenses. For, usually the hotel receives a total energy bill to be paid. In the old days, some hotels went for allocating this amount according to certain factors (ex.

Surface, Department Usage...). However, this practice proved to be misleading, since it might under-allocate energy expenses for some departments and over-allocate it for others. Nowadays, most of the hotels decide not to allocate such expenses any more. Rather, hotels report such expenses in separate schedules.

At this stage, departments of a typical hotel would be listed along with their various related direct expenses. Later, examples of fixed charges and undistributed expenses would be discussed. Last, a bracket would be opened to discuss one of the most important Direct Expenses in any hotel, which is Payroll and Related Expenses. For, hotels being described as labour intensive companies devote a big percentage of their financial resources to such an expense.

TYPICAL HOTEL DEPARTMENTS

Rooms Division Department: It is the place where guests receive several kinds of services ranging from reservation, registration, to checkout and settlement of their accounts. This department typically compromises a Rooms Division manager, an assistant manager(s), registration clerks, cashiers, mail and information clerk, and uniform service personnel. The various types of Rooms Division department direct expenses include:

- Commissions expenses: This account includes payments by the hotel to authorized agents that bring room business to the hotel. Usually at the end of each month, hotels sit with these agents in order to reconcile their monthly sales figures and authorize commission payment (usually in the form of a percentage of room revenue)
- Reservation expenses: This expense account represents any payment to various agents contracting to bring potential room revenue business to the hotel. These agents might have the form of Central Reservation Offices (Whether affiliate or non-affiliate), Intersell agencies...
- Contract cleaning expenses: This expense account represents payment to contracting outside cleaning agencies. Some hotels (especially small and middle size hotels) might opt for contract cleaning because of its attractive financial implications. If this is the case, these hotels might not be forced to have a housekeeping department, or might keep housekeeping staff to minimum. Such expenses should be determined in light of the contract signed between both parties (*i.e.* the hotel from one side and the cleaning company from the other.)
- Laundry and dry cleaning expenses: This cost applies to outside laundry and dry cleaning costs *for the Rooms Division department*. In most of the cases, such contracts are signed to benefit more than one revenue generator. In this case, the Rooms Division department shall report the laundry and dry cleaning expenses related only to the Rooms Division department.

- Guest transportation expenses: These expenses include the cost of transporting guests from and to the hotel via various means of transportation (ex: Mini-buses, buses, limousines...). If the guest transportation's volume business, staff, and costs are significantly high, then a separate department might be established.
- Linen expenses: This specific expense account includes the allocation of a portion of linen expenditure for a specific period of time. This practice goes along with one of the accounting principles: the matching principle. Some sub-accounts of linen expense might be:
  - Towels expenses
  - Facecloth expenses
  - Blankets expenses
  - Sheets expenses
    - Pillow expenses
- Guest supplies expenses: This account includes the various guest supplies provided free of charge to guests in their rooms. Some sub-accounts of guest supplies expenses might include:
  - Newspaper expenses
  - Guest stationary expenses
  - Shoe cloth expenses
  - Coffee expenses
  - Writing supplies expenses
  - Toilet requisites expenses
  - Flowers expenses
  - Hangers expenses
  - Matches expenses
  - Ice expenses
  - Candy expenses
- Cleaning supplies expenses: Such an account includes the cost of Rooms Division's cleaning supplies. Some sub-accounts of guest supplies expenses might include:
  - Brooms expenses
  - Soaps and polishes expenses
  - Cleaning cloths expenses
  - Mops expenses
  - Cleaning chemicals expenses
  - Dusters expenses
  - Brushes expenses
  - Insecticides expenses
  - Dustpans expenses
  - Pail expenses
  - Disinfectants expenses
  - Cleaning accessories expense

- Printing and stationary expenses: This expense account includes printed formats (ex: virgin registration records, reservation records, guest folios...), office supplies (ex: pens, pencils, rubbers, erasers...), printed manuals and guidelines for the use of the Rooms Division employees. Some sub-accounts of printing and stationary expenses might include:
  - Binders expenses
  - Floor plans expenses
  - Pencils and Pens expenses
  - Vouchers expenses
  - Rack card expenses
  - Reports expenses
  - Desk pad expenses
  - Envelopes expenses
  - Ink expenses
  - Folio expenses
- Uniforms expenses: This expense account includes the allocation of a portion of uniforms asset (if the hotel purchases uniforms) for a certain period of time along with the expense of repairing, and cleaning them. If the hotel rents uniforms rather than purchasing them, then the uniform expense shall include the renting cost, usually predetermined in light of the contract linking the hotel and the uniform renting company.

Food & Beverage Department: This department is responsible for the preparation and service of food and beverage to guests. It compromises the kitchen, restaurants, bars, and any premise in which Food and Beverage is served.

Telephone Department: This department is responsible to handle guest communication. This might be insured through connecting guests to desired locations, whether in-house, local or long distance calls. Moreover, this department is usually composed of a chief operator, supervisors, operators, and messengers. Last, with the automation revolution affecting right now most hotels, it became possible to separate calls of guests and communication handled by hotel employees, therefore, making it possible to have the telephone department as a minor revenue generating department. For, prior to automation, the separation of cost of calls was not possible and hence the telephone department might show frequently a loss since telephone direct costs are overstated.

Administrative & General Department: Actually looking at any hotel organization chart, Administrative and General Department (referred usually as A&G) does not exist. It is however a financial reporting centers including executives of the Hotel (ex: General Manager, Assistant General Managers...) and other employees involved with executive and financial activities (ex: Accounting personnel, resident Manager, Accounts Receivable clerks, Night

Auditors...). Moreover, if there is staff in the hotel not included in departments due to low business volume not justifying the establishment of a department, they might be included under the A& G department (ex. Data Processing Staff, Transportation Staff, and Personnel Staff...).

Marketing Department: This department is composed of a marketing manager, marketing assistant managers responsible for sales, convention, public relations, and advertising functions, along with marketing personnel. This department is a cost centre that indirectly supports revenue generators in their sole aim of generating hotel revenue. This can be insured, for example, through large group reservations, hence maximizing room revenue, or buffet, conference, and catering opportunities brought by this very department hence maximizing room revenue, F& B revenue, and the hotel revenue as a whole.

Property, Operation and Maintenance (POM): Concerned with the appearance and physical condition of the building, the repair and maintenance of equipment, and rubbish removal. Some positions of this department might include POM manager, POM assistant manager(s), electricians, plumbers, gardeners, painters, and interior design specialists...

Data Processing Department: This special department might be established in hotels operating under the fully automated system. Moreover, such hotels should have significant investment in computer equipment and staff to justify the establishment of a single department. If these conditions do not exist, than the Data Processing functions would be financially grouped under Administrative & General Department.

Human Resources Department: Similar to Data Processing Department, if the Dollar Amount and Staff incurred for employees' hiring, screening, interviewing, selecting, recruiting, and Training is significant, than a Human Resources Department may be established. Otherwise, Human Resources functions would be financially grouped under Administrative & General Department

Guest Transportation Department: If the Dollar Amount and Number of Staff employed in the transportation of Guests is significant, a separate Department might be established. Otherwise, guest transportation staff would be grouped under Rooms Division Department.

Financial Reporting Centers

A Financial Reporting Centre is an area of responsibility for which separate Cost Information must be collected Might be classified as Revenue Centers, Support Centers, and Other Financial Reporting Centers.

Revenue Centers : Generate Revenue through sales of Products and/or Services to Guests

- Rooms
- Food and Beverage
- Telephone
- Gift Shops

- Garage and Parking
- Other Operated Departments
- Rentals and other Income

Support Centers Þ those departments that have minimal Guest Contact and do not produce Sales. Yet, they do provide services to Revenue Centers, which, in turn, provide Services to Guests

- Administrative & General
- Marketing
- Property Operation and Maintenance
- Data Processing
- Human Resources

Other Financial Reporting Centers Þ include Energy Costs and Fixed Charges (Rent Expense, Property Taxes, Insurance Expense, Interest Expense, Depreciation and Amortization Expenses)

Each Financial Reporting Centre should be assigned an Identification Number. To illustrate, consider the following Example:

Financial Reporting Centre	*Identification Number*
Rooms	11
Food and Beverage	15
Telephone	17
Administrative & General	31
Marketing	36
Property Operation and Maintenance	38
Energy Costs	41
Fixed Charges	51

Furthermore, each Account should be assigned an Identification Number. Hotels commonly opt for either the Five-Digit (xx-xxx) or Eight-Digit Account Numbering Systems (xx-xxx-xxx)

Responsibility Accounting

Aim Þ provides Financial Information useful in evaluating the effectiveness of Managers and Department Heads. That's why only Direct Expenses should be charged to Specific Departments

Expenses Þ include the day-to-day Costs of Operating the Business, the Expired Costs of Assets through Depreciation and Amortization, and the "write-off" of pre-paid items. Expenses are classified as Direct expenses (Cost of Sales and Operating Expenses), Indirect Expenses (Fixed Charges and Undistributed Expenses) and Income Taxes

Direct Expenses : they are Costs incurred solely for the benefit of a particular Department

- Cost of Sales
- Payroll Expenses
- Payroll-related Expenses
- Operating Supplies

- China, Glassware, Silver, and Linen
- Laundry and Dry Cleaning

Indirect Expenses : They are incurred for the benefit of the Hotel as a whole, and cannot be identified with any particular Department

- Property Insurance
- Interest Expense
- Property Taxes
- Rent Expense
- Depreciation and Amortization
- Marketing Expense
- Administrative & General Expenses
- Property Operations and Maintenance
- Energy Costs

Income Taxes : It is neither a Direct Expense, nor an Indirect Expense. It should appear as a separate Line Item on a Hotel's Summary Income Statement

Departmental Expense Accounting:

Separate Expenses versus one Lump-sum Amount of Expenses

Payroll and Payroll-related Expenses:

1. Salaries and Wages (Payroll Expense) : Includes Salaries, Wages, Overtime Pay, and any Employee Bonuses and Commissions
2. Employee Benefits : Include Vacation and Holiday Pay
3. Payroll Taxes : Includes Social Security Taxes (Employer's Portion)
4. Employee Meals : Includes the Cost of Food furnished to Employees as a Convenience to the Employer
5. Worker's Compensation Insurance : Includes the Expense of Worker's Compensation Insurance
6. Employee Group Plans : Includes Life and Health Insurance, and Other Forms of Employee Group-plan Fringe Benefits

FINANCIAL ACCOUNTANCY

Financial accountancy (or financial accounting) is the branch of accountancy concerned with the preparation of financial statements for decision makers, such as stockholders, suppliers, banks, government agencies, owners, and other stakeholders. The fundamental need for financial accounting is to reduce principal-agent problem by measuring and monitoring agents' performance and reporting the results to interested users. Financial Accountancy is used to prepare accounting information for people outside the organisation or not involved in the day to day running of the company. Managerial accounting provides accounting information to help managers make decisions to manage the business. Financial Accountancy is governed by both local and international accounting standards.

BASIC ACCOUNTING CONCEPTS

The accounting equation (Assets = Liabilities + Owners' Equity) and financial statements are the main topics of financial accounting. The trial balance which is usually prepared using the Double-entry accounting system forms the basis for preparing the financial statements. All the figures in the trial balance are rearranged to prepare a profit and loss statement and balance sheet. There are certain accounting standards that determine the format for these accounts (SSAP, FRS, IFS). The financial statements will display the income and expenditure for the company and a summary of the assets, liabilities, and shareholders or owners' equity of the company on the date the accounts were prepared to.

Meaning of the Accounting Equation

The value of a company can be understood simply as the useful assets that ownership of a company entitles one to claim. This value is known as Owners' Equity. Some assets of a company, however, cannot be claimed as equity by the owners of a company because other people have legal claim to them - for example if the company has borrowed money from the bank. The value of a resource claimable by a non-owner is called a liability. All of the Assets of a company can be claimed by someone, whether owner or not, so the sum of a company's equity and its liabilities must equal the value of its Assets. Thus the accounting equation describes what portion of a company's assets can by claimed by the owners.

Various account types are classified as 'credit' or 'debit' depending on the role they play in the accounting equation.

Assets = Liabilities + Equity *or*

Assets - Liabilities - Equity = 0

Another way of stating it is:

Equity = Assets - Liabilities

which can be interpreted as: "Equity is what is left if all assets have been sold and all liabilities have been paid".

PROCESS OF MEASURING RISK MANAGEMENT

Risk management is the process of measuring risk and then developing and implementing strategies to manage that risk. Financial risk management focuses on risks that can be managed ("hedged") using traded financial instruments (typically changes in commodity prices, interest rates, foreign exchange rates and stock prices). Financial risk management will also play an important role in cash management.

CORPORATE FINANCE

This area is related to corporate finance in two ways. Firstly, firm exposure to business risk is a direct result of previous Investment and Financing decisions. Secondly, both disciplines share the goal of creating, or enhancing, firm value. All large corporations have risk management teams, and small firms practice informal, if not formal, risk management. Derivatives are the instruments most commonly used in Financial risk management. Because unique derivative contracts tend to be costly to create and monitor, the most cost-effective financial risk management methods usually involve derivatives that trade on well-established financial markets. These standard derivative instruments include options, futures contracts, forward contracts, and swaps.

Relationship with other areas in Finance

Corporate finance utilizes tools from almost all areas of finance. Some of the tools developed by and for corporations have broad application to entities other than corporations, for example, to partnerships, sole proprietorships, not-for-profit organizations, governments, mutual funds, and personal wealth management. But in other cases their application is very limited outside of the corporate finance arena. Because corporations deal in quantities of money much greater than individuals, the analysis has developed into a discipline of its own. It can be differentiated from personal finance and public finance.

Related Professional Qualifications

The new internationally recognised Corporate Finance Qualification (CF) is the only directly related professional qualification, although many others traditionally can lead to the field:

- Qualified accountant qualifications: Chartered Certified Accountant (ACCA), Chartered Accountant (CA), Certified Public Accountant (CPA)
- Other non-statutory accountancy qualifications: Chartered Cost Accountant (CCA Designation from AAFM), Certified Management Accountant (CMA), Chartered Management Accountant (ACMA)
- Business qualifications: Master of Business Administration (MBA), Doctor of Business Administration (DBA)
- Finance qualifications: Masters degree in Finance (MSF), Corporate Finance Qualification (CF), Chartered Financial Analyst (CFA), Association of Corporate Treasurers (ACT), Certified Market Analyst (CMA/FAD) Dual Designation, Master Financial Manager (MFM).

PERSONAL FINANCIAL PLANNER

A Financial Planner or Personal Financial Planner is a practicing professional who helps people deal with various personal financial issues through proper planning, which includes but is not limited to these major areas: tertiary education planning, retirement planning, investment planning, risk management and insurance planning, tax planning, estate planning and business succession planning (for business owners). The work engaged in by this professional is commonly known as *personal financial planning*. In carrying out the planning function, he is guided by a process known as the *financial planning process* which should result in creating a detailed strategy for making their clients as wealthy as possible.

Why would people plan their finances with the help of a financial planner? It is because of the complexity of knowing how to perform the following:

- To provide direction and meaning to financial decisions;
- To understand how each financial decision affects the other areas of his finances; and
- To adapt more easily to life changes in order to feel more secure.

This is particularly difficult to cope without professional help as the case in a fast changing environment.

DEFINITION

We may broadly define personal financial planning as a process of determining an individual's financial goals, purposes in life and life's priorities, and after considering his resources, risk profile and current lifestyle, to detail a balanced and realistic plan to meet those goals.

By 'process', it means financial planning is a step-by-step guide that is not specifically attributed to any particular financial product or service. In other words, any content-based practitioner, e.g. life insurance adviser, accountant, investment adviser, etc., can make use of the same steps listed in the process to perform the financial planning function for their client. The above definition uses the individual's goals and purpose in life as strategic guideposts for mapping a course of action on 'what need to be done' to reach meaningful goals in meaningful ways for him.

The goals and purposes in life are the reference points or outcomes to aim at when the financial plan is constructed. Along side the data gathering exercise, the purpose of each goal is determined to ensure that the goal is meaningful in the context of the individual's situation. Through a process of careful analysis by an experienced financial planner, these goals are then subjected to a reality check by considering the individual's current and future resources available to achieve them.

In the process, the constraints and obstacles to these goals are noted. The information will be used later to determine if there are sufficient resources available to get to these goals, and what other things need to be considered in the process. If the resources are insufficient or absent to meet any of the goals, the particular goal will be adjusted to a more realist level or is replaced with a new goal.

To plan for the future would usually require some forms of self-constrains in postponing some enjoyment today for the sake of the future. To be effective, the approach to financial planning should consider the individual's current lifestyle so that the 'pain' in postponing current pleasures is bearable over the term of the plan. It is in times where current sacrifices are involved that the strength of the plan's purpose for each goal is called upon to ensure that the pursuit of the goal will continue. The plan would consider the importance of each goal and prioritized them accordingly for taking action. It should be noted that many financial plans fail because these practical points were not sufficiently considered.

Scope

What does financial planning covers? Financial planning should ideally cover all areas of the client's financial needs and finally to end with the achievement his goals and objectives in each of the targeted areas. Usually, the scope of financial planning would include the following:

- Risk Management and Insurance Planning: To make provision against cash flow risks through sound risk management and insurance techniques:
- Investment and Planning Issues: Planning, creating and managing capital accumulation to generate future capital and cash flows for reinvestment and spending.
- Retirement Planning: Planning to ensure financial independence when one retires.
- Tax Planning: Planning for the reduction of tax liabilities and the freeing-up of cash flows for other purposes.
- Estate Planning: Planning for the creation, accumulation, conservation and distribution of assets.
- Cash Flow and Liability Management: Maintaining and enhancing personal cash flows through debt and lifestyle management.

THE PERSONAL FINANCIAL PLANNING PROCESS

The *personal financial planning process* is generally accepted as a six-step process as follows:

Step 1: Setting goals with the client This step (that is usually performed in conjunction with Step 2) is meant to identify where the client wants to go in terms of his finances and life.

Step 2: Gathering relevant information on the client This would include the qualitative and quantitive aspects of the client's financial and relevant non-financial situation.

Step 3: Analysing the information The information gathered is analysed so that the client's situation is properly understood. This include checking whether there are sufficient resources to reach the client's goals and what those resources are.

Step 4: Constructing a financial plan Based on the understanding of what the client wants in the future and his current financial status, a roadmap to the client goals is drawn to facilitate the achievements of those goals.

Step 5: Implementing the strategies in the plan Guided by the financial plan, the strategies outlined in the plan is implemented using the resources allocated for the purpose.

Step 6: Monitoring implementation and reviewing the plan The implementation process is closely monitored to ensure it stays in alignment to the client's goals. Periodic reviews are undertaken to check for misalignment and changes in the client's situation. If there are any deviation or significant changes to the client's situation, the strategies and goals in the financial plan are revised accordingly.

Job Function

Professionally, a financial planner is someone who specializes in the planning aspects of finance, in particular personal finance, as contrasted by a stock broker who is only concerned with the actual investments or a life insurance intermediary who advises on risk products. In today's context, he performs his job guided by the financial planning process, which is usually a six-step process, and considers the client's situation from all relevant angles and recommends solutions that are integrated. The six-step financial planning process has been adopted by the International Organization for Standardization (ISO) and the details can be obtained from the organisation. Financial planners are also known by the title financial advisor in some countries, although these two terms are technically not synonymous, and their roles have some functional differences.

Although, there are many types of 'financial planners', the use of the title today is more lean towards those who mainly consider the whole financial picture of a client and then provide solutions in a holistics and comprehensive manner manner. To differentiate from the other types of financial planners, they are sometimes called 'comprehensive' financial planners. Other financial planners may specialize in one or more areas, such as, insurance planning and retirement planning. There are also a small group of planners who termed themselves as fee-only financial planners. As the name implied, these planners make a living by planning and advising clients on their finance for a fee, which is their only source of earnings.

Licensing, Regulation and Self-regulation

Currently, the title of 'financial planner' is largely an unregulated term in many countries. This has allowed financial services personnel in these countries with no restrictive rules to use the title indiscriminately. Commonly, financial products intermediaries, such as life insurance and unit trusts agents, use the title to project a professional image to their client even when they are not trained in the professional aspects of financial planning. This has often led to abuse. Clients may be deceived to receive financial planning services that are unprofessional and from providers who are unethical.

To promote financial planning as a profession, financial professionals and practitioners from across the globe (starting from the United States) involved in the trade begin to form trade organisations to provide self-regulations and to maintain some orderliness in the industry. Some, such as the FPA, begin to organise high-level training programmes and certify members who successfully completed these programmes. However, the title of 'financial planner' continues to be of common usage among individuals in the financial industry in most countries where the financial planning concept exists at some level as there are little or no legal barriers to prevent them from using the title. Expectedly, the governments in many countries where the financial planning profession is taking roots begin to play an increasingly active role in tasking themselves to ensure the market is orderly. More stringent laws and guidelines were progressively introduced to keep the profession in check.

In Australia, the financial planning services are initially delinated by law by the granting of licence to deal in securities or advise on investments. Licences are issued under the stringent criteria by the Australian Securities and Investments Commission (ASIC), which has evolved these regulations vigorously over the years. Financial planning is now a highly regulated industry in Australia especially where financial advice to the public is involved. Practitioners who offer advice that could influence a client's decision to purchase a financial product must meet minimum training requirements and be licensed by the ASIC. The meaning of 'licenced' refers to Australian Financial Services Licence (AFSL) holders and representatives or authorised representatives of licence holders. Broadly, most people embarking in financial planning will start as an authorised representative of a licence holder.

Becoming a financial planner involves two main steps:

1. Meet the training requirements of Policy Statement 146
2. Select a licence holder to be affiliated with

The licence holder is the authorised representative, and will be ultimately responsible for the advice given by the planner and hence must make sure its representatives meet all compliance and training prerequisites. As at November 2005, there were approximately 4300 licence holders registered with ASIC and over 42,500 authorised representatives in Australia.

Then, in 2001, the Singapore government introduced the Financial Advisers Act (FAA) to regulate the conduct of financial advisory business in the country. However, the FAA do not specifically require a high level qualification before a financial practitioner can use the title 'financial planner'. The Act also defines a financial adviser to mean a firm with a corporate structure which is properly licenced by the Monetary Authority of Singapore (MAS) to perform financial advisory business. In both the Australia and Singapore situation, there is no law specifically on 'holding out' oneself to be a financial planner.

United States

In the United States of America, the NASD regulates and oversees the activities of more than 5,050 brokerage firms, approximately 172,050 branch offices and more than 663,050 registered securities representatives. A financial advisor or stock broker should be licensed to provide any consultation on investment in securities. Typical licenses needed to promote the sale of stocks are the: Series 7 (stock broker exam), Series 63 (state exam), and Series 65 or 66 RIA Registered Investment Advisor Law exam. Generally, any advisor who charges a fee for investment advise would need to also have the Series 65 or 66 license. Thus, anyone can call themselves a financial planner but they would still need NASD licenses to provide advice for a fee or be registered as an investment advisor with the SEC Securities and Exchange Commission in the USA. Many brokerage firms still claim an exemption for their employees who sell fee based products and services.

Licensing

The first country to introduce legislation that require a person to be licensed before he can hold himself out to be a 'financial planner' is Malaysia. This is quite unexpected as the financial planning concept is considered quite a new introduction in the Asian region as compared to those in the west, such as the United States and Australia where the profession is more established. The Securities Commission(SC) of Malaysia introduced legislation through amendments made to the Securities Industry Act in 2003 to regulate financial planning and the use of the title or related-title of 'financial planner' or to conduct activities related to financial planning.

In 2005, amendments to the Malaysian Insurance Act require those who carry out financial advisory business (including financial planning activities related to insurance) and/or use the title of financial adviser under their firm (which, like in Singapore, must be a corporate structure) to obtain a licence from Bank Negara (BNM) Some persons who offer financial advisory services, e.g. licenced life insurance agents, are exempted from licensing for them to engage in financial advisory business.

Among others, one of the basic requirements to apply for a financial planner or financial adviser licence in Malaysia is the key company officers, e.g. directors, must be a RFP designee (most, if not all Malaysian FChFP designees also hold the RFP designation). Subsequently, in Septermber 2006, the CFP qualification is included as one of the alternative that can be used by the financial adviser licence applicant. With this development, the demand for financial planning courses begin to take root in more concrete forms in Malaysia. The licence applicant must also be a member of a self-regulatory organisation (SRO)in financial planning that is recognised by the authorities. For this purpose, the two SROs that are currently recognised by both the Security Commission and Bank Negara is the Malaysia Financial Planning Council (MFPC) and the Financial Planning Association of Malaysia (FPAM). This requirement is to ensure there are some form of self-supervision in place for those practicing financial planning.

In some countries,e.g. United States, financial planners must be registered as an investment advisor first. This requires an employee within a firm to pass the series 65 or 66 Registered Investment Advisor Exam. Or, a private advisor or company can apply to the state and SEC for a RIA Registered Investment Advisor License or Status. It should be understood that being 'licenced' to practice financial planning is not the same as merely having a professional 'qualification' in financial planning.

A person may be professionally qualified in financial planning, but without a licence required by the law, he cannot practice the trade in that country or call himself a financial planner there. As of now, there are quite a bit of qualifications related to financial planning that can be found in world. The most prestigious financial planning designations are those which are not just of advanced standing and well-known, but are also recognised by the relevant authorities for licensing purpose. The FChFP, RFP,CFP, ChFC, RFC, FFSI, CWM, MFP, or PFS, FPS designations are advanced financial planning or closely related qualifications that are independently offered and regulated by esteemed financial industry organizations but not all are recognised for licensing purpose.

In some palces, individual employees within a licensed and Registered Investment Advisor firm such as a: brokerage, bank or insurance company may be exempt if providing complementary financial planning services in relation to their existing products and services. Moreover, financial planners should be extremely careful in providing estate planning or taxation advise for a fee as these fields are highly regulated by the local bar associations lawyers and public accountants CPAs. "Investment Advisor" also includes any person who uses the title "financial planner" and who, for compensation, engages in the business, whether principally or as part of another business, of advising others, either directly or through publications or writings, as to the value of securities or as to the advisability of investing in, purchasing or selling securities, or who, for compensation and as part of a regular business, publishes analyses or reports concerning securities.

From California Department of Corporations

A financial planner will be registered with the state if they have <25 million in AUM and with the SEC if they have >30 million in AUM, and they are required to present you with their ADV Part II or equivalent before you enter into a contract with them. No certification, tests or training ensure that any planner is suitable for you or any investor, and it is important to read their ADV Part II, interview them, and fully understand any contract that you enter with them.

History of Certifications

As a newly emerged profession, it is quite expected that there will be a lack of regulation in the financial planning industry, especially in the early years of development. The need for some forms of self-regulations and the demand that a financial planner should be competent and trustworthy have prompted several independent financial services organizations to introduce certifications and ethical benchmarks to meet these challenges in accordance to the need in each country. Those who meet the requirement of the certification process and ethical standards will be awarded a professional financial planning designation.

Probably the earliest and the most well-known of the financial planning certification service mark is the Certified Financial Planner(CFP), which has gained global recognition because of its active standard setting activities and worldwide presence. The CFP designation was first introduced in the United States in the earlier 70's to meet the need of the consumers. The CFP mark now belongs to the CFP Board of Standard's ("CFP Board"), USA, which have member association all over the world. CFP Board was founded in July 1985 as the International Board of Standards and Practices for Certified Financial Planners, Inc, (IBCFP) by the College for Financial Planning (College) and the Institute of Certified Financial Planners (ICFP).

The IBCFP became Certified Financial Planner Board of Standards Inc.(CFP Board) on February 1, 1994. As a professional regulatory organization acting in the public interest by fostering professional standards in personal financial planning, CFP Board establishes and enforces education, examination, experience and ethics requirements for CFP® certificants. The CFP service mark is promoted all over the world through its member associations, the FPAs.

Another well-known certification mark with a unique history is the Fellow Chartered Financial Practitioner (FChFP), which is conferred by the Asia-Pacific Financial Services Association (APFinSA). The FChFP designation is the first known professional designation in financial planning that is completely developed in Asia and the programs leading to the designation is tailored to each country's need by local professionals and practitioners who writes these courses. It is also among the earliest to be vigorously promoted in this region. The FChFP designation was pioneered by the National Association of Malaysian Life Insurance and Financial Advisors (NAMLIFA) and was first launched on 31st May 1996 to its members in Malaysia as an 8-module financial planning programme. The FChFP was adopted by APFinSA in 2001 (of which NAMLIFA is a member) as the highest professional financial services designation amongst its member associations in 11 countries. This development effectively made the FChFP designation a regionally recognised designation in financial planning.

Through the Insurance and Financial Practitioners Association of Singapore (IFPAS), Singapore was the second country to successfully introduce the FChFP designation to its practitioners in 2003. It was during this time that the original letters of the designation 'ChFP' was modified to 'FChFP' to prevent the public from confusing it with the CFP mark. The FChFP designation has since spread to all over the Asia-Pacific region and is quick gaining strength in places like Hong Kong, China and Taiwan.

The Registered Financial Planner (RFP)designation is conferred by the Malaysian Financial Planning Council (MFPC)which was registered in 2004. (Note: The MFPC's RFP designation should be differentiated from the RFP designation conferred by the Registered Financial Planners Institute from the United States.) The Malaysian RFP designation and the MFPC was created through the collaborative work of the Life Insurance Association of Malaysia (LIAM), National Association of Malaysian Life Insurance and Financial Advisors(NAMLIFA) and Malaysian Insurance Institute (MII) who also become the founding members of the Association or Charter Promoter Organisations (ChPOs). Since then, other organisations such as the Malaysian Association of Chartered Financial Consultant (MAChFC) have joint the Association as a member.

The Personal Financial Specialist(PFS) credential was established for CPAs in the United States who specialize in personal financial planning. The credential is awarded exclusively to AICPA members who have demonstrated considerable experience and expertise in that area. As of today, the AICPA has granted approximately 3,300 CPA/PFS credentials. In Australia, the financial planning specialisation, CPA (FPS), is available to those members of CPA Australia who can demonstrate their eligibility through experience and education within the financial services industry.

The objectives of the FPS designation is to:

- Achieve public recognition for those who hold the specialisation enhance the quality of financial planning services that members provide
- Increase practice development and career opportunities for CPAs

The FPS is only avail to CPAs and is based on a points system, where a minimum of 100 points must be accrued. It should be noted that while all CPA Australia members who provide financial product advice must be licensed by ASIC, it is not mandatory for a member to be licensed to first obtained the CPA (FPS) designation.

The Chartered Financial Consultant (ChFC) is another prestigious financial planning qualification, which is conferred by American College, USA). Since 1982, the ChFC has remained among the most extensive education available for professionals seeking a designation in financial planning. Todate, more than 41,000 individuals have attained this distinction. This designation has also spread to Asia, where designees are found in countries like Singapore, Malaysia, Indonesia, China and Hong Kong.

In Europe, the European Financial Planner (EFP) designation conferred by the European Financial Planning Association (EFPA) is gaining ground as a financial planning certification mark. The EFPA is the largest professional and educational organisation for financial planners and financial advisors in Europe and is the only Financial Planning Association created solely in the interest of european financial planning consumers and practitioners.

In one of the significant recent developments, several major financial services organisations with international/regional affiliations have grouped together to form the Federation of Financial Standards Associations(IFFSA). The organisations that originally initiated the IFFSA concept are the European Financial Planner EFPA and the Asia-Pacific Financial Services Association (APFinSA). It is expected that more organisations will join as associates of this new entity.

The rest of the certification qualifications related to financial planning include: Fellow, Financial Services Institute (conferred by LOMI, USA); The highest known conditions set for conferment of a financial planning credential seems to be those of the CWM Chartered Wealth Manager (conferred by the AAFM) designation which requires an accredited MBA, PhD or CFA to apply (Note: This entry requirement is not uniform and only applies to some places where the AAFM operates).

Education

In America, more than 150,000 financial services professionals have earned advanced degrees and designations from The American College. Their leading financial planning programs include ChFC programme and courses leading to the CFP certification awarded by the CFP Board of Standards. Another American organisation active in the promotion of financial planning courses is the International Association of Registered Financial Consultants(IARFC), which confers the Registered Financial Consultant (RFC) designation. The IARFC has introduced a financial planning self-study and examination process for Registered Financial Consultant applicants.

In Singapore, the Financial Planning Association of Singapore (FPAS) appoints educational providers to conduct tutorials for students interested in taking the CFP examinations. Two of its active education providers are Financial Perspectives and FTC. The Singapore College of Insurance(SCI) conducts localised courses leading to the ChFC designation which is awarded by The American College. Finally, the Insurance and Financial Practitioners Association of Singapore (IFPAS) uses the educational provider, Professional Education and Consultancy (PEC) to conduct tutorials for its FChFP students. These training companies, i.e. Financial Perspectives, FTC and PEC, also provide a host of other financial related trainings to the financial practitioners in Singapore.

As for Malaysia, the Financial Planning Association of Malaysia (FPAM) has active education providers such as IMS, IFPA, PNB, KDU and IBBM to conduct its CFP courses. The Malaysian Financial Planning Council (MFPC) also appoints education providers for its RFP courses. Some of them to date are MII, NAMLIFA, MIM-IMS, IBBM, OUM, Kolej Kasturi and Regent School of Economics. For the FChFP, the courses are conducted in-house by the National Association of Malaysian Life Insurance and Financial Advisors (NAMLIFA) and its branches throughout the country. Other Malaysian training providers active in supporting financial planning education in the non-designation domain include BrainStation Academy, AD Capital and Jon Wise.

Globally, cross-recognition agreements are being developed to facilitate the learning of financial planning. The 2 major accrediting agencies AACSB and ACBSP in the west, which accredit over 560 of the best business school programs, provides the Certification of MFP Master Financial Planner Professional from the American Academy of Financial Management, which is available to AACSB and ACBSP business school graduates with finance or financial services related concentrations.

MANAGERIAL FINANCE

Managerial Finance is that branch of finance that provides tools for a company's financial managers. It encompasses corporate finance and management accounting also known as cost accounting. Financial analysts provide analysis in the corporate finance field. And, cost analysts provide analysis in the cost accounting field. Therefore, the financial-cost analyst provides analysis in the managerial finance arena. These analysts require skills of both the internal corporate financial analyst and cost analyst.

CORPORATE FINANCE

Corporate finance is a specific area of finance dealing with the financial decisions corporations make and the tools as well as analysis used to make these decisions. The primary goal of Corporate finance is to enhance corporate value, without taking excessive financial risks. The discipline may be divided among long-term and short-term decisions and techniques. Capital investment decisions comprise the long-term choices about which projects receive investment, whether to finance that investment with equity or debt, and when or whether to pay dividends to shareholders. Short-term corporate finance decisions are called working capital management and deal with the balance of current assets and current liabilities; the focus here is on managing cash, inventories, and short-term borrowing and lending (e.g., the credit terms extended to customers).

The time frames, and the goal of the discipline, are inter-related: value is enhanced when return on capital, a function of working capital management, exceeds cost of capital, a function of previous capital investment decisions. Corporate finance is closely related to managerial finance, which is slightly broader in scope, describing the financial techniques available to all forms of business enterprise, corporate or not.

Capital Investment Decisions

Longer term Corporate finance decisions - generally relating to fixed assets and capital structure - are referred to as *Capital investment decisions*. The decision here will be based on several inter-related criteria. In general, management must "maximize the value of the firm" by investing in projects which are NPV positive, when valued using an appropriate discount rate; these projects must also be financed appropriately. If no such opportunities exist, maximizing shareholder value dictates that management return excess cash to shareholders. Capital investment decisions thus comprise an investment decision, a financing decision, and a dividend decision.

The Investment Decision

Management must allocate limited resources between competing opportunities ("projects") in a process known as capital budgeting. Making this capital allocation decision requires estimating the value of each opportunity or project: a function of the size, timing and predictability of future cash flows.

Project Valuation

In general, each project's value will be estimated using a discounted cash flow (DCF) valuation, and the opportunity with the highest value, as measured by the resultant net present value (NPV) will be selected. This requires estimating the size and timing of all of the incremental cash flows resulting from the project. These future cash flows are then discounted to determine their present value. These present values are then summed, and this sum is the NPV.

The NPV is greatly influenced by the discount rate. Thus selecting the proper discount rate - the project "hurdle rate" - is critical to making the right decision. The hurdle rate is the minimum acceptable return on an investment - i.e. the project appropriate discount rate. The hurdle rate should reflect the riskiness of the investment, typically measured by volatility of cash flows, and must take into account the financing mix. Managers use models such as the CAPM or the APT to estimate a discount rate appropriate for a particular project, and use the weighted average cost of capital (*WACC*) to reflect the financing mix selected. (A common error in choosing a discount rate for a project is to apply a WACC that applies to the entire firm. Such an approach may not be appropriate where the risk of a particular project differs markedly from that of the firm's existing portfolio of assets.)

In conjunction with NPV, there are several other measures used as (secondary) selection criteria in corporate finance. These are visible from the DCF and include payback, IRR, Modified IRR, equivalent annuity, capital efficiency, and ROI.

Valuing Flexibility

In many cases, for example R&D projects, a project may open (or close) paths of action to the company, but this reality will not typically be captured in a strict NPV approach. Management will therefore (sometimes) employ tools which place an explicit value on these options. So, whereas in a DCF valuation the most likely or average or scenario specific cash flows are discounted, here the "flexibile and staged nature" of the investment is modelled, and hence "all" potential payoffs are considered. The difference between the two valuations is the "option value" inherent in the project.

The two most common tools are Decision Tree Analysis (DTA) and Real options.

- The real options approach is used when the value of a project is contingent on the value of some other asset or underlying variable. (For example, the viability of a mining project is contingent on the price of gold; if the price is too low, management will abandon the mining rights, if sufficiently high, management will develop the Ore-body. Again, a DCF valuation would capture only one of these outcomes.) Here, using financial option theory as a framework, the decision to be taken is identified as corresponding to either a call option or a put option - valuation is then via the Binomial model or, less often for this purpose, via Black Scholes; see Contingent claim valuation. The "true" value of the project is then the NPV of the "most likely" scenario plus the option value.
- The DTA approach attempts to capture flexibility by incorporating likely events and consequent management decisions into the valuation. In the decision tree, each management decision in response to an "event" generates a "branch" or "path" which the company could follow. (For example, management will only proceed with stage 2 of the project given that stage 1 was successful; stage 3, in turn, depends on stage 2. In a DCF model, on the other hand, there is no "branching" - each scenario must be modelled separately.) The highest value path (probability weighted) is regarded as representative of project value.

THE FINANCING DECISION

Achieving the goals of corporate finance requires that any corporate investment be financed appropriately. As above, since both hurdle rate and cash flows (and hence the riskiness of the firm) will be affected, the financing mix can impact the valuation. Management must therefore identify the "optimal mix" of financing – the capital structure that results in maximum value.

The sources of financing will, generically, comprise some combination of debt and equity. Financing a project through debt results in a liability that must be serviced - and hence there are cash flow implications regardless of the project's success. Equity financing is less risky in the sense of cash flow commitments, but results in a dilution of ownership and earnings. The cost of equity is also typically higher than the cost of debt, and so equity financing may result in an increased hurdle rate which may offset any reduction in cash flow risk. Management must also attempt to match the financing mix to the asset being financed as closely as possible, in terms of both timing and cash flows.

The Dividend Decision

In general, management must decide whether to invest in additional projects, reinvest in existing operations, or return free cash as dividends to shareholders. The dividend is calculated mainly on the basis of the company's unappropriated profit and its business prospects for the coming year. If there are no NPV positive opportunities, i.e. where returns exceed the hurdle rate, then management must return excess cash to investors - these free cash flows comprise cash remaining after all business expenses have been met. (This is the general case, however there are exceptions. For example, investors in a "Growth stock", expect that the company will, almost by definition, retain earnings so as to fund growth internally. In other cases, even though an opportunity is currently NPV negative, management may consider "investment flexibility" and potential payoff and decide to retain cash flows.)

Management must also decide on the form of the distribution, generally as cash dividends or via a share buyback. There are various considerations: where shareholders pay tax on dividends, companies may elect to retain earnings, or to perform a stock buyback, in both cases increasing the value of shares outstanding; some companies will pay "dividends" from stock rather than in cash. Today it is generally accepted that dividend policy is value neutral.

Working Capital Management

Decisions relating to working capital and short term financing are referred to as *working capital management*. These involve managing the relationship between a firm's short-term assets and its short-term liabilities. The goal of Working capital management is to ensure that the firm is able to continue its operations and that it has sufficient cash flow to satisfy both maturing short-term debt and upcoming operational expenses.

Decision Criteria

By definition, Working capital management entails short term decisions - generally, relating to the next one year period - which are "reversible". These decisions are therefore not taken on the same basis as Capital Investment Decisions (NPV or related, as above) rather they will be based on cash flows and / or profitability.

- One measure of cash flow is provided by the cash conversion cycle - the net number of days from the outlay of cash for raw material to receiving payment from the customer. As a management tool, this metric makes explicit the inter-relatedness of decisions relating to inventories, accounts receivable and payable, and cash. Because this number effectively corresponds to the time that the firm's cash is tied up in operations and unavailable for other activities, management generally aims at a low net count.

- In this context, the most useful measure of profitability is Return on capital (ROC). The result is shown as a percentage, determined by dividing relevant income for the 12 months by capital employed; Return on equity (ROE) shows this result for the firm's shareholders. Firm value is enhanced when, and if, the return on capital, which results from working capital management, exceeds the cost of capital, which results from capital investment decisions as above. ROC measures are therefore useful as a management tool, in that they link short-term policy with long-term decision making.

Management of Working Capital

Guided by the above criteria, management will use a combination of policies and techniques for the management of working capital. These policies aim at managing the *current assets* (generally cash and cash equivalents, inventories and debtors) and the short term financing, such that cash flows and returns are acceptable.

- Cash management. Identify the cash balance which allows for the business to meet day to day expenses, but reduces cash holding costs.
- Inventory management. Identify the level of inventory which allows for uninterrupted production but reduces the investment in raw materials - and minimizes reordering costs - and hence increases cash flow; see Supply chain management; Just In Time (JIT); Economic order quantity (EOQ); Economic production quantity (EPQ).
- Debtors management. Identify the appropriate credit policy, i.e. credit terms which will attract customers, such that any impact on cash flows and the cash conversion cycle will be offset by increased revenue and hence Return on Capital (or *vice versa*).
- Short term financing. Identify the appropriate source of financing, given the cash conversion cycle: the inventory is ideally financed by credit granted by the supplier; however, it may be necessary to utilize a bank loan (or overdraft), or to "convert debtors to cash" through "factoring".

INTERNAL FINANCIAL REPORTING MANAGEMENT

Management is responsible for establishing and maintaining adequate internal control over financial reporting of the company. Internal control over financial reporting is a process designed to provide reasonable assurance regarding the reliability of financial reporting and the preparation of financial statements for external purposes in accordance with accounting principles generally accepted in the United States of America.

The company's internal control over financial reporting includes those policies and procedures that :

(i) Pertain to the maintenance of records that, in reasonable detail, accurately and fairly reflect the transactions and dispositions of the assets of the company;

(ii) Provide reasonable assurance that transactions are recorded as necessary to permit preparation of financial statements in accordance with accounting principles generally accepted in the United States of America, and that receipts and expenditures of the company are being made only in accordance with authorizations of management and directors of the company; and

(iii) Provide reasonable assurance regarding prevention or timely detection of unauthorized acquisition, use, or disposition of the company's assets that could have a material effect on the financial statements.

Because of its inherent limitations, internal control over financial reporting may not prevent or detect misstatements. Also, projections of any evaluation of effectiveness to future periods are subject to the risk that controls may become inadequate because of changes in conditions, or that the degree of compliance with the policies or procedures may deteriorate.

A primary responsibility of directors and officers is to ensure that the organization is accountable for its programs and finances to its contributors, members, the public and government regulators. Accountability requires that the organization comply with all applicable laws and ethical standards; adhere to the organization's mission; create and adhere to conflict of interest, ethics, personnel and accounting policies; protect the rights of members; prepare and file its annual financial report with the Internal Revenue Service and appropriate state regulatory authorities and make the report available to all members of the board and any member of the public who requests it. The development and maintenance of the organization's internal controls will help to ensure accountability.

WHAT ARE INTERNAL CONTROLS?

Internal controls are systems of policies and procedures that protect the assets of an organization, create reliable financial reporting, promote compliance with laws and regulations and achieve effective and efficient operations. These systems are not only related to accounting and reporting but also relate to the organization's communication processes, internally and externally, and include procedures for:

(1) Handling funds received and expended by the organization,

(2) Preparing appropriate and timely financial reporting to board members and officers,

(3) Conducting the annual audit of the organization's financial statements,

(4) Evaluating staff and programs,
(5) Maintaining inventory records of real and personal property and their whereabouts, and
(6) Implementing personnel and conflicts of interest policies.

Procedures for Monitoring Assets

Every organization should have procedures to monitor and record assets received, held and expended. These financial controls should be described in an accounting policies and procedures manual. The manual should be reviewed with and given to all directors and officers, trustees, employees and volunteers. It should include procedures for:

- Preparing an annual income and expense budget and periodic reports - at least quarterly, preferably monthly - comparing actual receipts and expenditures to the budget with timely variance explanations.
- Writing and signing checks or vouchers and receiving, recording, securing and depositing cash and other receipts. Such procedures should ensure that no single individual is responsible for receiving, recording and depositing funds or writing and signing checks. Checks and balances are essential to make embezzlement more difficult.
- Ensuring that grants and contributions received are properly recorded, accountings required as a condition of any grant are completed and restrictions on the use of such funds, such as contributions given for a restricted purpose (*e.g.* building fund, scholarships) and prohibitions on the use of the principal of an endowment, are obeyed.
- Requisitioning, authorizing, verifying, recording and monitoring all expenditures, including payment of invoices, petty cash and other expenditures. Such procedures should ensure that no single individual is permitted to request, authorize, verify and record expenditures. For example, the same person should not be responsible for cash disbursements and bank reconciliations. These functions should be assigned to different individuals.
- Accessing, inputting and changing electronic data maintained by the organization.

  Preserving electronic records and ensuring data compatibility when systems change and creating an appropriate records retention policy are part of this process.
- Providing for regular oversight by an audit committee or, if there is no audit committee, by the executive committee or by the board of directors itself.
- Reporting to the audit committee or board by employees and volunteers of allegations of fraud or financial improprieties.

- Ensuring that timely and appropriate financial reports are distributed to all directors and officers and reviewed by them, as well as the president, chief executive officer, treasurer and chief financial officer.
- Providing procedures for approving contracts to which the organization is a party, including securing competitive bids from vendors.
- Making clear the responsibilities of all individuals involved with the organization, including the board of directors and officers, employees, volunteers and consultants, maintaining an organizational chart and updating such information as necessary.
- Preparing for the annual audit process in a timely manner.
- Developing a prudent investment strategy and providing proper oversight of the investment assets.
- Complying with governmental and other reporting requirements, including watchdog agencies.
- Complying with obligations to members, employees and the public, including their right to a copy of the organization's annual financial report.

Various Roles in the Organization

There should be written job descriptions for directors, officers and trustees, employees, volunteers and consultants. The work of the organization will be more easily accomplished and problems will be avoided if all involved understand what is expected of them and the limits of their authority.

A comprehensive description of the chief executive officer's job should make clear his or her responsibilities in the day-to-day activities of the organization and set forth exactly what information is expected by the board and when it must be communicated. For example, if the board expects monthly financial reports and bi-monthly programmatic reports, making those expectations clear from the beginning will avoid ambiguity and will clarify the responsibility for accountability to the board. Likewise, all other employees should have written job descriptions and be advised of what is expected of them. Volunteers are no exception. They should be given job descriptions that clearly describe what is expected of them. For many organizations, volunteers are the only people who conduct programs and have contact with the public. If they do not understand their responsibilities or do not act professionally, the organization could be at risk.

Training

Appropriate training should be arranged for all involved. New directors, officers, employees and volunteers should be trained by those who are familiar with the organization and its operations. There are many organizations that provide free or low-cost training for board members and others within the organization, and there are numerous resources that provide guidance in developing training. For all involved, familiarity with the organization's internal controls is essential. Training is a wise investment!

Personnel Policies

Personnel policies, including vacation and sick leave, health insurance and other benefits, evaluations, ordinary and overtime compensation, conflicts of interest and code of ethics, and grievance procedures (including protections for "whistle blowers") should be in writing and given to all employees prior to hiring, with changes in policies communicated on a regular basis.

Conflicts of Interest Policies and Code of Ethics

Directors, officers, trustees and others who serve a nonprofit organization should not have any personal or business interest that may conflict with their responsibilities to the organization. To avoid such conflicts, it is wise to have a "conflicts of interest policy" that clearly states the procedures to be followed if a board member's personal or financial interests may be advanced by an action of the board. The conflicts of interest policy should require an individual to fully disclose any interest the individual and/or the individual's family has in any entity that does business with the organization and that any change in the information concerning potential conflicts should be provided to the organization immediately.

The policy may be set forth in the organization's by-laws. The policy must require that such individual may not participate in any decision to approve doing business with the individual or any entity in which the individual has an interest, and such decision must be made by a disinterested majority of the board of directors or trustees. The organization should also have a code of ethics addressing issues such as transparency, disclosure in fundraising solicitations, integrity in governance and diversity. There are many examples of written policies regarding conflicts of interest and other ethical matters available. Consult the resources cited in this booklet to assist you in drafting your organization's ethics and conflict of interest policies. The policies should be discussed with the organization's attorneys and auditors prior to adoption. All board members, employees, volunteers and consultants should be given copies of both policies and sign a statement acknowledging that they have read them.

The Audit Committee

Crucial to the governance of a not-for-profit organization is the establishment of an audit committee. Typically, an audit committee is composed of members of the board of directors who are independent of any financial interest in the organization and at least one of whom has expertise in accounting. The audit committee acts as a liaison to the organization's independent external auditor who is a certified public accountant ("CPA") or firm of CPAs. The audit committee's responsibilities should include the following:

- Selection and review of the independent external auditors and review of the annual fees to be paid for services rendered by them and each proposed audit plan developed by management and the external auditors.
- Review with the independent external auditors the organization's annual financial statements and reports. Consider whether they are complete and consistent with information understood by the committee members.
- Review and evaluate the management letter received from the independent external auditors and discuss recommendations for any changes necessary to remedy problems identified in the letter.
- Maintain communication between the board and independent external auditors by meeting on a regularly scheduled basis with an opportunity for the auditors and the audit committee to meet without management present. At the completion of the audit, review the audit fieldwork process with the auditors. Obtain an understanding of their evaluation of management and whether they encountered any difficulties or had any disagreements with management during their audit. Review all journal entries proposed by the auditors.

Audits are a factor in providing proper financial management oversight of an organization. The audit committee should interact with management to implement and monitor the internal control structure and to take steps that insure that the possible risks of fraud or embezzlement are mitigated. In order for an audit committee to function properly, it should be made up of people who are independent of the day-to-day management of the organization. For example, no paid CEO, executive director, chief financial officer or other employee should be on the committee. In addition to the audit committee's role in the preparation of the audit, its responsibilities include the following:

- Ensure that proper federal and state tax filings are completed timely, including payroll taxes, sales taxes and unrelated business income taxes.
- Understand the organization's internal controls and have policies in place to update them as needed.
- Periodically review the organization's insurance coverage and determine its adequacy.
- Make recommendations necessary to improve the organization's efficiency and/or remedy problems identified by the committee or others.
- Identify and monitor related party transactions and review the conflict of interest, ethics and related party disclosure policies periodically and update as needed.

- Monitor any legal matters that could impact the financial health and reporting of the organization.
- Institute and oversee any special investigatory work as needed.

In organizations with small boards, the entire board may serve the function of the audit committee. For larger organizations, it is more appropriate to create a separate audit committee that can devote its attention to this area. Whatever form the audit committee takes, at least one member should have an understanding of financial matters and should be comfortable reviewing financial reports and other financial records. No member of the audit committee should ever be involved in any conflict of interest transaction, and no member of the audit committee should be compensated in any manner by the organization other than director's fees paid generally to all directors, if any. The audit committee should be familiar with the organization's internal controls and report to the board as appropriate the adequacy of the internal controls and any concerns raised by the staff or outside auditors.

LONG-RUN MANAGEMENT DECISIONS

LONG-RUN MANAGEMENT OBJECTIVES AND CONSTRAINTS

To pursue our purpose of describing distinguishable classes of management decisions and related types of accounting information, it is useful to discuss first the objectives and constraints faced by management. The value of this approach is that, in general, different classes of management decisions can be identified with specific types of objectives and constraints.

The key to differences in types of objectives and constraints characterizing particular decision situations is, in turn, often explainable in relation to the time span of enterprise activities that will be influenced by the decision choice. One usually finds it helpful to separate management activities and decisions into long-run and short-run categories.

Long-run decisions: Long-run decisions are defined as those decisions whose outcomes commit the enterprise or directly influence its activities for many future periods. The long run is thought of as a span of time sufficiently long that a significant project or programme of the enterprise can be planned, implemented, and run its course. Short-run Short-run decisions are defined as decisions whose outcomes commit the enterprise or directly influence its actions for perhaps only one year at most. The latitude available in selecting alternatives in the short run is restricted considerably by the commitments made by the enterprise in past long-run decisions. Long-run Objectives. From an accounting perspective, a business enterprise in a market economy is best seen in terms of a sequence of economic operations. Usually, the enterprise starts with an endowment of cash, its money capital, constituting a claim against resources, products, and services available in the economy.

The enterprise expends a portion of that cash to acquire resources and uses those resources in the production of products or services. The products or services, in turn, are sold to other economic units that at some point remit cash to the enterprise in exchange. The new cash flows renew the enterprise's ability to acquire the same or different resources for employment in further production of products and services.

In this process there is usually a division of the enabling economic function, the enterprise function. Owners and creditors supply the necessary capital. Management identifies the most promising opportunities to provide products and services; it acquires, organizes, and directs the necessary resources to exploit identified opportunities. The contribution of suppliers of capital and the contribution of management complement each other. Each group identified presumably provides a unique opportunity for the other through the organizational unit, the business enterprise. Each group will presumably wish to withdraw its resources from the relationship if other opportunities appear more attractive. The implication of this possibility for management is significant. Profit Maximization. If it is expected that the enterprise will fail to earn returns for the suppliers of money capital that are at least equal to what they can earn in other opportunities of comparable risk, the enterprise will not attract the necessary money capital to function.

If the enterprise consistently fails to produce products and services whose values exceed the costs of resources used, it will actually dissipate its money capital and jeopardize its ability to survive. In either case, the opportunity for management to use its talents to the fullest is dimished by the faltering supply of money capital at the disposal of the enterprise. The best insurance against such a situation is for management to pursue a long-run objective of maximizing the value of the excess of the cash flows received for products and services provided to customers over the cash expended for resources used.

Only in this way can management ensure that sufficient money capital will be available to maximize its own opportunities to employ its talents. This basic goal of management is often referred to as the profit maximization goal. Profit Maximization and Other Goals. Long-run profit maximization is the preeminent goal of business enterprises in a market economy. But note the emphasis on "long-run." The statement would be shortsighted without that emphasis and would be contrary to the current stated policies of most significant business organizations.

Those policies often include such goals as:

- Betterment of employee morale,
- Employee education and training,
- Protection of the environment,
- Improved product quality,
- Community service,
- Contribution to basic research in a particular field.

In the short run, one would expect such goals to conflict frequently with the pursuit of maximum profits. But clearly all are related, or rather necessary, to achieve maximum profits in the long run. So, if a very broad view of long-run profitability is taken, then the single goal of long-run profit maximization generally embraces all so-called other goals. Constraints on Long-run Decisions. In the long run, management can conceivably alter virtually every aspect of a business, including its own (management's) composition.

A distinguishing feature of long-run decisions is that they are relatively free from internally imposed constraints. Nevertheless, because long-run decisions (commitments) must be made as of a point in time, certain externally imposed constraints apply-at least in part. Among the largely externally imposed constraints on long-run decisions are the laws and customs of society, the state of technology, the size of the population and labour force, worldwide and local supplies of natural resources, and so forth, which exist at the time of decision.

Of course, some of these constraints can be influenced to some degree by an individual enterprise; for example, the passage of a new law may be the result of lobbying efforts on the part of business, or changes in the customs of society may be influenced by advertising campaigns. But in general, as of the time of any given long-run decision, external constraints impose some limitation on the enterprise.

Although externally imposed constraints affect each enterprise to varying degrees, there are two specific constraints on long-run decisions that are usually unique to each individual enterprise.

First, at a given point in time, each enterprise faces a limited number of long-run opportunities that it can effectively exploit because of its location, its prior activities, and the composition of its management. Second, each enterprise faces a limited supply of money capital with which to embark on alternative long-run courses of action. Although management can alter these two restrictions in the long run, the alterations themselves may require the immediate commitment of scarce money capital and take some time to effect. Hence, at any given decision point, long-run alternatives are restricted by these two limitations.

Long-run Management Decisions and Related Accounting Information

Given the long-run profit maximization objective, the long-run success of the enterprise (management) hinges on management's ability to identify and implement the most promising product lines, projects, and programmes within the enterprise's capabilities and its environmental and money-capital limitations. The first requisite to success is active seeking of opportunities, either to provide new and better products or services or to develop new and better means of production.

The former requires involvement, at least at some minimal level, in research into present markets and consumer (or industrial) preferences, plus product development research. The latter requires at least some involvement with industrial engineering as well as organizational, institutional, and behavioural research.

All of these are essentially information-seeking activities contributed by specialists other than accountants. The contribution of accountants comes into play in another important requisite to long-run success of the enterprise-the selection of the most promising set from among the identified alternatives.

Capital-Budgeting Decisions: The essential feature of long-run opportunities (alternatives) is that they usually require considerable initial outlays of the enterprise's limited money capital for implementation. Initial outlays include expenditures for such things as long-lived assets to be employed in the programme, legal fees, and further costs of developmental and organizational research. Over many future periods, related additional outlays are required to produce benefits in the form of cash inflows or lower total outlays than the programmes they replace. Since long-run programmes generally require outlays of scarce money capital, the process of selecting the best set of alternatives is usually referred to as capital budgeting.

Capital budgeting: Capital budgeting is the process of choosing the best set from among the available long-run opportunities requiring significant outlays of money capital.

The Accounting Role in Capital Budgeting

Choosing the best set from available long-run opportunities requires that each opportunity be evaluated with respect to the long-run objective of the enterprise. We have already noted that the objective of management in the long run is to maximize the excess of cash receipts for products and services over cash outlays for resources used in production. We have also noted, however, that most long-run programmes involve initial outlays of cash to get started, followed by many periods of additional outflows and inflows.

Thus it is clear that in order to evaluate the desirability of long-run alternatives, some model is necessary that permits the decision maker to compare cash inflows and outflows of many future periods.

One such model is the present value model, which converts cash flows of disparate time periods into their equivalent values in cash as of the time of decision.

The attractiveness to management of a long-run programme, project, or product line ultimately hinges on its real economic features, that is, the physical capabilities, quality, and demand for a product; the kinds and quantities of resources required to carry out a programme; and the kind of organization structure and production techniques required for implementation. Such information, as noted earlier, comes from nonaccounting sources such as marketing personnel, industrial engineers, and organization development specialists. The role of the accountant in bringing these relevant economic attributes of an alternative into focus for management is to translate them into the cash inflows and outflows that they imply for present and future periods.

Example: Shoosh Ski Company has manufactured a well-known line of quality fibreglass skis for the last ten years. The company was one of the first to experiment with fibreglass skis and as a result of early technical gains has become very successful. Of late, however, the company faces a threat to its long-run success. Many competitors have entered the market, and the competition has reduced Shoosh's prospects for continued increases in its sales of skis.

The president of the company has been very unhappy with the prospect of a declining share of the market. In searching for alternatives, she has concluded that whereas many competitors make finished skis, few suppliers can produce high-quality metal edges used in making skis. Shoosh Company, however, has the know-how to do the job.

But to make the edges for sale to other ski manufacturers, Shoosh Company will need an immediate factory and equipment expansion that will have a ten-year life, costing $120,000, with no salvage value in the end. The company has enough money to pay for the expansion. But is it worth diverting the $120,000 from other possible uses in order to begin production of the new product?

The president understands the concept of present value and intends to use it in her decision. She has already determined that the company can invest the $120,000 in projects of risk equal to that of the plant expansion and receive an annual rate of interest of 10 per cent.

She therefore reasons that unless the present value (at 10 per cent) of the net cash inflows from the production and sale of edges equals or exceeds $120,000, that is, unless the net present value (at 10 per cent) of the factory expansion is equal to or greater than zero, the project is not worth implementing. With that she turns the project over to the company accountant, who must now provide the necessary information to value the choice.

The first step in determining the net present value of the factory expansion is estimation of the future cash inflows and outflows associated with the project. Unfortunately, in practice no one is going to tell the accountant directly what these amounts are going to be, except for the initial outlay of $120,000.

Instead he has to work with the sales manager, production engineer, plant manager, and others who will plan and control the new manufacturing operation in order to determine what new cash inflows and outflows to expect from the operation.

First he approaches the sales manager and requests estimates of how many pairs of edges will be sold and at what price in each of the next ten years. The sales manager estimates that $30 would be a competitive price for the edges (per pair). At that price he estimates that on the average 5,000 pairs of edges can be sold each year for the next ten years.

Meanwhile the production engineer has determined the quantities of material, labour, and miscellaneous other resources required for production in addition to the new factory facilities. He estimates the following resource requirements: Materials: Each pair of edges requires a 10' × 1/8" × 3/16" bar of cold rolled steel alloy.

- *Manufacturing labour*: Two hours of skilled labour will be required in total to complete each pair of edges.
- *Other costs-annual*: Supervisor's salary Cleanup, repairs, and maintenance Insurance, taxes, etc.

With the information based on physical production plans, the accountant turns to the personnel manager and the purchasing agent to determine the cash costs of the production requirements for the edges. He estimates the annual net cash inflow from production and sales of the edges. The accountant then presents the company president with decisionready information relevant to the factory expansion.

Assuming that the president has confidence in the accountant's ability to gather the necessary information and make the necessarily uncertain projections of cash flows as well or better than anyone else in the organization, she will undertake the plant expansion, since it has a positive net present value of $15,080.

Example: brings into focus two important aspects of all managerial activity. First, it illustrates an important feature of the accountant's role in the business enterprise, alluded to earlier. Notice that the accountant has actually prepared a ready-made decision value for the decision maker, that is, the net present value of the decision alternative. Recall that we noted earlier that there usually is (or should be) a close working relationship between the accountant and an internal decision maker.

As a result, the decision maker can communicate to the accountant features of his specific decision model, including such things as the time preference rate that he feels is appropriate for discounting the expected cash flows from a particular project, to which the accountant does not have access in the case of external parties.

Hence, at the discretion of the decision maker, the managerial accountant may perform not only the information-gathering step in the decision process but parts of the problem definition and evaluation steps as well. It is important to note, however, that as more of the decision process is assumed by the accountant, the risk increases that the accountant will intentionally or unintentionally introduce his own biases into the decision.

The accountant should of course maintain a detached attitude insofar as possible. But the decision maker should nevertheless be aware of this risk in determining the degree to which decision responsibility is delegated to the accountant.

The second important aspect of managerial accounting (also alluded to earlier) is the managerial accountant's responsibility as a translator. Since the management of the enterprise is almost always interested in the effects of the decisions on cash flows, an important part of the managerial accounting function is the translation of the resource flows connected with a product, project, or programme into financial or money flow implications. One of the most general sets of skills or tools employed by managerial accountants to execute their role as translators is cost behaviour analysis.

2

Accounting Cycle in Hospitality Industry

INTRODUCTION

In accountancy, an account is a label used for recording and reporting a quantity of almost anything. Most often it is a record of an amount of money owned or owed by or to a particular person or entity, or allocated to a particular purpose. It may represent amounts of money that have actually changed hands, or it may represent an estimate of the values of assets, or it may be a combination of these.

TYPES OF ACCOUNTS

1. Asset accounts: represent the different types of economic resources owned by a business, common examples of Asset accounts are cash, cash in bank, building, inventory, prepaid rent, goodwill.
2. Liability accounts: represent the different types of economic obligations by a business, such as accounts payable, bank loan, bonds payable, accrued interest.
3. Equity accounts: represent the residual equity of a business (after deducting from Assets all the liabilities) including Retained Earnings and Appropriations.
4. Revenue accounts: represent the hotel's gross earnings and common examples include Sales, Service revenue and Interest Income.
5. Expense accounts: represent the hotel's expenditures to enable itself to operate. Common examples are electricity and water, rentals, depreciation, doubtful accounts, interest, insurance.
6. Contra-accounts: from the term contra, meaning to deduct, the value of which are opposite the 5 above mentioned types of accounts. For instance, a contra-asset account is Accumulated depreciation. This label represent deductions to a relatively permanent asset like Building.

ACCOUNTING PROCESS

The accounting process is a series of activities that begins with a transaction and ends with the closing of the books. Because this process is repeated each reporting period, it is referred to as the *accounting cycle* and includes these major steps:

1. Identify the transaction or other recognizable event.
2. Prepare the transaction's source document such as a purchase order or invoice.
3. Analyze and classify the transaction. This step involves quantifying the transaction in monetary terms (e.g. dollars and cents), identifying the accounts that are affected and whether those accounts are to be debited or credited.
4. Record the transaction by making entries in the appropriate journal, such as the sales journal, purchase journal, cash receipt or disbursement journal, or the general journal. Such entries are made in chronological order.
5. Post general journal entries to the ledger accounts.
   The above steps are performed throughout the accounting period as transactions occur or in periodic batch processes. The following steps are performed at the end of the accounting period:
6. Prepare the trial balance to make sure that debits equal credits. The trial balance is a listing of all of the ledger accounts, with debits in the left column and credits in the right column. At this point no adjusting entries have been made. The actual sum of each column is not meaningful; what is important is that the sums be equal. Note that while out-of-balance columns indicate a recording error, balanced columns do not guarantee that there are no errors. For example, not recording a transaction or recording it in the wrong account would not cause an imbalance.
7. Correct any discrepancies in the trial balance. If the columns are not in balance, look for math errors, posting errors, and recording errors. Posting errors include:
   - Posting of the wrong amount,
   - Omitting a posting,
   - Posting in the wrong column, or
   - Posting more than once.
8. Prepare adjusting entries to record accrued, deferred, and estimated amounts.
9. Post adjusting entries to the ledger accounts.
10. Prepare the adjusted trial balance. This step is similar to the preparation of the unadjusted trial balance, but this time the adjusting entries are included. Correct any errors that may be found.
11. Prepare the financial statements.
    - Income statement: prepared from the revenue, expenses, gains, and losses.
    - Balance sheet: prepared from the assets, liabilities, and equity accounts.

- Statement of retained earnings: prepared from net income and dividend information.
- Cash flow statement: derived from the other financial statements using either the direct or indirect method.

12. Prepare closing journal entries that close temporary accounts such as revenues, expenses, gains, and losses. These accounts are closed to a temporary income summary account, from which the balance is transferred to the retained earnings account (capital). Any dividend or withdrawal accounts also are closed to capital.
13. Post closing entries to the ledger accounts.
14. Prepare the after-closing trial balance to make sure that debits equal credits. At this point, only the permanent accounts appear since the temporary ones have been closed. Correct any errors.
15. Prepare reversing journal entries (optional). Reversing journal entries often are used when there has been an accrual or deferral that was recorded as an adjusting entry on the last day of the accounting period. By reversing the adjusting entry, one avoids double counting the amount when the transaction occurs in the next period. A reversing journal entry is recorded on the first day of the new period.

    Instead of preparing the financial statements before the closing journal entries, it is possible to prepare them afterwards, using a temporary income summary account to collect the balances of the temporary ledger accounts (revenues, expenses, gains, losses, etc.) when they are closed. The temporary income summary account then would be closed when preparing the financial statements.

ACCOUNTING INFORMATION SYSTEM

An accounting information system (AIS) is the system of records a business keeps to maintain its accounting system. This includes the purchase, sales, and other financial processes of the business.

The purpose of an AIS is to accumulate data and provide decision makers (investors, creditors, and managers) with information to make decisions. While this was previously a paper-based process, most modern businesses now use accounting software. In an Electronic Financial Accounting system the steps in accounting cycle are dependent upon the system itself. Example: some systems allow direct journal posting to the various ledgers and others do not.

ACCOUNTING REFORM

Accounting reform is an expansion to accounting rules that goes beyond the realm of financial measures for both individual economic entities and national economies. It is advocated by those who consider the focus of the present standards and practices wholly inadequate to the task of measuring and reporting the activity, success, and failure of modern enterprise, including government.

The basic bookkeeping concepts underlying contemporary accounting date back about 500 years to Renaissance Italian practices. Obviously, the vast majority of articulations by modern standard setters have little in common with the accounting practices then used. Real debate concerns concepts such as whether to report transactions, such as asset acquisitions, at their cost or to report them at their current market values.

The former, traditional approach, appeals for its reliability but can quickly lose its relevance due to inflation and other factors; the latter, increasingly common approach, appeals for its relevance but may be less reliable due to its resort to appraisals or other subjective measures. This trade off is essentially impossible to overcome. The relative virtue of either approach depends on the subject matter in question.

PROFESSIONAL MANAGEMENT CIRCLES

Limited reforms within professional management circles have led in the past to activity-based costing, economic value added, regret and risk measures. Not only do most businesses raise capital based on numbers derived from current standards, there are extensive lobbying efforts by the accounting industry to keep those standards roughly as they are: complex, loopholed, and unable to be applied or audited easily by laymen. Heads of the U.S. Securities and Exchange Commission since the 1980s have consistently complained that this lobbying makes it impossible for them to apply meaningful reform, even in the wake of accounting scandals, e.g. that which felled Arthur Andersen in 2002.

NATIONAL ECONOMIES

Any comprehensive scheme of accounting reform is a major professional and academic enterprise; Typically it requires examination of the role of each of the fundamental factors of production, an analysis of capital indicating how many types there are and how each supports each factor of a production process.

A comprehensive scheme that would affect, for instance, the United Nations standards for national accounts, the rules of the Bank for International Settlements, or listing requirements on the major stock exchanges, would have to defend any change against critics that advocated lesser reforms - making it extraordinarily difficult to achieve simultaneous consent. Marilyn Waring, who deeply criticized the UN account system for systematically under-valuing the social and economic contributions of women, stated also that she had to read literally an entire room full of books in order even to understand the standards applied today.

It seems unlikely that most advocates of reform have the stamina to do so, nor the background required to debate each issue with economists or accountants that build their careers on the detailed extension and improvement of standards that already exist. Most critics considered reform prospects bleak. The critique from ecological economics was even more fundamental, claiming that most means of measuring well-being indicated that the developed nations were in a state of "uneconomic growth" through the 1980s and 1990s, due mostly to failures of measurement, most or all of which could be tracked back to the practice of using the Gross National Product as a means of making money supply decisions.

This is perhaps the most obvious and widely-held critique of current national accounting and economic growth reporting systems - the creators of the GNP and GDP measures themselves advise against its use as a single measure of economic growth - but politicians and press typically do so without caveat nor apology. Robert Costanza, Paul Hawken, Amory Lovins and others who advocate a consistent global system for valuing natural capital, note that failures in this area are particularly grim: promoting extinction, loss of biodiversity, climate change and destructive weather for the sake of such "growth". John McMurtry characterized this as "the cancer stage of capitalism". What makes "economic sense" under current standards, they argue, is in fact leading to ecological catastrophe, social conflict, and economic chaos.

One barrier to accounting reform are governments themselves. They have the authority to determine what are accepted accounting principles, while using questionable accounting practices themselves. Governments, for example, pay off operating costs with longer-term debt and thus overstate budgetary surpluses or conceal operating deficits. This is not unlike the allegedly fraudulent practices of some corporations.

Accounting Software

Accounting software is computer software that records and processes accounting transactions within functional modules such as accounts payable, accounts receivable, payroll and trial balance. It functions as an accounting information system. It may be developed in-house by the hotel or organization using it, may be purchased from a third party, or may be a combination of a third-party application software package with local modifications. It varies greatly in its complexity and cost. Since the mid 1990s, the market has been undergoing considerable consolidation, with many suppliers ceasing to trade or being bought by larger groups.

Modules

Accounting software is typically composed of various modules, different sections dealing with particular areas of accounting. Among the most common are:

Core Modules

- *Accounts receivable*—where the hotel enters money received
- *Accounts payable*—where the hotel enters its bills and pays money it owes

- *General ledger*—the hotel's "books"
- *Billing*—where the hotel produces invoices to clients/customers
- *Stock/Inventory*—where the hotel keeps control of its inventory
- *Purchase Orders*—where the hotel orders inventory
- *Sales Orders*—where the hotel records customer order for the supply of inventory Non Core Modules
- *Debt Collection*—where the hotel tracks attempts to collect overdue bills (sometimes part of accounts receivable)
- *Expense*—where employee business-related expenses are entered
- *Inquiries*—where the hotel looks up information on screen without any edits or additions
- *Payroll*—where the hotel tracks salary, wages, and related taxes
- *Reports*—where the hotel prints out data
- *Timesheet*—where professionals (such as attorneys and consultants) record time worked so that it can be billed to clients

Personal Accounting

Mainly for home users that use accounts payable type accounting transactions, managing budgets and simple account reconciliation at the inexpensive end of the market suppliers include:

Low End

At the low end of the business markets, inexpensive applications software allows most general business accounting functions to be performed. Suppliers frequently serve a single national market, while larger suppliers offer separate solutions in each national market.

Many of the low end products are characterized by being "single-entry" products, as opposed to double-entry systems seen in many businesses. Some products have considerable functionality but are not considered GAAP or FASB compliant. Some low-end systems do not have adequate security nor audit trails.

Mid Market

The mid-market covers a wide range of business software that may be capable of serving the needs of multiple national accountancy standards and allow accounting in multiple currencies. In addition to general accounting functions, the software may include integrated or add-on management information systems, and may be oriented towards one or more markets, for example with integrated or add-on project accounting modules.

Software applications in this market typically include the following features:

- Industry-standard robust databases (eg Microsoft SQL, Oracle, Pervasive)
- Industry-standard reporting tools (eg Cognos, Crystal)

- Tools for configuring or extending the application (eg an SDK, access to program code, the ability to be controlled via Visual Basic for Applications (VBA))

High End

The most complex and expensive business accounting software is frequently part of an extensive suite of software often known as Enterprise resource planning or *ERP* software. These applications typically have a very long implementation period, often greater than six months. In many cases, these applications are simply a set of functions which require significant integration, configuration and customisation to even begin to resemble an accounting system.

The advantage of a high-end solution is that these systems are designed to support individual hotel specific processes, as they are highly customisable and can be tailored to exact business requirements. This usually comes at a significant cost in terms of money and implementation time.

Vertical Market

Some business accounting software is designed for specific business types. It will include features that are specific to that industry. The choice of whether to purchase an industry-specific application or a general-purpose application is often very difficult. Concerns over a custom-build application or one designed for a specific industry include:

- Smaller development team
- Increased risk of vendor business failing
- Reduced availability of support

This can be weighed up against:

- Less requirement for customisation
- Reduced implementation costs
- Reduced end-user training time and costs

Some important types of vertical accounting software are:

- Banking
- Construction
- Medical
- Point of Sale (Retail)

Use by Non Accountants

With the increasing dominance of having financial accounts prepared with Accounting Software, as well as some suppliers claims that anyone can prepare their own books, accounting software can be considered at risk of not providing appropriate information as non-accountants prepare accounting information. As recording and interpretation is left to software and expert systems, the necessity to have a Systems Accountant overseeing the accountancy system becomes ever more important. The set up of the processes and the end result must be vigorously checked and maintained on a regular basis in order to develop and maintain the integrity of the data and the processes that manage this data.

FORENSIC ACCOUNTING

Forensic accounting is the specialty practice area of accounting that describes engagements which result from actual or anticipated disputes or litigation. 'Forensic' means suitable for use in Court, and it is to that standard and potential outcome that forensic accountants generally have to work. Forensic accountants often have to give expert evidence at the eventual trial. All of the larger accounting firms, as well as many medium-sized and boutique firms have specialist forensic accounting departments. Within these groups, there may be further sub-specialisations: some forensic accountants may for example just specialise in insurance claims, personal injury claims, fraud, construction, or royalty audits. Engagements relating to civil disputes may fall into several categories: calculating and quantifying losses and economic damages, whether suffered through tort or breach of contract; disagreements relating to hotel acquisitions - perhaps earn outs or breaches of warranties; and business valuation. Forensic accountants often assist in professional negligence claims where they are assessing and commenting on the work of other professionals.

Engagements relating to criminal matters typically arise in the aftermath of fraud. They frequently involve the assessment of accounting systems and accounts presentation - in essence assessing if the numbers reflect reality. Forensic accountants may be involved in recovering proceeds of crime and in relation to confiscation proceedings concerning actual or assumed proceeds of crime or money laundering. In the UK, relevant legislation is contained in the Proceeds of Crime Act 2002. Many forensic accountants are also Certified Fraud Examiners and/or Certified Public Accountants. Forensic accountants utilize an understanding of business information and financial reporting systems, accounting and auditing standards and procedures, evidence gathering and investigative techniques, and litigation processes and procedures to perform their work.

Forensic accountants are also increasingly playing more proactive risk reduction roles by designing and performing extended procedures as part of the statutory audit, acting as advisors to audit committees, and assisting in investment analyst research.

CREATIVE ACCOUNTING

Creative accounting and earnings management are euphemisms referring to accounting practices that may or may not follow the letter of the rules of standard accounting practices but certainly deviate from the spirit of those rules. They are characterized by excessive complication and the use of novel ways of characterizing income, assets or liabilities. The terms "innovative" or "aggressive" are also sometimes used. The term as generally understood refers to systematic misrepresentation of the true income and assets of corporations or other organizations.

"Creative accounting" is at the root of a number of accounting scandals, and many proposals for accounting reform - usually centering on an updated analysis of capital and factors of production that would correctly reflect how value is added. Newspaper and television journalists have hypothesized that the stock market downturn of 2002 was precipitated by reports of accounting irregularities at the Enron, Worldcom, and other business entities in the United States. One commonly accepted incentive for the systemic over-reporting of corporate income which came to light in 2002 was the granting of stock options as part of executive compensation packages. Since stock prices reflect earning reports, stock options could be most profitably exercised when income is exaggerated, and the stock can be sold at an inflated profit.

The most notable activist is Abraham Briloff (professor emeritus of CUNY Baruch) who for years wrote a column for *Barron's* that constantly analyzed breaches of ethics and audit professionalism among CPA firms. His most famous book is called *Unaccountable Accounting*. The profession, in turn, was not kind to Dr. Briloff but much of what he advocated has been forced on the industry in the wake of the Enron scandal. A lesser usage is in professional humor, when accountants poke fun at each other's more esoteric accountancy practices. According to critic David Ehrenstein, the term "Creative Accounting" was first used in 1968 in the film *The Producers* by Mel Brooks.

Creative Accounting Tactics

Although not technically wrong, many annual and quarterly reports and presentations dive heavily into theoretical scenarios where "one-time charges" to earnings are excluded. What this means is for example, a law suit settlement amount would be taken out of the reported profit in one big chunk, even if it is paid out little by little over time (this practice is called reserving). Often, when explaining the quarterly results, a CEO might say "Well if we didn't take this charge for the law suit, we would have made this much money". Very often, the hypothetical situations proposed get even more complicated. The main "creative" aspect to this is when a "one time" "exceptional" charge really is something that is very common to the business.

- Banks are able to lend out most of the money they receive in deposit (they also can lend money they borrow from other banks). However, to protect against bad loans, banks must keep aside a supply of money called a "reserve". The bank, within general guidelines, gets to set the size of this reserve to what it feels is prudent compared to how risky its outstanding loans are. However, when the bank wants to make it look like it made more money this quarter than last, one way to do that is to take money from the reserve and call it profit with the excuse that the loans are safer now than before and that amount was no longer needed.
- One of the main genres of "creative accounting" is known as slush fund accounting, whereby some earnings from this quarter are

hidden away just in case the profit from next quarter is not enough for the management to make their bonuses. This happened most famously at Freddie Mac. As of 2004 there is a large investigation underway to see if retroactive insurance policies from insurers such as General Re of Berkshire Hathaway were used for slush fund accounting. The question is if these insurance policies truly transferred some risk or were merely a slush fund.

- Creative accounting is not limited to large firms with banks of accountants. Smaller companies often use creative accounting, but for tax saving purposes rather than meeting bonuses or shareholder expectations. Salaries are sometimes included in profits to benefit from corporation tax rates being lower than personal tax rates and spouses are sometimes put on the books as employees though they may never have worked for the hotel. As smaller companies are generally subject to less onerous rules - and many of them fall below the limit required for a full annual audit every year - much of the creative accounting in this sector does not get a lot of publicity.

TRIAL BALANCE

If the journal entries are error-free and were posted properly to the general ledger, the total of all of the debit balances should equal the total of all of the credit balances. If the debits do not equal the credits, then an error has occurred somewhere in the process. The total of the accounts on the debit and credit side is referred to as the *trial balance.*

To calculate the trial balance, first determine the balance of each general ledger account as shown in the following example:

General Ledger

			Cash				*Accounts Receivable*				
.Sep	1	7500	Sep	15	100	Sep	17	700	Sep	25	425
	17	400		28	500						
	25	425									
Bel.		6825				Bel.	275				
	Parts Inventory					*Accountable payble*					
Sep	8	250C	Sep	18	275	Sep	28	500	Sep	8	250C
Bal.		2225							Bal.		2000
		Capital					*Revenue*				
		Sep	1		750C		Sep	17	1100		
		Bal.			7500		Bal.		1100		
Expenses											
Sep	15	1000									
Sep	18	275									
Bal.		1275									

Once the account balances are known, the trial balance can be calculated as shown:

Trial Balance

Account Title	*Debits*	*Credits*
Cash	6825	
Accounts Receivable	275	
Parts Inventory	2225	
Accounts Payable		2000
Capital		7500
Revenue		1100
Expenses	1275	
	10600	10600

In this example, the debits and credits balance. This result does not guarantee that there are no errors. For example, the trial balance would not catch the following types of errors:

- Transactions that were not recorded in the journal
- Transactions recorded in the wrong accounts
- Transactions for which the debit and credit were transposed
- Neglecting to post a journal entry to the ledger

If the trial balance is not in balance, then an error has been made somewhere in the accounting process. The following is listing of common errors that would result in an unbalanced trial balance; this listing can be used to assist in isolating the cause of the imbalance.

1. Summation error for the debits and credits of the trial balance
2. Error transferring the ledger account balances to the trial balance columns
    - Error in numeric value
    - Error in transferring a debit or credit to the proper column
    - Omission of an account
3. Error in the calculation of a ledger account balance
4. Error in posting a journal entry to the ledger
    - Error in numeric value
    - Error in posting a debit or credit to the proper column
5. Error in the journal entry
    - Error in a numeric value
    - Omission of part of a compound journal entry

The more often that the trial balance is calculated during the accounting cycle, the easier it is to isolate any errors; more frequent trial balance calculations narrow the time frame in which an error might have occurred, resulting in fewer transactions through which to search.

Journal entries

Closing Entries

At the end of the accounting period, the balances in temporary accounts are transferred to an income summary account and a retained earnings account, thereby resetting the balance of the temporary accounts to zero to begin the next accounting period.

First, the revenue accounts are closed by transferring their balances to the income summary account. Consider the following example for which September 30 is the end of the accounting period. If the revenue account balance is $1100, then the closing journal entry would be:

Date	*Accounts*	*Debit*	*Credit*
9/30	Revenue	1100	
		Income Summary	1100

Next, the expense accounts are closed by transferring their balances to the income summary account. If the expense account balance is $1275, then the closing entry would be:

Date	*Accounts*	*Debit*	*Credit*
9/30	Income Summary	1275	
		Expenses	1275

At this point, the net balance of the income summary account is a $175 debit (loss). The income summary account then is closed to retained earnings:

Date	*Accounts*	*Debit*	*Credit*
9/30	Retained Earnings	175	
		Income Summary	175

Finally, the dividends account is closed to retained earnings. For example, if $50 in dividends were paid during the period, the closing journal entry would be as follows:

Date	*Accounts*	*Debit*	*Credit*
9/30	Retained Earnings		50
		Dividends	50

Once posted to the ledger, these journal entries serve the purpose of setting the temporary revenue, expense, and dividend accounts back to zero in preparation for the start of the next accounting period.

Note that the income summary account is not absolutely necessary - the revenue and expense accounts could be closed directly to retained earnings. The income summary account offers the benefit of indicating the net balance between revenue and expenses (i.e. net income) during the closing process.

Reversing Entries

When an adjusting entry is made for an expense at the end of the accounting period, it is necessary to keep track of this expense so that the transaction will be allocated properly between the two periods. *Reversing entries* are a way to handle such transactions.

Consider the case in which a note is issued on the 16th of September, with interest payable on the 15th of October. If the total interest to be paid at the end of the 30 day period is $100, then half of the amount would be allocated to the month of September using the following adjusting journal entry:

Period-End Adjusting Entry

Date	*Accounts Title*	*Debit*	*Credit*
9/30	Interest Expense	50	
		Interest Payable	50
		15 days of accrued interest.	

On October 15, the 30 days of interest will be paid as a $100 lump sum. If the bookkeeper remembers that half of that interest already was recorded as an expense in September, then he or she can record only $50 as the interest expense for October. Alternatively, a *reversing entry* can be made at the beginning of October as follows:

Reversing Entry

Date	*Accounts Title*	*Debit*	*Credit*
10/1	Interest Payable	50	
		Interest Expense	50
		Reversing entry for	
		15 days of interest accrued in Sep.	

Note that the above journal entry is exactly the reverse of the adjusting entry made on September 30. Once this reversing entry is posted, the affected ledger accounts will appear as follows:

Ledger Accounts After Reversing Entry

	Interest Payable					*Interest Expense*		
Oct	1	50	Sep	3C	50	Oct	1	50
			Bal.	0		Bal.	50	

The interest payable account carried a credit balance of $50 over to the new period, and this balance became zero when the October 1 reversing entry was posted. Because the interest expense ledger account was closed at the end of the reporting period on September 30 (as were all expense accounts), its balance was reset to zero at that time. After the posting of the reversing entry on October 1, the interest expense ledger account had a credit balance (i.e. a negative expense balance) of $50.

On Oct 15, the note matures and the $100 interest is due. Because the reversing entry was made on Oct 1, the Oct 15 entry is for the full $100 that is due on the note, and is recorded as follows:

October 15 Journal Entry

Date	*Accounts Title*	*Debit*	*Credit*
10/15	Interest Expense	100	
		Interest Payable	100
		Interest for Sep 16 through Oct 15.	

The ledger accounts will appear as follows once the journal entries through October 15 are posted:

	Interest Payable						*Interest Expense*				
Oct	1	50	Sep	3C	50	Oct	15	100	Oct	1	50
			Oct	15	100						
				Bal.	100		Bal.	50			

The net interest expense for October then is $50, as it should be since the other $50 already was reported in September.

As can be seen in the ledger accounts, the net effect is that a $50 interest expense will be realized in October, and the full $100 of interest will be paid to the holder of the note.

Reversing entries are a useful tool for dealing with certain accruals and deferrals. Their use is optional and depends on the accounting practices of the particular firm and the specific responsibilities of the bookkeeping staff.

LEDGER BOOK

A ledger is the principal book for recording transactions in the hotel. Originally, the term referred to a book remaining regularly in one place, and so it was used of the copies of the Scriptures and service books kept in a church. According to Charles Wriothesley's *Chronicle* (1538):

The curates should provide a booke of the bible in Englishe, of the largest volume, to be a lidger in the same church for the parishioners to read on.

It is an application of this original meaning that is found in the commercial usage of the term for the principal book of account in a business house. Apart from these applications to various forms of books, the word is used for

- A small line immediately above or below the musical staff to contain a note such as middle C on the leger line just below the a staff with a treble clef, or an octave higher than concert A, or Hi A on the highland bagpipe, just above the staff with a treble clef. (often spelled leger)
- The horizontal timbers in a scaffold lying parallel to the face of a building, which support the "put logs" (also known by ligger);
- A flat stone to cover a grave, often inscribed as a memorial;
- A stationary form of tackle and bait in angling.

In the form "lieger", the term was formerly frequently applied to a "resident", as distinguished from an "extraordinary" ambassador.

LEDGER POSTINGS

The process of posting account payable transactions in Peoplesoft creates balanced accounting entries that can be transferred to a General Ledger system. Peoplesoft creates accounting entries for all payments. Posting payments in Peoplesoft Payables creates balanced accounting entries for all payment-related transactions. Payment-related transactions include manual payments, drafts, electronic funds transfers, system created and cancelled payments. After these accounting entries are generated, they are available for General Ledger journal generation.

The Payment posting run is activated by the production of cheques. Debits are made to creditor control accounts and the corresponding credit is made to the bank account. Note the accounting examples shown below. Entries are also made as necessary to foreign currency gain and loss accounts. Overall, the effect of this run is a 'clearing' of the creditors control to the extent of the total amount being paid in the cheque run. The Voucher posting run carried out by the Accounts Payable System posts transactions for claims and credit notes that have been budget checked. The creditors control accounts are recorded and the various expense accounts indicated by individual document lines are charged. The document posting run reports expenditure movements on non-salary expense account codes within each cost centre.

The University cash flow is monitored to ensure that sufficient funds are available to cover the cheques. The following examples illustrate the current accounting treatment for authorised and verified accounts payable.

1. A voucher claim is processed for the supply of five different items purchased for direct use. The claim has a system status of *postable* and is automatically selected by the system for posting to the ledger and acquittal of commitment.
   DR Expense (e.g., materials, services, publications, etc.) $1,000
   CR Creditors Control $1,000
   Individual document lines are posted to department/section and by expense account.
2. Two of the five items purchased are found to be faulty and are returned to the supplier. A credit note is issued for the full cost of the two items, and is authorised and verified.
   DR Creditors Control $400
   CR Expense $400
   The credit note line amount produces a credit adjustment to the account charging of the associated claim line. The vouchers are posted to the actuals (cash) ledger.
3. A cheque is drawn to pay the supplier the net amount owing.
   DR Creditors Control $600
   CR Bank $600
   The vouchers are posted to the actuals (cash) ledger.

Voucher Processing

In order for a voucher to be eligible for posting, it must meet the following criteria.

- All save validations passed
- Passed budget checking
- If Purchase Order Voucher - Matched (if applicable)
- Purchase Order must be posted (if applicable)
- Approved
- Entry Status set to postable
- The post checkbox clicked on
- Not already posted

Once a voucher has been posted, only its non-accounting information can be modified. If a change to accounting information is required for a posted voucher, you must first unpost it.

Payment Posting–Processing

Running payment posting allows you to create accounting entries for payments applied to vouchers. These accounting entries are then available for general ledger journal creation using the Journal generator. The Vouchers and Payments should be posted on any weeknight. Journal generators and General Ledger Interfaces should also be run on weeknights. If a voucher is unposted, any posted payments for that voucher will be automatically unposted.

To post a payment, use the following path in ESP Go ® Administer Procurement ® Create Payments ® Process ® Payment Posting Request ® Add or Update/Display

GENERAL LEDGER

The general ledger, sometimes known as the nominal ledger, is the main accounting record of a hotel business which uses double-entry bookkeeping. It will usually include accounts for such items as current assets, fixed assets, liabilities, revenue and expense items, gains and losses. The general ledger is a summary of all of the transactions that occur in the hotel. It is built up by posting transactions recorded in the general journal. There are seven basic categories in which all accounts are grouped:

1. Asset
2. Liability
3. Owner's equity
4. Revenue
5. Expense
6. Gains
7. Losses

The balance sheet and the income statement are both derived from the general ledger. Each account in the general ledger consists of one or more pages. The general ledger is where posting to the accounts occurs. Posting is the process of recording amounts as credits, (right side), and amounts as debits, (left side), in the pages of the general ledger. The listing of the account names and the sum of the account balances is called a trial balance. The purpose of the trial balance is, at a preliminary stage of the financial statement preparation process, to ensure the equality of the total debits and credits.

The general ledger should include the date, description and balance or total amount for each account. It is usually divided into at least seven main categories. These categories generally include assets, liabilities, owner's equity, revenue, expenses, gains and losses. The main categories of the general ledger may be further subdivided into sub-ledgers to include additional details of such accounts as cash, accounts receivable, accounts payable, etc. Because each bookkeeping entry debits one account and credits another account in an equal amount, the double-entry bookkeeping system will ensure that the general ledger will always be in balance; thus maintaining the accounting equation:

Assets = Liabilities + Shareholders' Equity

The accounting equation is the mathematical structure of the balance sheet.

ACCOUNTING AND BOOKKEEPING ENTRIES

The bookkeeping and accounting entries that are required are limited to those listed below. No others are needed. The customary accounts-payable and accounts-receivable ledgers are eliminated entirely where the procedures outlined are followed. The preliminary invoice which is prepared on the first or second day following the month of advertising shows the estimated billing price of the newspaper space for the prior month.

At the outset, it is known that this is not an accurate invoice. It is sent to the client for the primary purpose of collecting the monies due with a minimum of effort on behalf of the agency and the client.

In addition to serving this function, the preliminary invoice serves as a basis for entering the sales of space and the cost thereof. As a matter of accounting principle, the client is indebted to the agency as soon as the advertising appears, and certainly the agency is indebted to the publisher at such time. Therefore, for proper accounting, newspaper-space billing should be entered on the agency's books on or before the last day of the month in which the advertising was published.

Usually, it is not feasible for an agency to send the preliminary estimated bill to its client until the first or second day of the month following the advertising because it is desirable that all advertising ordered during the month be included. There is no objection to giving this invoice the date of the last day of the month of advertising, even though it is actually prepared on the first or second day of the following month. By dating the preliminary estimated invoice as of the last day of the month of advertising, it can be properly entered in the agency's books and records as of the month of advertising. The estimated invoices are usually prepared from approved estimates, media recommendations or signed schedules, since such records form a basis for securing the needed information without the necessity of again calculating the billing price of the space ordered in each newspaper.

These figures were already developed in preparing the estimate, schedule or media recommendation. To determine the cost of the space billed to the client on the preliminary estimated invoice, it is usual to multiply the billing price by eighty-five percent, since by far the majority of newspapers allow a fifteen percent agency commission. A cost figure which equals eighty-five percent of the billing price as shown on the estimated invoice is sufficiently accurate for recording this invoice and the cost of the space billed. A Sales and Cost Journal is one of the principal books of original entry of an advertising agency. All invoices sent to clients are entered in this record. A preliminary invoice would be entered in a Sales and Cost Journal. Note that the sale is recorded under newspaper billings, and the cost of the space is recorded under newspaper costs.

The final accounting entries will be made from totals taken from this Sales and Cost Journal at the end of each month and they will be discussed later. When the final detailed invoice is prepared, after all space has been measured and the insertion orders audited against publishers' bills, the totals as shown on this final invoice are entered in the Sales and Cost Journal. Note that from the gross totals on this invoice there has been subtracted the amount of the preliminary invoice, leaving a balance in both the billing-price column and the cost column. The balance in the billing-price column represents the amount still due to the agency by the client, and the balance in the cost column represents the adjustment of the estimated cost as originally shown on the preliminary invoice.

At the end of the month, each column in the Sales and Cost Journal is totaled, and the total of the column headed "costs, newspapers" represents a charge to "cost of newspaper sales" and a credit to "accounts payable" control account. The total of the column "sales, newspapers" represents a charge to "accounts receivable" control and a credit to "newspaper sales."

In examining these accounting entries, it is important to note that "accounts payable" control account is never credited until the client is billed. The "accounts payable" control account is supported in detail by the files of insertion orders and the preliminary invoices which have not been finally billed. In other words, the total cost of the space as billed on preliminary invoices for which no final billing has been completed, plus all insertion orders which have been billed but have not been paid, minus all insertion orders which have been paid but which have not been billed, represents the detail of the control account "accounts payable, space".

Magazines and Trade Papers: Billing, Paying and Accounting

The methods used to bill, pay and account for magazine space are similar to those used for performing the same functions in connection with newspaper space. For that reason, only the differences in the two procedures will be discussed in this chapter.

Contracts

Contracts for magazine space specify the amount of space to be used and in many cases specify the dates on which advertisements are to appear. They specify the type of space contracted for, such as inside front or back cover, the number of colors in which the advertisement is to be printed, etc. This is because magazines go to press so far in advance of publication date that they require this information in order to make up the magazine properly and reserve the required space for the advertiser. The contract issued to cover magazine space then, unlike the contract for newspaper space, completely describes the space contracted for, and for many purposes could be considered as a definite order.

Insertion Orders

An insertion order is issued by the agency to cover each month's advertising in a magazine. The magazine insertion orders are similar to the newspaper insertion orders except that it is unnecessary to provide for recording the amount of space used to publish the advertisement, since magazine advertisements are printed from plates and the advertisements always require the entire amount of space ordered by the agency.

Checking the Space

Many magazines' terms provide that the agency make payment for the space prior to the publication date. For this reason, it is not possible to verify the appearance of the advertising before paying the magazine's bill; and since the agency collects from its clients on or before the date that it is required to pay the publisher, the client must be billed before the advertising has actually appeared.

Two carbon copies of magazine insertion orders are required in the bookkeeping process. One copy is sent to the checking department where it remains until after the magazine has been received and the advertisement checked. The bookkeeping copy of the insertion order is sent to the accounting department immediately after it is issued. This copy of the insertion order is filed in a tickler file under the date on which the client should be billed (about fifteen days prior to the date on which the agency must pay the publisher). After the advertisement has been billed to the client and perhaps after the agency has paid the publisher, a copy of the magazine is received in the checking department and the advertisement is checked. The checking copy of the insertion order is then initialed by the checker to indicate that the advertisement appeared in proper form in the magazine, after which it is sent to the accounting department.

Billing the Advertising

Weekly magazines usually require payment from the agency on the tenth, fifteenth or thirtieth of the month of issue. Some monthly magazines require payment during the month preceding issue; others require payment during the month of issue. On the billing date, the bookkeeping copy of the insertion order is taken from the tickler file and an invoice is typed by reference to the insertion order which contains all the particulars required for billing. The date on which the invoice was prepared is noted on the insertion order and it is filed in a billed-and-unpaid file. No adjustment of the original billing is required in connection with magazine space for, unlike newspaper space, the advertisements in magazines always require the amount of space ordered by the agency.

Payments to Publications

When the bills are received from magazine publishers, the insertion orders covering the space are located in the billed-and-unpaid file. The publisher's bill is audited against the insertion order and the check is prepared. The date of the payment is entered on the insertion order which is then filed in a paid-and-billed file. In some instances, agencies pay magazine publishers before they bill clients. This condition occurs where the agency does not have sufficient credit with the publisher. The publisher may require in such cases that the agency pay for space on closing date (the date that the magazine goes to press).

Since under normal terms the agency cannot bill its client until ten or fifteen days prior to the date, on which the magazine would normally require the agency to pay for the space, it becomes imprudent for the agency to bill the client in time to receive the money to make the payment to the magazine publisher on closing date. When this condition occurs, the copy of the insertion order is taken from the unpaid-and-unbilled file, the payment is made and the date of the payment is indicated on the insertion order, which is then filed in a paid-but-unbilled file under the proper billing date. On the proper billing date the invoice is prepared and sent to the client. The billing date is noted on the insertion order which is then filed in the billed-and-paid file.

Radio Time: Billing, Paying and Accounting

Radio advertising requires "time on the air," radio performers and, in some cases, scripts, sound effects, recording, etc. Time on the air is purchased from either independent stations or networks, that is, groups of stations such as the National Broadcasting Company, American Broadcasting Company, Mutual Broadcasting System or Columbia Broadcasting System.

Advertising agencies, in some cases, purchase only the time on the air from the radio station or network; and they purchase the talent, sound effects and other required items separately. In other instances, the advertising agency purchases time on the air, the required talent, sound effects and production materials directly from the radio station or network. When this is done, it is called a "package," and the broadcast is referred to as a "package show."

The advertising agency receives a fifteen percent commission from the radio station on all charges for time on the air. Where package shows are purchased, or in other cases where either talent or production materials are purchased by advertising agencies from radio stations or networks, the radio station or network allows no commission to the agency on either talent or production materials; but it is usual for the agency to add 17.65 or 15 percent to the cost of talent and production materials purchased from networks or stations when computing the billing price of these items. (When 17.65 percent is added to the cost, the commission realized on the selling price—117.65 percent of the cost—is fifteen percent of the selling price.)

Contracts

Contracts for radio time or for package shows are prepared by the radio station or network that is selling the time to the agency. Note the difference between this and the procedure followed in publication advertising where the contract is prepared by the agency and sent to the publication.

Radio time and radio package shows are sold in units of weeks of broadcasting and regularly cover thirteen-week periods, or multiples thereof. In many cases, the cost of the "time on the air" is reduced as the volume of time used increases; thus, the rate for each week's broadcasting is less per broadcast when twenty-six weeks' time is contracted for than when only thirteen weeks* time is used.

Usually, where better rates are offered for longer periods of time, contracts between stations and agencies provide that, if the contract period is extended, then the rate per broadcast will be retroactively adjusted. If, for example, the station has better rates for a twenty-six-week period than for a thirteen-week period, and only a thirteen-week commitment is entered into originally, and the contract is renewed for an additional thirteen weeks, then there will be a retroactive rate adjustment to the first thirteen weeks of broadcasting, and the next thirteen weeks of broadcasting will be at the twenty-six-week rate.

Where talent is purchased separately by the agency, of course a separate contract is entered into between the agency and the talent. The contract for live talent, when it is made separately, must cover a period running concurrently with that covering the radio time on the air; for obviously the talent is useless without the time on the air. Just as obviously, time on the air is planned with specific talent which is purchased for a particular programme.

The contract between the station or network and the agency will be specific even as to small detail. It will cover the time that the radio show will be broadcast each day, on what day or days of the week the show will be broadcast, and all of the contingencies that could be anticipated, such as interruptions in the programme, omissions of broadcasts, etc.

Often the contracts between radio stations or networks and advertising agencies are non-cancellable contracts. This suggests the enormous contingent liability or commitment that an agency can have in connection with a radio show covered by a fifty-two-week contract. Before an agency signs a contract with a radio station or network, it is of course necessary that the agencies have a firm commitment from its client.

It is suggested that the client be required to sign a contract with the agency containing exactly the same terms and conditions as the contract that the agency is required to sign with the radio station or network. This is for the station's benefit as much as for the agency's. It also benefits the client, since it is certainly desirable that the client understand just what his commitment is—particularly in the case of radio advertising where the non-cancellable commitments can run into vast sums even in short periods of time.

In certain types of radio advertising, the agency is required to furnish the station or network with scripts, recordings or other materials for the show. Where this is the case, the agency is obligated to secure the needed items and furnish them to the radio station or network in advance of the broadcast date.

Usually, agencies have separate departments for the production of radio advertising, including scriptwriters and copywriters. The difference between the two titles is that scriptwriters write stories and copywriters write advertising copy. Some radio advertising of course requires no scriptwriting, sound effects, or other services or materials.

In the early days of radio advertising, advertisers and agencies attempted to verify the programs broadcast by each station by appointing individuals in each city to listen to the broadcast of the station located in that city and to file a report on the quality of broadcast, the content of the broadcast and the elapsed time required. This type of verification proved to be expensive and cumbersome. Some agencies and advertisers still check radio broadcasts through the advertisers' dealers or through separate third-party organizations of one type or another. But most advertisers and agencies rely on the honesty of the broadcasting station which furnishes affidavits certifying the fact that each broadcast charged for was actually performed.

Billing Work Sheets

After the agency has entered into a contract with a radio station or network, the essential information required for accounting purposes should be extracted from the contract so that it will be readily available from week to week and month to month as it becomes necessary to refer to such data for bookkeeping and accounting purposes. It is best to compile this information in an orderly fashion so that it can be more efficiently used by the agency's bookkeepers and clerks. A billing work sheet is a convenient form for extracting the needed information from radio contracts. Billing work sheets should clearly set forth all of the following information:

- Client name
- Station name.
- Station address.
- Name of the programme.
- Term of the contract.
- Commission rate.
- Cash discount terms.
- Times and days of the broadcasts.
- Rate per broadcast.

The billing work sheet should provide ample space for computing the amount due the station and the amount to be billed to the client for each week or month of the contract period. Some radio stations bill agencies on a weekly basis, others on a monthly one.

Where the agency is billed on a weekly basis, it sends invoices to clients each week; where it is billed on a monthly basis, it bills its client on the same basis. If weekly bills are sent, the computations and invoices are prepared on the last day of the week; monthly invoices are prepared on the last day of each month.

When the agency prepares the invoice to its client to cover either a week's or a month's broadcasting, those invoices are prepared on the basis of full performance, since on the last day of the week or month of broadcasting, the billing clerks have not yet received bills from radio stations and therefore cannot account for interruptions and omissions. The procedure for handling such omissions and interruptions will be described later. Billing work sheets should be arranged alphabetically by client, with each client's billing work sheets arranged alphabetically by station call letters.

Invoices to Clients

As was stated previously, invoices for clients are prepared by reference to the file of radio-billing work sheets. Invoices could be prepared by referring directly to contracts with radio stations, but these contracts are legalistic in form. Therefore, to excerpt the needed information would require considerable time.

It is for this reason that the billing work sheet is prepared as soon as the contract has been completed, so that then this work sheet can be referred to month in and month out until the contract has expired. A separate invoice should be prepared for each programme. This means that there could be two or more invoices covering broadcasting from the same radio station, since one client may purchase several programs from one station and each programme could be covered by a separate contract.

At least three copies of each radio-time invoice should be prepared by the advertising agency. The original is to be sent to the client; the file and bookkeeping copies are to be retained by the advertising agency. After the invoices have been prepared, all radio-time invoices for one client should be grouped together and attached to a summary invoice. Billing amount but the cost amount as well. In addition, space is provided on the bookkeeping copy of each invoice to record adjustments to the original invoice and payments to radio stations.

Payments to Radio Stations

When the agency first prepares the invoice that it sends to its client for the radio-time charges, that invoice is prepared on the basis of the number of broadcasts contracted for; at this time no adjustment is made for interruptions, omissions, etc. The bookkeeping copy of the client's invoice is designed to act in the same manner as a payment voucher.

In other words, it is used as the authorization for the payment to the radio station. This is because the agency, having billed its client for the radio time, can authorize payment in an amount not exceeding the legitimate cost of the items so billed. Of course it is necessary for the agency to verify the cost of these items by comparing the figures shown on the bookkeeping copy of the invoice with those shown on the radio station's bill to the agency. It is also necessary to examine the affidavit from the station to determine that all broadcasts scheduled actually were performed.

Bookkeeping copies of radio-time invoices to clients are filed by the agency in a file called "Billed but Unpaid Items." It is important to note that when an invoice is prepared, that invoice is entered in the Sales and Cost Journal and the cost of the radio time is thereby credited to accounts payable. Accounts-payable radio time is never credited until a client is billed, since this credit originates from entering clients' bills to the Sales and Cost Journal, as will be seen in greater detail by examination of the chapter "Chart of Accounts and Accounting Records." No radio station should be paid without a client's having been billed, as will be seen in the following:

When a bill is received from a radio station, affidavits verifying the broadcasts should accompany such bills. The bills from the radio stations are then audited against bookkeeping copies of invoices sent to clients (found in the "Billed-but-Unpaid" files). If no bill has been sent to a client for the item billed by the radio station, an invoice should be prepared before the radio station's bill is passed for payment. If the station's bill allows credits for interruptions or omissions, etc., then that information should be posted on the bookkeeping copy of the agency's invoice.

The check number and the amount paid to the radio station is to be noted on the bookkeeping copy of the client invoice, and the check is sent to the radio station. Duplicate copies of checks issued to radio stations are filed and the total of such duplicates at the end of the month is charged to "accounts payable, radio time." The bookkeeping copies of the original radio-time invoices sent to clients are now examined to determine if any billing adjustment is required.

FINANCIAL STATEMENTS

Financial statements (or financial reports) are a record of a hotel financial flows (revenues/expenses) and levels (assets/liabilities). Because these statements are often complex an extensive set of Notes to the Financial Statements and management discussion and analysis is usually included. The notes will typically describe each item on the Balance Sheet, Income statement and Cash flow statement in further detail. In many cases the notes are much longer than the financial statement they are elucidating.

The reason financial statements are required by many statutes is to require management of the enterprise to report to the owners and government. Debtholders, suppliers and employees, as well as internal mangement are other users of the statements. The POV of the statements though, is for the owner's use. Accounting is the language of finance. Financial statement presentation rules are the grammar. The statements are necessary for owners to asses management and make rational economic decisions.

Once the adjusting entries have been made or entered into a worksheet, the financial statements can be prepared using information from the ledger accounts. Because some of the financial statements use data from the other statements, the following is a logical order for their preparation:

- Income statement
- Statement of retained earnings
- Balance sheet
- Cash flow statement

Income Statement

The income statement reports revenues, expenses, and the resulting net income. It is prepared by transferring the following ledger account balances, taking into account any adjusting entries that have been or will be made:

- Revenue
- Expenses
- Capital gains or losses

Statement of Retained Earnings

The retained earnings statement shows the retained earnings at the beginning and end of the accounting period. It is prepared using the following information:

- Beginning retained earnings, obtained from the previous statement of retained earnings.
- Net income, obtained from the income statement
- Dividends paid during the accounting period

Balance Sheet

Balance sheet which describes a hotel's assets, liabilities and net equity at both a specific point of time and at the beginning of the period of time. It is constructed using the following information:

- Balances of all asset accounts such cash, accounts receivable, etc.
- Balances of all liability accounts such as accounts payable, notes, etc.
- Capital stock balance
- Retained earnings, obtained from the statement of retained earnings

Cash Flow Statement

The cash flow statement explains the reasons for changes in the cash balance, showing sources and uses of cash in the operating, financing, and investing activities of the hotel. Because the cash flow statement is a cash-basis report, it cannot be derived directly from the ledger account balances of an accrual accounting system. Rather, it is derived by converting the accrual information to a cash-basis using one of the following two methods:

- *Direct method:* Cash flow information is derived by directly subtracting cash disbursements from cash receipts.
- *Indirect method:* Cash flow information is derived by adding or subtracting non-cash items from net income.

Analogy of Financial statements

Knowing is not the same as understanding, so it is helpful to present an analogy.

- Think of an investment as a water reservoir. The value of the investment is the volume of water in it. The shareholder equity on the balance sheet measures this value.
- Streams empty into the reservoir, adding more water. These inflows are measured by revenues on the income statement.
- Streams run out of the reservoir, depleting it. These outflow are measured by expenses on the income statement.
- When a neighbour joins in the investment as a partner, he digs a canal from his own reservoir so it drains into yours. This additional water is measured by an increase in the share capital.
- When employees install an underground pipe to drain the reservoir into one of their own, the value of the investment falls. This draw is for stock options. Historically this drain has not been measured, and even now is not fully measured.

While measuring the volume of water in the reservoir at a point in time (balance sheet) is relatively easy, keeping track of the streams' volumes at every second of the year is difficult. Accountants may choose to ignore some streams: they may not know some streams exist: water may be evaporating, and unmeasurable. As a result the income statement is easily wrong. Regardless, the net sum of inflows less outflows should equal the difference in the reservoir (beginning vs. ending). The statement of changes in shareholder equity attempts this reconciliation.

None of the financial statements measures your own personal share of the reservoir when you have partners. It is up to the individual investor to measure, not the business totals, but his share. The methods to use 'equity per share' is shown at shareholders' equity.

Government Financial Statements

The rules for measurement and presentation of a government's financials may be different from those required for business and even for non-profit organizations. They may use either accrual accounting, or cash accounting, or a combination of the two. Because most governments may not lawfully spend money previously approved in a budget, the financial results are usually presented side by side with the budget.

Audit

Although the legal statues differ, most jurisdictions require an audit of the financials, by independent accountants, of all hotel businesses. Private ones can waive the requirement. Note that the auditors do not certify financial statements, that is done by the hotel's directors. All an auditor does is give an opinion on whether they are "true and fair" (or meet other particular requirements that the auditor is engaged to opine on).

There has been much legal debate over who an auditor is liable to. Since audit reports tend to be addressed to the current shareholders, it is commonly thought that they owe a legal duty of care to them. But this may not be the case as determined by common law precedent. In Canada, auditors are liable only to investors using a prospectus to buy shares in the primary market. In the UK, they have been held liable to potential investors when the auditor was aware of the potential investor and how they would use the information in the financial statements. Nowadays auditors tend to include in their report liability restricting language, discouraging anyone other than the addressees of their report from relying on it. Liability is an important issue: in the UK, for example, auditors have unlimited liability.

In the United States, especially in the post-Enron era there has been substantial concern about the accuracy of financial statements. Corporate officiers (the CEO and CFO) are personally liable for attesting that financial statements "do not contain any untrue statement of a material fact or omit to state a material fact necessary to make the statements made, in light of the circumstances under which such statements were made, not misleading with respect to the period covered by th[e] report". Making or certifiing misleading financial statements exposes the people involved to substantial civil and criminal liability. For example Bernie Ebbers (former CEO of WorldCom) was sentenced to 25 years in federal prison for allowing WorldCom's revenues to be overstated by $11 billion over five years.

Standards and Regulation

To ensure that financial statements prepared by different companies can be adequately compared, they must be prepared according to certain rules. Countries under the common law legal system usually follow guidelines set in generally accepted accounting principles ("GAAP"). National accounting bodies in each country have developed their own specific sets of accounting principles. Different countries have developed their own accounting principles over time, making international comparisons of companies difficult. Recently there has been a push towards standardising accounting rules made by the International Accounting Standards Board ("IASB"). IASB develops International Financial Reporting Standards that have been adopted by Australia, Canada and the European Union (for publicly quoted companies only), are under consideration in South Africa and other countries. The United States Federal Accounting Standards Board has made a commitment to converge the US GAAP and IFRS over time.

Inclusion in Annual Report

To entice new investors, most public companies assemble their financial statements on fine paper with pleasing graphics and photos in an annual report to shareholders, attempting to capture the excitement and culture of the organization in a "marketing brochure" of sorts. Usually the hotel's chief executive will write a letter to shareholders, describing the financial year in the most favorable light. In the United States, prior to the advent of the internet, the annual report was the main way that a corporation communicated with individual shareholders. Blue chip companies went to great expense to produce and mail out attractive annual reports to every shareholder. The annual report was often prepared in the style of a coffee table book. Financial statements and records have been produced for as far back as there has been human writing. The people in the old Mesopotamian societies operated both insurance and credit corporations, and had the obvious need of record keeping.

MODERN ACCOUNTANCY

The first book on accounting was written by a Croatian merchant Benedetto Cotrugli, who is also known as Benedikt Kotruljeviæ, from the city of Dubrovnik. During his life in Italy he met many merchants and decided to write, Della Mercatvra et del Mercante Perfetto (On Trade and the Perfect Merchant) in which he elaborated on the principles of modern, double-entry book-keeping. He finished his lifework in 1458. However, his work was not published until 1573, as a result of which his contributions to the field have been overlooked by the general public.

For this reason, Luca Pacioli, also known as Friar Luca dal Borgo, is credited for the "birth" of accounting. His Summa de arithmetica, geometrica, proportioni et proportionalita (Venice 1494), a synthesis of the mathematical knowledge of his time, includes the first published description of the method of keeping accounts that Venetian merchants used at that time, known as the double-entry accounting system. Although Pacioli codified rather than invented this system, he is widely regarded as the "Father of Accounting". The system he published included most of the accounting cycle as we know it today. He described the use of journals and ledgers, and warned that a person should not go to sleep at night until the debits equalled the credits! His ledger had accounts for assets (including receivables and inventories), liabilities, capital, income, and expenses — the account categories that are reported on an organization's balance sheet and income statement, respectively. He demonstrated year-end closing entries and proposed that a trial balance be used to prove a balanced ledger. His treatise also touches on a wide range of related topics from accounting ethics to cost accounting.

The first known book in the English language on accounting was published in London by John Gouge (or Gough) in 1543. It is described as A Profitable Treatyce called the Instrument or Boke to learn to knowe the good order of the kepyng of the famouse reconynge, called in Latin, Dare and Habere, and, in English, Debitor and Creditor.

A short book of instructions was also published in 1588 by John Mellis of Southwark, in which he says, "I am but the renuer and reviver of an ancient old copie printed here in London the 14 of August 1543: collected, published, made, and set forth by one Hugh Oldcastle, Scholemaster, who, as appeareth by his treatise, then taught Arithmetics, and this booke in Saint Ollaves parish in Marko Lane." John Mellis refers to the fact that the principle of accounts he explains (which is a simple system of double entry) is "after the forme of Venice".

A book described as The Merchants Mirrour, or directions for the perfect ordering and keeping of his accounts formed by way of Debitor and Creditor, after the (so termed) Italian manner, by Richard Dafforne, accountant, published in 1635, contains many references to early books on the science of accountancy. In a chapter in this book, headed "Opinion of Book-keeping's Antiquity," the author states, on the authority of another writer, that the form of book-keeping referred to had then been in use in Italy about two hundred years, "but that the same, or one in many parts very like this, was used in the time of Julius Caesar, and in Rome long before."

An early Dutch writer appears to have suggested that double-entry book-keeping was even in existence among the Greeks, pointing to scientific accountancy having been invented in remote times.

There were several editions of Richard Dafforne's book - the second edition in 1636, the third in 1656, and another in 1684. The book is a very complete treatise on scientific accountancy, beautifully prepared and containing elaborate explanations. The numerous editions tend to prove that the science was highly appreciated in the 17th century. From this time on, there has been a continuous supply of literature on the subject, many of the authors styling themselves accountants and teachers of the art, and thus proving that the professional accountant was then known and employed.

The requirements for entry in the profession of accounting vary from country to country. Accountants may be licensed by a variety of organisations, such as the British qualified accountancy bodies including Association of Chartered Certified Accountants (ACCA) and Institute of Chartered Accountants, and are recognized by titles such as Chartered Certified Accountant (ACCA or FCCA) and Chartered Accountant (UK, Australia, New Zealand, Canada, India, Pakistan, South Africa), Certified Public Accountant (Ireland, Japan, US, Singapore, Hong Kong, the Philippines), Certified Management Accountant (Canada, U.S.), Certified General Accountant (Canada), or Certified Practising Accountant (Australia). Some Commonwealth countries (Australia and Canada) often recognise both the certified and chartered accounting bodies. The majority of "public" accountants in New Zealand and Canada are Chartered Accountants; however, Certified General Accountants are also authorized by legislation to practise public accounting and auditing in all Canadian provinces, except Ontario and Quebec, as of 2005. There is, however, no legal requirement for an accountant to be a paid-up member of one of the many Institutes and other bodies which are effectively a form of professional trade union. Unlike the Law Society, which can legally stop a solicitor from practising, accountancy institutes do not have such authority. However, auditors are regulated.

Before the Enron and other accounting scandals, there were five large firms and were called the Big Five. Since Arthur Andersen's assurance practice split (after the firm was found guilty in the Enron scandal), with a plurality joining KPMG in the US and Deloitte & Touche outside of the US, Arthur Andersen left from the group. Previous to this there were also groupings referred to as the "Big Six" (Arthur Andersen, plus Coopers & Lybrand before its merger with Price Waterhouse) and the "Big Eight" (Ernst and Young prior to their merger were Ernst & Whinney and Arthur Young and Deloitte & Touche was formed by the merger of Deloitte, Haskins and Sells with the firm Touche Ross).

Enron turned out to be only the first of a series of accounting scandals that enveloped the accounting industry in 2002.

This is likely to have far-reaching consequences for the U.S. accounting industry. Application of International Accounting Standards originating in International Accounting Standards Board headquartered in London and bearing more resemblance to UK than current US practices is often advocated by those who note the relative stability of the UK accounting system (which reformed itself after scandals in the late 1980s and early 1990s). Accounting reform of a far more comprehensive sort is advocated by those who see issues with capitalism or economics, and seek ecological or social accountability.

According to Accountancy Age's 2005 league table, fee income amongst the Top 50 accounting firms in the UK rose from £6.3bn to £7.0bn. This followed two successive years in which fee income had declined, largely a result of the sale by some of the larger firms of their consultancy arms. As detailed in the next section, fee income in most business areas - audit, tax, corporate finance and consultancy - rose in the 2005 survey, with insolvency and wealth management being the only segments where revenue fell.

PricewaterhouseCoopers remains the largest firm with fee income totalling £1,780m followed by Deloitte (£1,350m), KPMG (£1,066m) and Ernst & Young (£945m). The combined revenue of the Big Four accounted for £5.0bn, 72% of the fee income of the Top 50, down from 78-79% in the years up to the 2002 survey and the third year in succession a decline in their share has occurred (Chart 1). Ernst & Young's fee income is the smallest of the largest four firms, but still over three times that of the next largest firm, Grant Thornton. The amount of fee income tapers off amongst the mid-tier firms so that in total there were only 25 firms that each generated more than £15m of revenue in the 2005 survey.

3

Cost Accounting

INTRODUCTION

Cost accounting is the process of tracking, recording and analyzing costs associated with the products or activities of an organization. In modern accounting, costs are measured in accordance with the Generally Accepted Accounting Principles (GAAP). GAAP reporting records historical events and assigns a monetary value to each event that has taken place. Costs are measured in units of currency by convention. Cost accounting could also be defined as a kind of management accounting that translates the Supply Chain (the series of events in the production process that, in concert, result in a product) into financial values. Managers use cost accounting to support decision making to reduce a hotel's costs and improve its profitability.

Cost accounting has long been used to help managers understand the costs of running a business. Modern cost accounting originated during the industrial revolution, when the complexities of running a large scale business led to the development of systems for recording and tracking costs to help business owners and managers make decisions. In the early industrial age, most of the costs incurred by a business were what modern accountants call "variable costs" because they varied directly with the amount of production. Money was spent on Labour, raw materials, power to run a factory, etc. in direct proportion to production. Managers could simply total the variable costs for a product and use this as a rough guide for decision-making.

Some costs tend to remain the same even during busy periods, unlike variable costs which rise and fall with volume of work. Over time, the importance of these "fixed costs" has become more important to managers. Examples of fixed costs include the depreciation of plant and equipment, and the cost of departments such as maintenance, tooling, production control, purchasing, quality control, storage and handling, plant supervision and engineering. In the early twentieth century, these costs were of little importance to most businesses. However, in the twenty-first century, these costs are often more important than the variable cost of a product, and allocating them to a broad range of products can lead to bad decision making.

Managers must understand fixed costs in order to make decisions about products and pricing.

For example: A hotel produced railway coaches and had only one product. To make each coach, the hotel needed to purchase $60 of raw materials and components, and pay 6 laborers $40 each. Therefore, total variable cost for each coach was $300. Knowing that making a coach required spending $300, managers knew they couldn't sell below that price without losing money on each coach. Any price above $300 became a contribution to the fixed costs of the hotel. If the fixed costs were, say, $1000 per month for rent, insurance and owner's salary, the hotel could therefore sell 5 coaches per month for a total of $3000 (priced at $600 each), or 10 coaches for a total of $4500 (priced at $450 each), and make a profit of $500 in both cases.

COST FUNCTION

The econometrical model which is used to analyse costs is a model in which explanatory variable represents total costs and endogenous variables represent factors that influence their level. Production quantity is the most important factor which determines the level of total costs.

TOTAL COST

In economics, and cost accounting, total cost describes the total economic cost of production and is made up of variable costs, which vary according to the quantity of a good produced and include inputs such as labour and raw materials, plus fixed costs, which are independent of the quantity of a good produced and include inputs that cannot be varied in the short term, such as buildings and machinery. Total cost in economics includes the total opportunity cost of each factor of production in addition to fixed and variable costs.

The rate at which total cost changes as the amount produced changes is called marginal cost. This is also known as the marginal unit variable cost. If one assumes that the unit variable cost is constant, as in cost-volume-profit analysis developed and used in cost accounting by the accountants, then total cost is linear in volume, and given by: total cost = fixed costs + unit variable cost * amount.

FIXED COST

In economics, fixed costs are business expenses that are not dependent on the activities of the business They tend to be time-related, such as salaries or rents being paid per month. This is in contrast to variable costs, which are volume-related. In management accounting, fixed costs are defined as expenses that do not change in proportion to the activity of a business, within the relevant period. For example, a retailer must pay rent and utility bills irrespective of sales. Along with variable costs, fixed costs make up one of the two components of total cost. In the most simple production function, total cost is equal to fixed costs plus variable costs.

AREAS OF CONFUSION

Fixed costs should not be confused with sunk costs. From a pure economics perspective, fixed costs may not be fixed in the sense of invariate; they may change but are fixed in relation to the quantity of production for the relevant period. For example, a company may have unexpected and unpredictable expenses unrelated to production. On the other hand, production output may vary sharply without changing the fixed costs.

Strictly speaking, there is not absolute fixed cost in long-run if the relevant range is long enough. Investments in facilities, equipment, and the basic organisation that can't be significantly reduced even for short periods of time without making fundamental changes are referred to as committed fixed costs. Discretionary fixed costs usually arise from annual decisions by management to spend on certain fixed cost items. In business planning and management accounting, usage of the terms fixed costs, variable costs and others will often differ from usage in economics, and may depend on the intended use.

Some cost accounting practices such as activity-based costing will allocate fixed costs to business activities, in effect treating them as variable costs. This can simplify decision-making, but can be confusing and controversial. In accounting terminology, fixed costs will broadly include almost all costs which are not included in cost of goods sold, and variable costs are those captured in costs of goods sold. The implicit assumption required to make the equivalence between the accounting and economics terminology is that the accounting period is equal to the period in which fixed costs do not vary in relation to production. In practice, this equivalenceies does not always hold, and depending on the period under consideration by management, some overhead expenses can be adjusted by management, and the specific allocation of each expense to each category will be decided under cost accounting.

TOTAL VARIABLE COST

Total variable cost is the opportunity cost incurred in the short-run production that depends on the quantity of output. As the name clearly implies, total variable cost is variable, it changes. If a firm produces a little output, then total variable cost is less. If a firm produces a lot of output, then total variable cost is more. A firm can avoid variable cost in the short run by reducing production to zero. This bit of information often comes in handy when the price received by a firm is so low that it falls short off covering variable cost at any positive quantity of production. As such, the firm might find it most "profitable" to cut losses by shutting down production and avoiding variable cost, until the price increases.

Variable Inputs

Total variable cost is usually, not always but usually, associated with inputs that are variable in the short run. For example, The Wacky Willy Company operates in the short run with labour as a variable input and capital as a fixed input. The cost associated with labour is a prime candidate to be a variable cost. This includes hourly wage payments to the workers and any hourly fringe benefits paid on behalf of the workers.

While labour is usually isolated as the variable input in the short run, most short-run production has other variable inputs, too. The Wacky Willy Company uses an assortment of other variable inputs, all of which are part of variable cost—including cuddly cloth, squeezeably soft stuffing, and thread that make up the Stuffed Amigos; electricity needed to run the machinery; and boxes, plastic wrapping, and other packing materials used to ship the Stuffed Amigos to customers. When The Wacky Willy Company makes more Stuffed Amigos, they incur a greater cost for these variable inputs.

Cost of Stuffed Amigos

The table to the right summarises the total variable cost of producing Wacky Willy Stuffed Amigos. The left-hand column is the quantity of Stuffed Amigos coming off the assembly line each minute, ranging from 0 to 10.

For reference, the right-hand column is the total cost of producing Stuffed Amigos, the combination of total variable and total fixed cost. The centre column is the total variable cost of producing each quantity, which is exactly $0 if no Stuffed Amigos are produced and rises to $43 if 10 Stuffed Amigos are produced. This is the essence of variable cost. Greater production entails greater total variable cost.

- The most obvious point is that total variable cost increases with increased production. Producing more Stuffed Amigos means higher total variable cost. This makes sense. To produce more Stuffed Amigos, The Wacky Willy Company needs to hire more labour and buy more materials. Because these inputs incur a cost, total variable cost rises with extra production.
- Moreover, total variable cost is zero when no Stuffed Amigos are produced. The Wacky Willy Company incurs no variable cost when they employ no workers and buy no materials—their variable inputs.
- A last note is that the incremental increase in total variable cost is NOT the same for each quantity. In other words, total variable cost does not rise at a constant rate. This incremental change in total variable cost reflects marginal cost, a key concept in the short-run production and supply decision of a firm.

Total Variable Cost Curve

The total variable cost curve graphically represents the relation between total variable cost incurred by a firm in the short-run product of a good or service and the quantity produced. The total variable cost curve for Wacky

Willy Stuffed Amigos production is emphasised in the graph to the right. Because total variable cost increases with the quantity produced, the total variable cost curve has a positive slope.

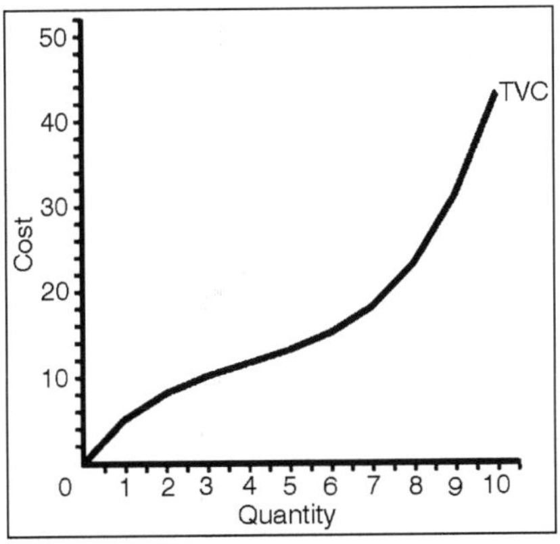

The most striking feature of the total variable cost curve is its shape. The total variable cost curve emerges from the origin, then twists and turns its way to $43. This curve begins relatively steep, then flattens, before turning increasingly steep once again. The slope of the total variable cost curve flattens as the first four Stuffed Amigos are produced due to increasing marginal returns found in Stage I of production.

The slope of the total variable cost curve becomes increasingly steeper after the fourth Stuffed Amigo is produced. This range of output corresponds with decreasing marginal returns, and the extremely important law of diminishing marginal returns, found in Stage II of production.

Average Variable Cost

Total variable cost can be used to derive a related variable cost concept–average variable cost. Average variable cost is simply variable cost per unit of output, which can be found by dividing total variable cost by the quantity of output.

If, for example, total variable cost is $43 and the quantity of output produced is 10 Stuffed Amigos, then average variable cost, that is the variable cost per unit produced, is $4.30 (= $43/10). The connection between total variable cost and average variable cost is mathematically represented by this equation:

A Fixed Alternative

Total variable cost is one of two components of total cost. The other is total fixed cost. Total fixed cost is the opportunity cost incurred in the short-run production by a firm that does NOT depend on the quantity of output.

A firm can produce a little output or a lot, increase or decrease production, or even stop producing altogether, but fixed cost remains unchanged. Total fixed cost is closely connected to the use of fixed inputs.

This means that total fixed cost is unaffected by the law of diminishing marginal returns. The connection between total cost, total variable cost, and total fixed cost is often summarised in this handy equation:

Total cost = Total fixed cost + Total variable cost

DETERMINANTS OF COST

The determinants of cost varies so much from firm to firm and from problem to problem that no general set is applicable to all. Nevertheless, there are a few determinants which are important enough in modern manufacturing enterprises so as to deserve special mention.

They are:

- Rate of output (*i.e.*, utilisation of fixed plant).
- Size of plant.
- Prices of input factors (materials and labour).
- Technology.
- Size of lot.
- Stability of output.
- Efficiency (of management as well as labour).

The word "cost" that we are using has different meanings in different settings. The kind of cost concepts to be used in a particular situation depends upon the business decision to be made. Hence an understanding of the meaning of various concepts is essential for clear business thinking. One way of getting clear-cut distinctions among different notions of cost is to set up several alternative bases of classifying costs and show the relevance of each for different kinds of problems. Although there are difficulties, workable approximations can be made if these concepts of cost can be developed by having (1) a clear understanding of the management problem and of the concept of cost that is relevant for it; (2) familiarity with the business and its records (2) familiarity with the business and its records an (2=3) ingenuity and boldness. These special cost-estimates are based mainly on the accounting and statistical records of the company, though sometimes they need to be supplemented by collection of special data.

COST MANAGEMENT

Cost management is the process by which companies control and plan the costs of doing business. Individual projects should have customised cost management plans, and companies as a whole also integrate cost management into their overall business model. There is no single accepted definition for this term, because it has such broad applications and possible strategies.

When properly implemented, cost management will translate into reduced costs of production for products and services, as well as increased value being delivered to the customer. For a company's management to be effective overall, cost management must be an integral feature of it. It is easiest to understand this concept if it is explained in the context of a single project.

For instance, before a project is started, the anticipated costs should be identified and measured. These expenses should then be approved before any purchasing occurs. During the process of completing a project, all incurred costs should be noted and kept in a record of some kind, to help ensure that the costs are controlled and kept in line with initial expectations, to the extent that this is possible. Taking this approach to cost management will help a company determine whether they accurately estimated expenses at first, and will help them more closely predict expenses in the future. Any overspending can also be monitored in this way, and either eliminated in future projects or specifically approved if the expense was necessary. Cost management cannot be used in isolation; projects must be organised and tailored with this strategy in mind. Starting a project with cost management in mind will help to avoid certain pitfalls that may be present otherwise.

If the objectives of the project are not clearly defined at first, or are changed during the course of the project, cost over-runs will be more likely. If costs are not fully researched before the project, they may be underestimated, thereby inflating the expectation of the project's success unrealistically. Construction projects are subject to their own particular challenges; these can include constraints in the form of laws and regulations that must be planned around.

If the project is completely and clearly defined, this will facilitate effective management of the costs it will incur. Effective cost management strategies will help a team deliver a finished project within the allocated budget, while also making it as valuable as possible to the company. There is always the possibility of unexpected costs, but preparation in the form of cost management will likely make them much easier to deal with when they occur.

BREAK-EVEN ANALYSIS

Break-even analysis is a technique widely used by production management and management accountants. It is based on categorising production costs between those which are "variable" and those that are "fixed". Total variable and fixed costs are compared with sales revenue in order to determine the level of sales volume, sales value or production at which the business makes neither a profit nor a loss.

THE BREAK-EVEN CHART

In its simplest form, the break-even chart is a graphical representation of costs at various levels of activity shown on the same chart as the variation of income with the same variation in activity. The point at which neither profit nor loss is made is known as the "break-even point" and is represented on the chart by the intersection of the two lines:

The line OA represents the variation of income at varying levels of production activity. OB represents the total fixed costs in the business. As output increases, variable costs are incurred, meaning tha t total costs also increase. At low levels of output, Costs are greater than Income. At the point of intersection, P, costs are exactly equal to income, and hence neither profit nor loss is made.

FIXED COSTS

Fixed costs are those business costs that are not directly related to the level of production or output. In other words, even if the business has a zero output or high output, the level of fixed costs will remain broadly the same. In the long term fixed costs can alter–perhaps as a result of investment in production capacity or through the growth in overheads required to support a larger, more complex business.

Examples of fixed costs:

- Rent and rates.
- Depreciation
- Research and development.
- Marketing costs.
- Administration costs.

VARIABLE COSTS

Variable costs are those costs which vary directly with the level of output. They represent payment output-related inputs such as raw materials, direct labour, fuel and revenue-related costs such as commission. A distinction is often made between "Direct" variable costs and "Indirect" variable costs. Direct variable costs are those which can be directly attributable to the production of a particular product or service and allocated to a particular cost centre.

Raw materials and the wages those working on the production line are good examples. Indirect variable costs cannot be directly attributable to production but they do vary with output. These include depreciation, maintenance and certain labour costs.

SEMI-VARIABLE COSTS

Whilst the distinction between fixed and variable costs is a convenient way of categorising business costs, in reality there are some costs which are fixed in nature but which increase when output reaches certain levels.

These are largely related to the overall "scale" and/or complexity of the business. For example, when a business has relatively low levels of output or sales, it may not require costs associated with functions such as human resource management or a fully-resourced finance department.

However, as the scale of the business grows then more resources are required. If production rises suddenly then some short-term increase in warehousing and/or transport may be required. In these circumstances, we say that part of the cost is variable and part fixed.

THE COST-ACCOUNTING STATEMENTS

The cost-accounting statements illustrated in this chapter are intended as guides. They show the general formats of reports that have been successfully used by modern advertising agencies. The individual client operating statement is a statement form on which the agency operations with one client are summarized. The amount of billings, costs and commissions for each type of advertising medium is shown, and the total of each class of direct expense is recorded. The gross profit from the operations is the difference between the commissions and fees on the one hand, and the direct expense on the other. This is the most significant one on the statement form and will be discussed further. Next, the statement shows the share of the general and administrative expense prorated to the client which, when deducted from the gross profit, produces the net profit resulting from the transactions with the particular client.

The over-all operating or profit-and-loss statement for the agency as a whole shows what has happened, and the individual client operating statement shows why it has happened. Since the individual client operating statement summarizes the result of the transactions with each client, it is necessary to support the statement with more detailed. Hie media billings and costs are self-explanatory and generally need no further analysis; however, when the actual figures for the period are at considerable variance with the budget or forecast, the detail of the actual figures can be secured by an examination of the Sales and Cost Journal. A separate page in the Sales and Cost Journal records the billings and costs from each client's business. The sheets contain separate columns for each medium so that the total billings or costs for any particular medium can be analyzed quickly by reference to the Sales and Cost Journal.

TIME RECORDS

The direct expenses include two classifications: salaries and expenses. The individual client operating statement shows the total cost of the time of each class of employee (executives, contact men, secretaries, copy, art, production, media selection, radio and other direct salaries). It is necessary to know how much of each employee's time was devoted to each client's work. No estimate allocating time be tween the various accounts served is reliable; and unless reliable figures are developed, the whole purpose of cost accounting vanishes. It is necessary for each creative employee in an agency to keep reasonably accurate time records, so that an accurate allocation of time costs can be made. It is not practical for every employee of the agency to keep a time record to show how many hours were devoted daily to each client. Some employees perform tasks that cannot be directly attributed to any one client's business. Others devote a few minutes at a time to each of several client's affairs.

A cost-accounting system should not be so burdensome that it consumes substantial amounts of time of valuable employees. For this reason, it is not desirable for an employee who does not devote at least a half-hour at a time to a client's account to keep time records. Employees who can keep reasonably accurate time records include contact men, research employees, copywriters, radio continuity writers, radio script writers, art directors and artists. Employees who may or may not be able to keep accurate time records without excessive effort include production-department employees, space buyers and checking-department employees.

Time records may be kept either on a daily, weekly or semimonthly basis. The shorter the interval, the more accurate the record is likely to be; for when weekly or semimonthly recording forms are used, the employee is likely to wait until the last day of the period before he fills out the record. The semimonthly form is usually the most convenient for accumulating the hours devoted to each client's account. If a daily or weekly form is used, it is suggested that the daily or weekly time reports be summarized onto a monthly schedule similar in form to the semimonthly time report. This semimonthly time report, it will be noted, contains clients' names from top to bottom along the left-hand margin of the sheet. It provides columns for each day in the semimonthly period. Where this form is used, the names of all the clients of the agency are mimeographed and the forms are distributed to all agency employees who keep these time records. At the end of each day, the employee records the amount of time devoted to each client's account.

A daily allocation in hours and half-hours is thought to produce sufficiently accurate time records. For the purpose of discussing the recording of agency employees* time and the allocating of this time to the various accounts served, employees are first divided into two classes called direct and indirect. Direct employees consist of those who work directly on clients' accounts. Indirect employees are those whose time only indirectly benefits the agency's clients. People in this latter class include bookkeepers and clerks, stenographers, receptionists, sometimes production employees, space buyers, etc. Usually the people in the first class keep time records allocating their time to the several accounts served, while the people in the second class usually do not. Direct employees sometimes devote part of their time to administrative work or to other duties that do not directly concern a particular client's business. In reporting the time devoted during the day, two methods are used. One method is to record only the hours devoted to clients' accounts, making no entry on the time sheet for the time devoted to work of a general or indirect character. When this method is followed, the total time reported by the employee, divided into the employee's compensation, produces a cost rate per hour. The costs applying to each client's account are then computed by multiplying the hourly cost rate by the number of hours reported as having been spent on each client's account. Since under this method the individuals make no report on administrative or general time, the only time reported is that devoted directly to clients' business. By charging each client on this basis, the cost of unallocated time is automatically absorbed by charges to clients, the absorption being proportionate to the portion of time devoted to each client.

Example: If an employee reports one hundred hours for a monthly period divided as follows:

Client	
A	40
B	50
G	10

and if the employee's monthly salary is $1,000, the hourly rate would be $10. Client A would be charged with $400, client B with $500 and client C with $100. Since the total of these allocated costs equals the employee's compensation, the time that the employee devoted to administrative or other classifications of work has automatically been allocated to clients in the proration shown. The other method used is to provide for showing on the time report the time devoted to indirect work. When this is done, the employee indicates the type of work performed and notes the number of hours devoted to each class of work such as administrative, accounting, sales promotion. When an individual's time reports include time devoted to general classifications of work not directly involving clients, the salary costs of the individual are prorated both to each client and to other classifications. The costs in the other classifications are charged to overhead and the overhead expenses are then prorated to the clients' accounts as described later.

Agency employees who have not been in the habit of keeping time records usually are reluctant to do so, feeling that they should not be subject to this menial work or to such detailed scrutiny of their efforts. In this connection, it is interesting to note that physicians, surgeons, dentists, attorneys, architects and accountants keep accurate records of the time devoted and services rendered to each client. Agency employees will find that the keeping of time records is of great help in eliminating waste and inefficiency. Time records are essential to the success of any advertising agency cost-accounting system. To keep these records requires only a few minutes a day on the part of each employee. The high-priced executive sometimes can assign this duty to his secretary, but in any event, the recording of time should be daily.

SCHEDULE OF DIRECT SALARIES

On the individual client operating statement, the total of each class of direct salaries is shown as it applies to each client's account. Obviously, if the cost of a particular class of direct salaries greatly exceeds the budgeted cost, management will want to know why. For this and other reasons, it is necessary that the total of each salary classification be broken down to show the items making up the total. A separate schedule supporting the individual client operating statement is used for this purpose; it is called "Schedule of Direct Salaries." This schedule shows the cost of each employee's salary that applies to the particular account. The items are arranged so as to group employees by classes of work. This grouping automatically provides for securing the total cost of each class of direct salaries, which total is shown on the individual client operating statement. The Schedule of Direct Salaries includes both the actual salary costs as they apply to each client, and the budgeted cost.

For this reason, the schedule form provides columns for reporting the current month's costs, the budgeted amount for the current month, the year-to-date actual cost and the budgeted amount for the year to date. The cost figures shown on the Schedule of Direct Salaries are the costs computed on the basis of the time devoted to each account as they are found from an examination of time records.

SCHEDULE OF DIRECT EXPENSES

The individual client operating statement shows the total of each class of direct expenses incurred in handling the client's account. When the actual figures vary in any important degree from the anticipated costs as shown by the budget figures, alert management will want to know the reason for the difference. The cost-accounting system that is described here has been developed so that all needed figures can be secured with a minimum of effort. The agency's expenses are recorded in a voucher register which is described in the chapter "General Books and Chart of Accounts." The Expense Voucher Register provides for recording expenses in such a manner that those items incurred directly because of one client's account are segregated. A recap of these items provides the detailed information for preparing the schedule of direct expenses. This schedule may include as much detail as management requires. Usually, it is set up in the manner, which provides for a heading covering each classification of expense, followed by a listing of the important items of expense incurred during the period, with the total of the expenses in each class. This total agrees with the amount reported for the item on the individual client operating statement. Where a classification of direct expense varies materially from the budget allowance for such items, management will examine the schedule of direct expenses.

Sometimes even the schedule is not in sufficient detail to provide the necessary information; in such cases, the data supporting the Expense Voucher Register of the agency are gathered together and submitted to management so as to show all of the details in connection with the particular item under scrutiny.

Allocation of Indirect Expenses

The overhead expenses of an advertising agency include the costs and expenses that do not directly result from the handling of one client's business. These expenses include indirect salaries. The indirect salaries include administrative, executive, accounting, secretaries, typists, bookkeepers, clerks. They may include production employees, media-department employees and part of the time of contact men or other creative people. Expense in this classification includes such items as rent, light, local telephone, stationery, dues and subscriptions, insurance, legal, auditing, etc. Various means have been employed to allocate general and administrative expenses as properly applying to the cost of serving each client.

In the cost-accounting system described, it is desirable to make an allocation of general and administrative expenses to the individual client operating statements, but it is not entirely essential. The choice of allocating or not allocating expenses in connection with the preparation of individual client operating statements must be management's choice and must be dependent on how management can best understand and interpret.

Where no allocation is made, the individual client operating statement ends with the gross-profit. In thinking of this figure, management must allow for both general and administrative expense and profit.

Where the expenses are allocated, the amount of such expense applying to each client is shown on the individual client operating statement, being deducted from the gross profit to produce the net operating profit resulting from handling each client's account. However, if an allocation of general and administrative expense is to be made, it is necessary to provide a basis for making such an allocation. In determining the basis for such allocation, the first question that must be answered is how scientific should the basis for allocation be? Ideally no one basis for allocation could apply to all items.

Example: The cost of preparing bills to clients and checks to publishers could be distributed on the basis of the number of transactions rather than on the relative dollar volume of the billing or payments. On the other hand, rent might be distributed in the same ratio as a distribution of salary costs of direct employees. A discussion of the various methods for distributing overhead or general and administrative expenses could fill a volume in itself. Here it will be limited merely to listing the various methods that have been used by agencies. These have been discussed in greater detail in the chapter on budgets.

1. Distribution of items on the basis of direct salaries.
2. Volume. (This distribution is made by first determining what part of the agency's commissions and fees was earned as the result of handling each individual client's business. The expenses are then allocated, using these ratios.)
3. Insertion orders. (Expenses may be allocated on the basis of the number of insertion orders issued.)
4. Purchase-order basis. (Expenses may be distributed on the basis of the number of purchase orders issued.)

COST-ACCOUNTING REPORTS MEAN

One of the peculiarities of the agency business grows out of the fact that the income for work performed is usually recorded on the books months after the completion of the work. This is because clients must be contacted and advertising plans conceived and developed long before they can appear in magazines and newspapers, as outdoor posters or as radio shows. Perhaps the greatest lag between the time of doing the work and the time of recording the income is in connection with foreign advertising. Sometimes this lag is more than one year, but there is always a considerable time lapse between doing the work and recording the income; for this reason, cost-accounting statements must be interpreted with care.

Obviously, the cost of serving a new client would not be covered by the income received during the first few months. Costs applying to new clients' accounts are always likely to be distorted in proportion to the income shown on the cost-accounting statement. One month's cost-accounting figures are always likely to be misleading in themselves. Therefore, the accumulative for the year to date are much more important than the figures for the current month. No conclusions should be made based on one or two months' operations; so where a few months' figures indicate the need for action it is generally best to adopt a "wait and see" attitude until longer experience can prove or disprove the tentative conclusions.

The gross-profit on the individual client operating statement is perhaps the most significant one on the report. The gross profit is the difference between the commissions and fees and the direct expenses. If the records are accurately kept there can be little or no question as to the accuracy of the gross-profit. Agencies should expect to realize a net profit (before Federal tax) of about three percent of gross billings or twenty percent of the commissions and fees. The gross-profit figure must be sufficiently large to provide for general and administrative expenses and profit. If the three-percent profit on gross billings (twenty percent of commissions and fees) is accepted as a reasonable, then after deducting this amount from the gross profit there must still remain an allowance sufficiently large to pay the agency's general and administrative expenses.

While it is difficult to generalize about advertising-agency costs and expenses because agencies differ so widely from one another in size and type of service performed, perhaps a rough guide can be given. General and administrative expenses in an advertising agency could vary from a low of ten percent of commissions and fees to a high of thirty percent of commissions and fees.

For the purpose of discussing methods of interpreting individual client operating statements, the following ratios are given as an example:

Commissions and Fees 100%
Direct Expenses 55
Gross Profit 45%
Indirect Expenses 25
Net Profit 20%

In the case of this example, a minimum gross profit of twenty-five percent is needed to meet indirect expenses alone, while forty-five percent is needed to meet indirect expenses and provide for a profit of twenty percent of commissions and fees.

Cost accounting in the agency business furnishes management with facts on which intelligent decisions can be based. Just how each person uses these facts varies considerably. A few suggestions can be made, however.

After one determines which accounts are profitable and which are not, both the unusually profitable account and the unusually unprofitable account should be investigated; for if an account is unusually profitable, it could be that the agency is not performing all the services that it should. If an account is not a profitable one, this does not necessarily mean that the agency should resign the business; rather, the facts should be studied to determine what, if anything, can be done to turn the loss into a profit.

The first investigation should be directed to determining whether or not the agency is spending too much money in consideration of the services to be performed. Sometimes high-priced personnel are assigned to small accounts that cannot economically justify the assignment. In such cases, different employees could be assigned. In other cases, it may be that the employees assigned to certain accounts are devoting too much time to them. This can be determined by a study of the work performed in comparison with that on other accounts. It may be that the client is receiving services that he does not require, and perhaps whole areas of work can be eliminated.

If a careful investigation discloses that the cost on an account cannot be reduced, then it is time to determine whether or not the operation for the period under study is a typical operation with the particular client. Perhaps some unusual work was performed; or it could be that the income for the particular period was less than average. If it is determined that the period under study is typical, and that, based on past operations, a continued loss could be expected as a result of the operations with the particular client, then if there is no feasible way of reducing the cost of performing the service, it is entirely practicable to request a service fee from the client to augment the commission income.

Perhaps the most significant facts which can be secured from an examination of the cost-accounting statements are found by comparing the budget figures with the actual figures for the period.

Usually, where a budget is carefully prepared, the difference between the two figures is caused by the fact that the operations took a different turn from that anticipated. Such differences continually occurring indicate the lack of control over the operations of the business. Adequate steps should be taken to set up controls that will work. Many agencies provide incentive systems offering bonuses or other incentives to key men, department heads, contact men, etc. They then hold these department heads, contact men and others responsible for operating an account within the budget.

In the routine preparation of cost-accounting statements, the agency's accounting department should compare the budget figures with the actual figures. Where important differences exist between the two figures, an analysis should be made to find the cause, and an explanation of each difference should be submitted to management along with the statements. The above are a few of the ways in which the facts secured from a cost-accounting system can be profitably used, but each individual will develop his own techniques for interpreting and using these facts.

There are no hard and fast rules that can be applied to determine the cost ratios for such items as contact cost, copy cost, art cost, etc. Neither are there established ratios which one can use to compare an agency's costs in connection with indirect expenses for items such as rent, supplies, dues and subscriptions, etc., because agencies' operations differ widely from one another just as the character of the agencies differs. The cost to service one account will vary widely from the costs incurred to service another.

A few surveys have been made of the agency business in an effort to establish general over-all ratios, and some figures are available from these surveys. The American Association of Advertising Agencies makes an annual survey of agency costs and operations, but the survey is limited to a study of the operations of some of the Association's members, and the results of the study are made available only to members of the American Association of Advertising Agencies. *Printers' Ink* recently inaugurated a study of agency operations and costs. The figures are available and may serve as general guides and ratios. In comparing the figures of a particular agency with general operating ratios, caution must be used, for it is difficult to find an agency that is "average."

BILLING, PAYING AND ACCOUNTING

The principles of accounting discussed in this chapter are used also in connection with other media. The differences of methods are in the detail rather than in the principles. Here, the matters of principle are discussed at some length. These principles were established with the following objectives in mind:

1. To achieve complete internal control for protection against errors and defalcations.
2. To function with the greatest simplicity and efficiency possible.
3. To gain promptness in completing operations.

The methods discussed have been carefully developed and tested over long periods of time. They have provided the ultimate in flexibility and ease of operation and at the same time have provided adequate controls to assure the greatest accuracy. One of the cardinal principles used throughout these procedures is that once a document has been prepared, it is not to be copied or recopied. Instead, the original document is used for various purposes by filing either the original or carbon copies and adding information to the document to complete a transaction.

It is sufficient here to repeat that when an advertising campaign is developed, a detailed list is prepared to show the space to be used in each newspaper, the dates for each ad, the size of each ad, the rate per line or inch, and the cost of each ad. The media recommendation, or a more formal schedule sometimes referred to as an estimate, is presented to the client for approval since the agency wants the client to be responsible to the agency before it makes commitments with papers. After clients have approved schedules or media recommendations, they are referred to as approved schedules or approved estimates. The approved estimate, schedule or media recommendation—depending on the form used by the agency—is sent to the media department so that contracts can be issued to the various papers.

Contracts

It is customary for agencies to protect their clients by issuing contracts to papers so as to assure the advertiser the best rates available. Usually, contracts with newspapers cover a period of one year. When a space-buying department receives a copy of an approved schedule or estimate, the first job of the department is to check the files to see if a contract has already been issued to each of the publications listed. Bear in mind that to protect a client, the agency must issue a specific contract with each publication in behalf of the specific client. Publishers do not recognize blanket contracts. These conditions set up the terms under which the agency buys the space. The recommended contract form provides for mailing in window envelopes and for the insertion of all the pertinent information in convenient order for later reference.

The contract should include: The name of the publisher, the name of the client for whom the space is being contracted, the name of the client's product that is to be advertised in the publication, the contract period, the position requested in the publication such as financial page, sports page, etc., the rate Usually, a contract for newspaper space calls for space as required for a period of one year. In some cases, a minimum quantity of space may be specified, such as five thousand lines. This practice is followed where the paper has a sliding-scale rate structure so that it becomes necessary to contract for a minimum quantity of space in order to secure a desired per-line rate. For example, where a client is to use more than five thousand lines of space, and the paper has one rate for less than five thousand lines and a lower rate for more, the contract would be issued for "five thousand lines or more."

There is a box on the upper right-hand portion of the contract headed "Rates for This Contract." There is considerable space provided in three vertical columns. The one on the extreme left has no heading. The second one has a heading "Contract Rate," and the third has the heading "Next Lower Rate."

This entire box with its three columns is used to show the various rates for different kinds of space. It is not uncommon for a newspaper to have five or six different rates. Papers always have different daily and Sunday rates. Some publishers publish both morning and evening papers and offer a combination rate where both the morning and evening editions are used. An additional combination rate may be offered for morning, evening and Sunday combinations. There may be still another rate for special positions, such as financial page, sports page, etc. If a client contemplates using different types of space which call for different rates, this information is noted in the box headed "Rates for This Contract."

This acknowledgment when filled in and returned by the publication amounts to an acceptance of the contract and all of its terms. Usually the acknowledgment when received is pasted or clipped to one of the copies of the contract that is retained by the agency. The usual thing is to make at least four copies of the contract, although additional copies may be required depending on the client's requirements and the organization of the agency.

Sometimes clients request copies of all contracts issued by the agency. In this case, a copy of the contract of course must be made for the client. The space-buying department of the agency needs to retain one copy of each contract, and the accounting department of the agency requires one copy of the contract. These three carbon copies are in addition to the original copy that is sent to the publisher.

The question of rates demands special consideration. It has been stated that many publications offer special rates where large quantities of space are used. This type of rate structure is called a sliding-scale rate structure. A newspaper may offer one rate for space used up to five thousand lines during a contract year. A lower rate may be offered for five to ten thousand lines and still a lower rate for ten to twenty thousand lines, with the lowest rate being offered for space used in excess of twenty thousand lines in a contract year.

There are both advantages and disadvantages in using the lower rates. When it is known that a client is going to earn a rate lower than the highest rate offered by the paper, and if the contract is issued for the total quantity of space that the client is expected to use during the contract year, the publisher will sometimes bill the space at the lower rate.

Example: If a paper offers, say, a twenty-five-cents-per-line rate for space up to five thousand lines and a twenty-cent rate for space in excess of five thousand lines used in one year, then if a contract is issued for five thousand or more lines to be used during the contract year, the publication in many cases will bill the agency at the twenty-cent rate. If the contract were issued for space as required during the contract year without specifying a minimum of five thousand lines, then the publication would undoubtedly bill the agency at the twenty-five cents-per-line rate.

The advantage in using the low rate is that if the paper bills the agency at the low rate, the agency then bills the client at this rate, and if the client uses the space anticipated, no adjustment need be made. On the other hand, a disadvantage is involved if the client fails to use enough space to justify the low rate, in which case the paper will bill the agency for the additional five cents per line on all space used during the contract year. The agency must then bill the client for this additional charge. This additional charge may be difficult to explain to the client and may lead to disputes and difficulties that would never have arisen if the client had been billed for the high rate initially and then, if he qualified for it, had received a credit for the next lower rate.

STANDARD COST ACCOUNTING

In modern cost accounting, the concept of recording historical costs was taken further, by allocating the hotel's fixed costs over a given period of time to the items produced during that period, and recording the result as the total cost of production. This allowed the *full cost* of products that were not sold in the period they were produced to be recorded in inventory using a variety of complex accounting methods, which was consistent with the principles of Generally Accepted Accounting Principles (GAAP) as established by the Financial Accounting Standards Board for reporting results of publicly owned companies. It also enabled managers to effectively ignore the fixed costs, and look at the results of each period in relation to the "standard cost" for any given product.

For example: if the railway coach hotel normally produced 40 coaches per month, and the fixed costs were still $1000/month, then each coach could be said to incur an overhead of $25 ($1000/40). Adding this to the variable costs of $300 per coach produced a full cost of $325 per coach.

This method tended to slightly distort the resulting unit cost, but in mass-production industries that made one product line, and where the fixed costs were relatively low, the distortion was very minor.

For example: if the railway coach hotel made 100 coaches one month, then the unit cost would become $310 per coach ($300 + ($1000/100)). If the next month the hotel made 50 coaches, then the unit cost = $320 per coach ($300 + ($1000/50)), a relatively minor difference.

An important part of standard cost accounting is a variance analysis which breaks down the variation between actual cost and standard costs into various components (volume variation, material cost variation, Labour cost variation, etc.) so managers can understand *why costs were different than planned* and take appropriate action to correct the situation.

WEAKNESSES OF STANDARD COST ACCOUNTING FOR MANAGEMENT DECISION MAKING

As time went on, standard cost accounting lost its usefulness for management decision making due to a variety of reasons:

- The practice of paying workers on a 'set-piece' basis changed in favour of paying on an hourly rate.

- Modern companies tend to have relatively low truly variable costs (primarily raw material, commissions or casual workers) and very high fixed costs (worker salaries, engineering costs, quality control, etc.).
- Equipment has become more complex and specialized and may be a very significant proportion of total costs.
- Changes in the level of full cost inventory create swings in profitability that are difficult to explain or understand. An increase in inventory can "absorb" costs of production and increase profits, while a decrease in inventory level will decrease profits.
- Organizations with a wide range of products or services have processes which are common to several finished items, making cost allocation irrelevant or misleading.

As a result of the above, using standard cost accounting to analyze management decisions can distort the unit cost figures in ways that can lead managers to make decisions that do not reduce costs or maximize profits. For this reason, managers often use the terms "direct costs" and "indirect costs" to replace the standard costing, to better reflect the way allocation of overhead is actually calculated. Indirect costs (often large) are usually allocated in proportion to either labour cost, other direct costs, or some physical resource utilization.

For example: If the railway coach hotel now paid its workforce a fixed monthly rate of $8,000 (total) and its other fixed costs had risen to $2,600/ month, the total fixed costs would then be $10,600/month. The unit cost to make 40 coaches per month would still be $325 per coach ($60 material + ($10,600/40)), but producing 100 coaches would result in a unit cost of $166 per coach ($60 + ($10, 600/100)), provided the hotel had the capacity to increase production to that level.

Managers using the standard cost for 40 coaches per month would likely reject an order for 100 coaches (to be produced in one month) if the selling price was only $300 per unit, seeing that it would result in a loss of $25 per unit. If they analyzed the fixed vs. variable cost distinction, they would see clearly that filling this order would result in a contribution to fixed costs of $240 per coach ($300 selling price less $60 materials) and would result in a net profit for the month of $13,400 (($240 x 100) - 10,600).

THE DEVELOPMENT OF THROUGHPUT ACCOUNTING

As companies have become more complex and begun producing a variety of products, the use of cost accounting to make decisions to maximize profitability has come under question. Managers learned in the 1980's about the theory of constraints and began to understand that *every production process has a limiting factor* somewhere in the chain of production. As managers learned to identify the constraints, they learned to use throughput accounting to manage them and *maximize the throughput dollars* from each unit of constrained resource.

For example: The railway coach hotel was offered a contract to make 15 open-topped streetcars each month, using a design which included ornate brass foundry work, but very little of the metalwork needed to produce a covered railway coach. The buyer offered to pay $280 per streetcar. The hotel had a firm order for 40 railway coaches each month for $350 per unit.

The hotel accountant determined that the cost of operating the foundry vs. the metalwork shop each month was as follows:

Overhead Cost	*Total Cost by Department*	*Hours Available*	*Cost per hour per month*
Foundry	$ 7,300.00	160	$45.63
Metalshop	$ 3,300.00	160	$20.63
Total	$10,600.00	320	$33.13

The hotel was at full capacity making 40 railway coaches each month. And since the foundry was expensive to operate, and purchasing brass as a raw material for the streetcars was expensive, the accountant determined that the hotel would lose money on any streetcars it built. He showed an analysis of the estimated product costs based on standard cost accounting and recommended that the hotel decline to build any streetcars.

Standard Cost Accounting Analysis	*Streetcars*	*Railway Coach*
Monthly Demand	15	40
Price	$280	$350
Foundry Time (hrs)	3.0	2.0
Metalwork Time (hrs)	1.5	4.0
Total Time	4.5	6.0
Foundry Cost	$136.88	$ 91.25
Metalwork Cost	$ 30.94	$ 82.50
Raw Material Cost	$120.00	$ 60.00
Total Cost	$287.81	$233.75
Profit per Unit	$ (7.81)	$116.25

However, the operations manager had just made improvements in the foundry equipment, and she knew there was idle time for the workers making coaches there. The constraint was the metalwork shop. She made an analysis of profit and loss if the hotel took the contract using throughput accounting to determine the profitability of products by maximizing "throughput" (revenue less variable cost) in the metal shop.

Throughput Cost Accounting Analysis	*Decline Contract*	*Take Contract*
Coaches Produced	40	34
Streetcars Produced	0	15
Foundry Hours	80	113
Metalshop Hours	160	159
Coach Revenue	$14,000	$11,900

Streetcar Revenue	$ 0	$ 4,200
Coach Raw Material Cost	$(2,400)	$(2,040)
Streetcar Raw Material Cost	$ 0	$(1,800)
Throughput Value	$11,600	$12,260
Overhead Expense	$(10,600)	$(10,600)
Profit	$1,000	$1,660

The president saw that the metalshop capacity was limiting the hotel's profitability. They could make only 40 railway coaches per month. But by taking the contract for the streetcars, the hotel could make nearly all the railway coaches ordered, and also meet all the demand for streetcars. The result would increase throughput in the metal shop from $6.25 to $10.38 per hour of available time, and increase profitability by 66 percent.

ACTIVITY-BASED COSTING

Activity-based costing (ABC) is a system for assigning costs to products based on the activities they require. In this case, activities are those regular actions performed inside a hotel. "Talking with customer regarding invoice questions" is an example of an activity performed inside most companies.

Accountants assign 100% of each employee's time to the different activities performed inside a hotel (many will use surveys to have the workers themselves assign their time to the different activities). The accountant then can determine the total cost spent on each activity by summing up the percentage of each worker's salary spent on that activity.

Each product or service is produced and delivered via the activities performed in the hotel. The accountant can then assign the different activities to the different products using an appropriate allocation method.

A hotel can use the resulting activity cost data to determine where to focus their operational improvement efforts. For example, a job based manufacturer may find that a high percentage of their workers are spending their time trying to figure out a hastily written customer order. Via ABC, the accountants now have a currency amount that will be associated with the activity of "Researching Customer Work Order Specifications". Senior management can now decide how much focus or money to budget for the resolutions of this process deficiency. Activity-based management includes (but is not restricted to) the use of activity-based costing to manage a business.

OPPORTUNITY COST

In economics, opportunity cost, or economic cost, is *the cost of something in terms of an opportunity forgone* (and the benefits that could be received from that opportunity), or *the most valuable forgone alternative*, i.e. the second best alternative. For example, if a city decides to build a hospital on vacant land that it owns, the opportunity cost is *some other thing* that might have been done with the land and construction funds instead. In building the hospital, the city has forgone the opportunity to build a sporting center on that land, or a parking lot, or the ability to sell the land to reduce the city's debt, and so on.

Opportunity cost need not be assessed in monetary terms, but rather can be assessed in terms of *anything* that is of value to the person or persons doing the assessing. For example, a person who chooses to watch, or to record, a television Programmeme cannot watch (or record) any other at the same time. (The rule still applies if the recording device can simultaneously record multiple Programmemes; there is going to be a limit, and if the number of desired Programmemes exceeds the capacity of the recorder, some of them will not be saved, and thus cannot be seen.) In any case, at the time the person chooses to watch a Programmeme, either live or on a recording, they cannot watch something else, and if they are not able to record another Programmeme showing at the same time, the opportunity to view it is lost (presuming the particular Programmeme is not repeated). Or another example, someone having a video game can choose to watch a Programmeme or play the video game on the TV; they can't do both simultaneously.

Whichever one they choose is a lost opportunity to experience the other. Assessing opportunity costs is funda-mental to assessing the *true cost* of any course of action. In the case where there is no explicit accounting or monetary the land for a parking lot, *or* the money that could have been made from selling the land, *or* the loss of any of the various other possible uses — but not all of these in aggregate, because the land cannot be used for more than one of these purposes.

However, most opportunities are difficult to compare. Opportunity cost has been seen as the foundation of the marginal theory of value. In some cases it may be possible to have more of everything by making different choices; for instance, when an economy is within its production possibility frontier. In microeconomic models this is unusual, because individuals are assumed to maximise utility, but it is a feature of Keynesian macroeconomics. In these circumstances opportunity cost is a less useful concept.

Pitfalls in the Calculation of Opportunity Costs

One has to be careful in calculating the opportunity cost of any course of action. There are two pitfalls in the way of such a calculation: some relevant costs may be ignored in the calculation or some costs that should not be included may be included. For example: Sunk costs should not be included in opportunity costs because once that cost is incurred, sunk costs are not part of the firm's alternatives because they cannot be put to alternative use. In a brief summary, an opportunity cost is the benefit lost from making one choice over another.

Marginal Cost

In economics and finance, marginal cost is the change in total cost that arises when the quantity produced changes by one unit.

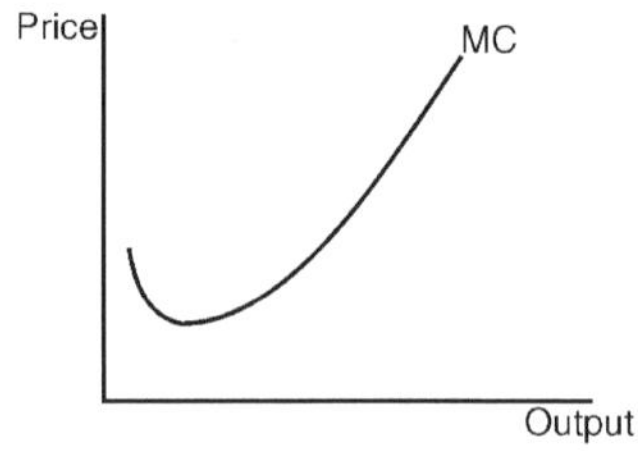

Fig. A typical Marginal Cost Curve

Mathematically, the marginal cost (MC) function is expressed as the derivative of the total cost (TC) function with respect to quantity (Q). Note that the marginal cost may change with volume, and so at each level of production, the marginal cost is the cost of the next unit produced.

$$MC = \frac{dTC}{dQ}$$

In general terms, marginal cost at each level of production includes any additional costs required to produce the next unit. If producing additional vehicles requires, for example, building a new factory, the marginal cost of those *extra* vehicles includes the cost of the new factory. In practice, the analysis is segregated into short and long-run cases, and over the longest run, all costs are marginal. At each level of production and time period being considered, marginal costs include all costs which vary with the level of production, and other costs are considered fixed costs.

It is a general principle of economics that a (rational) producer should always produce (and sell) the last unit if the marginal cost is less than the market price. As the market price will be dictated by supply and demand, it leads to the conclusion that marginal cost equals marginal revenue. These general principles are subject to a number of other factors and exceptions, but marginal cost and marginal cost pricing play a central role in economic definitions of efficiency.

Marginal cost pricing is the principle that the market will, over time, cause goods to be sold at their marginal cost of production. Whether goods are in fact sold at their marginal cost will depend on competition and other factors, as well as the time frame considered. In the most general criticism of the theory of marginal cost pricing, economists note that monopoly power may allow a producer to maintain prices above the marginal cost; more specifically, if a good has low elasticity of demand (consumers are insensitive to changes in price) and supply of the product is limited (or can be limited), prices may be considerably higher than marginal cost. Since this description applies to most products with established brands, marginal pricing may be relatively rare; an example would be in markets for commodities.

A number of other factors can affect marginal cost and its applicability to real world problems. Some of these may be considered market failures. These may include information assymetries, the presence of negative or positive externalities, transaction costs, price discrimination and others.

Cost Functions and Relationship to Average Cost

In the most simple case, the total cost function and its derivative are expressed as follows, where f(Q) is a cost function relating cost to production volume and FC represents fixed costs:

$$TC = FC + f(Q)$$

$$MC = \frac{dTC}{dQ} = \frac{d(FT + f(Q))}{dQ}\frac{df(Q)}{dQ}$$

Since (by definition) the fixed costs do not vary with production volume, the marginal cost *is not related to* fixed costs; the term drops out of the differentiated equation. This can be compared with average cost or AC, which is the total cost divided by the number of units produced and *does* include fixed costs.

$$AC = \frac{FC + f(Q)}{Q}$$

This result has important implications, since it indicates that the producer should choose to produce (sell) even if the market price is less than average cost, because the marginal revenue (the income received from selling the marginal unit) is greater than or equal to marginal cost. For example, an electric powerplant should produce and sell electricity when it is paid $20 per megawatt if its marginal cost is $15, despite the fact that its average cost (including the cost of building the plant, salaries, etc) is $25 per megawatt. Although the plant is "losing money", it has lost $5 *less* than if it had not sold the last marginal unit.

Transaction Cost

In economics and related disciplines, a transaction cost is a cost incurred in making an economic exchange. For example, most people, when buying or selling a stock, must pay a commission to their broker; that commission is a transaction cost of doing the stock deal. Or consider buying a banana from a store; to purchase the banana, your costs will be not only the price of the banana itself, but also the energy and effort it requires to find out which of the various banana products you prefer, where to get them and at what price, the cost of travelling from your house to the store and back, the time waiting in line, and the effort of the paying itself; the costs above and beyond the cost of the banana are the transaction costs. When rationally evaluating a potential transaction, it is important to consider transaction costs that might prove significant. A number of kinds of transaction cost have come to be known by particular names.

- *Search and information costs* are costs such as those incurred in determining that the required good is available on the market, who has the lowest price, etc.
- *Bargaining costs* are the costs required to come to an acceptable agreement with the other party to the transaction, drawing up an appropriate contract and so on. In game theory this is analyzed for instance in the game of chicken.

- *Policing and enforcement costs* are the costs of making sure the other party sticks to the terms of the contract, and taking appropriate action (often through the legal system) if this turns out not to be the case.

The term "transaction cost" is frequently thought to have been coined by Ronald Coase, who used it to develop a theoretical framework for predicting when certain economic tasks would be performed by firms, and when they would be performed on the market. However, the term is actually absent from his early work up to the 1970s. While he did not coin the specific term, Coase indeed discussed "costs of using the price mechanism" in his 1937 paper *The Nature of the Firm*, where he first discusses the concept of transaction costs. The term "Transaction Costs" itself can instead be traced back to the monetary economics literature of the 1950s, and does not appear to have been consciously 'coined' by any particular individual.

Arguably, transaction cost reasoning became most widely known through Oliver E. Williamson's *Transaction Cost Economics*. Today, transaction cost economics is used to explain a number of different behaviors. Often this involves considering as "transactions" not only the obvious cases of buying and selling, but also day-to-day emotional interactions, informal gift exchanges, etc.

The determinants of transaction costs are according to Williamson frequency, specificity, uncertainty, limited rationality, and opportunistic behaviour.

At least two definitions of the phrase "transaction cost" are commonly used in literature. Transaction costs have been broadly defined by Steven N. S. Cheung as any costs that are not conceivable in a "Robinson Crusoe economy" — in other words, any costs that arise due to the existence of institutions. To Cheung, "transaction costs", if the term is not so popular in economics literatures, should be called "institutional costs". But many economists seem to restrict the definition to exclude costs internal to an organization. The latter definition parallels Coase's early analysis of "costs of the price mechanism" and the origins of the term as a market trading fee.

Starting with the broad definition, many economists then ask what kind of institutions (firms, markets, franchises, etc.) minimize the transaction costs of producing and distributing a particular good or service. Often these relationships are categorized by the kind of contract involved. This approach sometimes goes under the rubric of New Institutional Economics.

IT's Relationship to Transaction Costs

Implementing a new information technology is generally seen as a means for reducing the transaction costs of an organization. However, in practice, implementing new IT often results in higher transaction costs. This is because the amount of information that needs to be processed by the organisation increases. This can result in information overload. Antonio Cordella and Kai

A. Simon call the cost of processing this information coordination cost. If these costs exceed the benefits of IT, then the implementation becomes something negative and expensive.

To reduce coordination costs, organizations can do one of two things:

- Improve information processing capabilities. This can be done either through implementing new information systems or creating lateral relations.
- Use IT to reduce the need for coordination through increased slack resources (which reduces the need for extreme precision) or increased reliance on self-contained tasks which provides more of the information to a single point of contact rather than requiring communications and coordination among multiple units. The decreased amount of information to process means lower coordination costs and lower transaction costs.

Technologies like enterprise resource planning (ERP) can provide technical support for these strategies.

Relationship to Transaction Costs

Firms, or more generally, organizations, develop and become larger over time, using more and more computers to work. This growth in the number of computers leads to a growth of software use (operating systems and their applications, for example) and, as a result, to the growth in the number of software use/access licenses to be purchased and managed. For the owners of software intellectual property rights, this process leads to a greater supervision of users to regulate/enforce lawful access to software.

The situation occurs when all of the software used by an organization is proprietary. This results in some costs — transaction costs — that are not usually taken into account by administrators and managers. The use of FLOSS - Free/Libre/Open Source Software leads to a reduction in transaction costs in terms of computation costs and in terms of the number of managed contracts, which can be numerically reduced by half.

MARGINAL COSTING

This method is used particularly for short-term decision-making. Its principal tenets are:

- *Revenue (per product)*—Variable Costs (per product) = Contribution (per product)
- *Total Contribution*—Total Fixed Costs = Total Profit or (Total Loss)

Thus it does not attempt to allocate fixed costs in an arbitrary manner to different products. The short-term objective is to maximise contribution per unit. If constraints exist on resources, then Managerial Accounting dictates that marginal cost analysis be employed to maximise contribution per unit of the constrained resource.

OTHER COSTING METHODS

More varieties of costing methods have been proposed in order to tailor for different aspects of the business. Some of the uprising ones include inventory costing method, process costing method, average costing method, target costing method. Still, the standard methods and normal costing methods are the most established methods in the world of public accounting. For management accountants in private industry, throughput accounting is rapidly becoming the standard for use in decision making in a fast-paced business environment.

COST-BENEFIT ANALYSIS

PRIVATE *VS.* PUBLIC GOODS

A private good is defined in economics as a good that exhibits these properties:

- Excludable—it is reasonably possible to prevent a class of consumers from consuming the good.
- Rivalrous—consumptions by one consumer prevents simultaneous consumption by other consumers. Private goods satisfies an individual want while public good satisfies a collective want of the society.

A private good is the opposite of a public good, as they are almost exclusively made for profit. An example of the private good is bread: bread eaten by a given person cannot be consumed by another and it is easy for a baker to refuse to trade a loaf.

One of the most common ways of looking at goods in the economy is the classic division based on:

- Is there a competition involved in obtaining a given good?
- Is it possible to exclude a person from consumption of a given good?
- Is it possible to exclude a person from consumption of a given good?

PUBLIC GOOD

In economics, a public good is a good that is non-rivalrous and non-excludable. Non-rivalry means that consumption of the good by one individual does not reduce availability of the good for consumption by others; and non-excludability that no one can be effectively excluded from using the good. In the real world, there may be no such thing as an absolutely non-rivaled and non-excludable good; but economists think that some goods approximate the concept closely enough for the analysis to be economically useful.

For example, if one individual visits a doctor there is one less doctor's visit for everyone else, and it is possible to exclude others from visiting the doctor. This makes doctor visits a rivaled and excludable private good. Conversely, breathing air does not significantly reduce the amount of air available to others, and people cannot be effectively excluded from using the air. This makes air a public good, albeit one that is economically trivial, since air is a free good.

A less straight-forward example is the exchange of MP3 music files on the Internet: the use of these files by any one person does not restrict the use by anyone else and there is little effective control over the exchange of these music files and photo files. Non-rivalness and non-excludability may cause problems for the production of such goods. Specifically, some economists have argued that they may lead to instances of market failure, where uncoordinated markets driven by parties working in their own self interest are unable to provide these goods in desired quantities.

These issues are known as public goods problems, and there is a good deal of debate and literature on how to measure their significance to an economy, and to identify the best remedies. These debates can become important to political arguments about the role of markets in the economy. More technically, public goods problems are related to the broader issue of externalities. Graphically, non-rivalry means that if each of several individuals has a demand curve for a public good, then the individual demand curves are summed vertically to get the aggregate demand curve for the public good.

This is in contrast to the procedure for deriving the aggregate demand for a private good, where individual demands are summed horizontally.

Terminology, and Types of Public Goods

	Excludable	Non-excludable
Rivalrous	Private goods food, clothing, cars, personal electronics national health service	Common goods (Common-pool resources) fish stocks, timber, coal,
Non-rivalrous	Club goods cinemas, private parks, satellite television	Public goods free-to-air television, air, national defence

Paul A. Samuelson is usually credited as the first economist to develop the theory of public goods. In his classic 1954 paper *The Pure Theory of Public Expenditure,* he defined a public good, or as he called it in the paper a "collective consumption good" ...[goods] which all enjoy in common in the sense that each individual's consumption of such a good leads to no subtractions from any other individual's consumption of that good...

This is the property that has become known as Non-rivalry. In addition a pure public good exhibits a second property called Non-excludability: that is, it is impossible to exclude any individuals from consuming the good. The opposite of a public good is a private good, which does not possess these properties.

A loaf of bread, for example, is a private good: its owner can exclude others from using it, and once it has been consumed, it cannot be used again. A good which is rivalrous but non-excludable is sometimes called a common pool resource.

Such goods raise similar issues to public goods: the mirror to the public goods problem for this case is sometimes called the tragedy of the commons. For example, it is so difficult to enforce restrictions on deep sea fishing that the world's fish stocks can be seen as a non-excludable resource, but one which is finite and diminishing. The definition of non-excludability states that it is impossible to exclude individuals from consumption. Technology now allows radio or TV broadcasts to be encrypted such that persons without a special decoder are excluded from the broadcast; however, an unencrypted Many forms of creative works have characteristics of public goods.

For example, a poem can be read by many people without reducing the consumption of that good by others; in this sense, it is non-rivalrous. Similarly, the information in most patents can be used by any party without reducing consumption of that good by others.

Creative works may be excludable in some circumstances, however: the individual who wrote the poem may decline to share it with others by not publishing it. Copyrights and patents both encourage and inhibit the creation of such non-rival goods by providing temporary monopolies, or, in the terminology of public goods, providing a legal mechanism to enforce excludability for a limited period of time.

For public goods, the "lost revenue" of the producer of the good is not part of the definition: a public good is a good whose consumption does not reduce any other's consumption of that good. The economic concept of public goods should not be confused with the expression "the public good", which is usually an application of a collective ethical notion of "the good" in political decision-making.

Another common confusion is that public goods are goods provided by the public sector. Although it is often the case that Government is involved in producing public goods, this is not necessarily the case. Public goods may be naturally available.

They may be produced by private individuals and firms, by non-state collective action, or they may not be produced at all. The theoretical concept of public goods does not distinguish with regard to the geographical region in which a good may be produced or consumed.

However, some theorists use the term global public good to mean a public good which is non-rival and non-excludable throughout the whole world, as opposed to a public good which exists in just one national area. Knowledge has been held to be an example of a global public good.

Collective Good

Collective goods are defined public goods that could be delivered as private goods, but are usually delivered by the government for various reasons, including social policy, and finances from public funds like taxes.

Note: Some writers have used the term public good to refer only to non-excludable pure public goods. They may then call excludable public goods club goods.

Examples

Common examples of public goods include: defence and law enforcement, public fireworks, lighthouses, clean air and other environmental goods, and information goods, such as software development, authorship, and invention. Some goods require special governmental incentives to be produced.

The provision of a lighthouse has often been used as the standard example of a public good, since it is difficult to exclude ships from using its services. No ship's use detracts from that of others, but since most of the benefit of a lighthouse accrues to ships using particular ports, lighthouse maintenance fees can often profitably be bundled with port fees. This has been sufficient to fund actual lighthouses.

Technological progress can create new public goods. The most simple examples are street lights, which are relatively recent inventions. One person's enjoyment of them does not detract from other persons' enjoyment, and it currently would be prohibitively expensive to charge individuals separately for the amount of light they presumably use. On the other hand, a public good's status may change over time.

Technological progress can significantly impact excludability of traditional public goods: encryption allows broadcasters to sell individual access to their programming. The costs for electronic road pricing have fallen dramatically, paving the way for detailed billing based on actual use. There is some question as to whether defence is a public good. Murray Rothbard argues, "national defence is surely not an absolute good with only one unit of supply. It consists of specific resources committed in certain definite and concrete ways-and these resources are necessarily scarce. A ring of defence bases around New York, for example, cuts down the amount possibly available around San Francisco. Jeffrey Rogers Hummel and Don Lavoie note," Americans in Alaska and Hawaii could very easily be excluded from the U.S., government's defence perimetre, and doing so might enhance the military value of at least conventional U.S., forces to Americans in the other forty-eight states. But, in general, an additional ICBM in the U.S., arsenal can simultaneously protect everyone within the country without diminishing its services."

The Free Rider Problem

Public goods provide a very important example of market failure, in which market-like behaviour of individual gain-seeking does not produce efficient results. The production of public goods results in positive externalities which are not remunerated. If private organisations don't reap all the benefits of a public good which they have produced, their incentives to produce it voluntarily might be insufficient. Consumers can take advantage of public goods without contributing sufficiently to their creation. This is called the free rider problem, or occasionally, the "easy rider problem".

The free rider problem depends on a conception of the human being as homo economicus: purely rational and also purely selfish-extremely individualistic, considering only those benefits and costs that directly affect him or her. Public goods give such a person an incentive to be a free rider. For example, consider national defence, a standard example of a pure public good. Suppose homo economicus thinks about exerting some extra effort to defend the nation.

The benefits to the individual of this effort would be very low, since the benefits would be distributed among all of the millions of other people in the country. There is also a very high possibility that he or she could get injured or killed during the course of his or her military service. On the other hand, the free rider knows that he or she cannot be excluded from the benefits of national defence, regardless of whether he or she contributes to it. There is also no way that these benefits can be split up and distributed as individual parcels to people. The free rider would not voluntarily exert any extra effort, unless there is some inherent pleasure or material reward for doing so. In the case of information goods, an inventor of a new product may benefit all of society, but hardly anyone is willing to pay for the invention if they can benefit from it for free.

Possible Solutions

Assurance Contracts

An assurance contract is a contract in which participants make a binding pledge to contribute to building a public good, contingent on a quorum of a predetermined size being reached. Otherwise the good is not provided and any monetary contributions are refunded.

A dominant assurance contract is a variation in which an entrepreneur creates the contract and refunds the initial pledge plus an additional sum of money if the quorum is not reached. In game-theoretic terms this makes pledging to build the public good a dominant strategy: the best move is to pledge to the contract regardless of the actions of others.

Coasian Solution

The Coasian Solution, named for the economist Ronald Coase and unrelated to the Coase theorem, proposes a mechanism by which potential beneficiaries of a public good band together and pool their resources based on their willingness to pay to create the public good.

Coase argued that if the transaction costs between potential beneficiaries of a public good are sufficiently low, and it is therefore easy for beneficiaries to find each other and pool their money based on the public good's value to them, then an adequate level of public goods production can occur even under competitive free market conditions. However, Coase famously wrote:

- "The world of zero transaction costs has often been described as a Coasian world. Nothing could be further from the truth. It is the world of modern economic theory, one which I was hoping to persuade economists to leave."

In some ways, the formation of governments and government-like communities, such as homeowners associations can be thought of as applied instances of practicing the coasian solution by creating institutions to reduce the transaction costs.

A similar alternative for arranging funders of public goods production, which is especially applicable to information goods, is to produce the good but refuse to release it to the public until some form of payment to cover costs is met. Author Stephen King, for instance, authored a new novel downloadable for free on his website while stating that he would not release subsequent unless a certain amount of money was raised.

Sometimes dubbed holding for ransom, this method of public goods production is a modern application of the street performer protocol for public goods production. Unlike assurance contracts, this relies on social norms to ensure that the threshold is reached and partial contributions are not wasted.

Government Provision

If voluntary provision of public goods will not work, then the obvious solution is making their provision involuntary. This saves each of us from our own tendency to be a free rider, while also assuring us that no one else will be allowed to free ride. One frequently proposed solution to the problem is for governments or states to impose taxation to fund the production of public goods.

This does not actually solve the theoretical problem because good government is itself a public good. Thus it is difficult to ensure the government has an incentive to provide the optimum amount even if it were possible for the government to determine precisely what amount would be optimum. These issues are studied by public choice theory and public finance. Sometimes the government provides public goods using "unfunded mandates". An example is the requirement that every car be fit with a catalytic converter. This may be executed in the private sector, but the end result is predetermined by the state: the individually involuntary provision of the public good clean air. Unfunded mandates have also been imposed by the U.S., federal government on the state and local governments, as with the Americans with Disabilities Act, for example.

Subsidies and Joint Products

A government may subsidise production of a public good in the private sector. Unlike government provision, subsidies may result in some form of a competitive market. The potential for cronyism can be limited with secret bidding for the subsidies or application of the subsidies following clear general principles.

Depending on the nature of a public good and a related subsidy, principal agent problems can arise between the citizens and the government or between the government and the subsidised producers; this effect and counter-measures taken to address it can diminish the benefits of the subsidy. Subsidies can also be used in areas with a potential for non-individualism: For instance, a state may subsidise devices to reduce air pollution and appeal to citizens to cover the remaining costs. Similarly, a joint-product model analyses the collaborative effect of joining a private good to a public good.

For example, a tax deduction can be tied to a donation to a charity. It can be shown that the provision of the public good increases when tied to the private good, as long as the private good is provided by a monopoly.

Privileged Group

The study of collective action shows that public goods are still produced when one individual benefits more from the public good than it costs him to produce it; examples include benefits from individual use, intrinsic motivation to produce, and business models based on selling complement goods.

A group that contains such individuals is called a privileged group. A historical example could be a downtown entrepreneur who erects a street light in front of his shop to attract customers; even though there are positive external benefits to neighbouring nonpaying businesses, the added customers to the paying shop provide enough revenue to cover the costs of the street light.

The existence of privileged groups may not be a complete solution to the free rider problem, however, as underproduction of the public good may still result. The street light builder, for instance, would not consider the added benefit to neighbouring businesses when determining whether to erect his street light, making it possible that the street light isn't built when the cost of building is too high for the single entrepreneur even when the total benefit to all the businesses combined exceeds the cost.

An example of the privileged group solution could be the Linux community, assuming that users derive more benefit from contributing than it costs them to do it. Another example is those musicians and writers who create music and writings for their own personal enjoyment, and publish because they enjoy having an audience.

Financial incentives are not necessary to ensure the creation of these public goods. Whether this creates the correct production level of writings and music is an open question.

Merging Free Riders

Another method of overcoming the free rider problem is to simply eliminate the profit incentive for free riding by buying out all the potential free riders. A property developer that owned an entire city street, for instance, would not need to worry about free riders when erecting street lights since he owns every business that could benefit from the street light without paying.

Implicitly, then, the property developer would erect street lights until the marginal social benefit met the marginal social cost. In this case, they are equivalent to the private marginal benefits and costs. While the purchase of all potential free riders may solve the problem of underproduction due to free riders in smaller markets, it may simultaneously introduce the problem of underproduction due to monopoly. Additionally, some markets are simply too large to make a buyout of all beneficiaries feasible – this is particularly visible with public goods that affect everyone in a country.

Introducing an Exclusion Mechanism

Another solution, which has evolved for information goods, is to introduce exclusion mechanisms which turn public goods into club goods. One well-known example is copyright and patent laws. These laws, which in the 20th century came to be called intellectual property laws, attempt to remove the natural non-excludability by prohibiting reproduction of the good. Although they can address the free rider problem, the downside of these laws is that they imply private monopoly power and thus are not Pareto-optimal. For example, in the United States, the patent rights given to pharmaceutical companies encourage them to charge high prices and to advertise to convince patients to persuade their doctors to prescribe the drugs.

Likewise, copyright provides an incentive for a publisher to act like The Dog in the Manger, taking older works out of print so as not to cannibalise revenue from the publisher's own new works. The laws also end up encouraging patent and copyright owners to sue even mild imitators in court and to lobby for the extension of the term of the exclusive rights in a form of rent seeking.

These problems with the club-good mechanism arise because the underlying marginal cost of giving the good to more people is low or zero, but, because of the limits of price discrimination those who are unwilling or unable to pay a profit-maximizing price do not gain access to the good. If the costs of the exclusion mechanism are not higher than the gain from the collaboration, club goods can emerge naturally.

James M. Buchanan showed in his seminal paper that clubs can be an efficient alternative to government interventions. On the other hand, because of the inherent inefficiency of club good provision, it is sometimes preferable to treat even naturally excludable club goods as public goods, and produce them by some other mechanism. Examples of such "natural" club goods include natural monopolies with very high fixed costs, private golf courses, cinemas, cable television and social clubs. This explains why many such goods are often provided or subsidised by governments, cooperatives or volunteer associations, rather than being left to be supplied by profit-minded entrepreneurs. These goods are often known as social goods.

Joseph Schumpeter claimed that the "excess profits," or profits over normal profit, generated by the copyright or patent monopoly will attract competitors that will make technological innovations and thereby end the monopoly. This is a continual process referred to as "Schumpeterian creative destruction", and its applicability to different types of public goods is a source of some controversy.

The supporters of the theory point to the case of Microsoft, for example, which has been increasing its prices, predicting that these practices will make increased market shares for Linux and Apple largely inevitable. A nation can be seen as a club whose members are its citizens. Government would then be the manager of this club. This is further studied in the Theory of the State.

Social Norms

If enough people do not think like free-riders, the private and voluntary provision of public goods may be successful. A free rider might litter in a public park, but a more public-spirited individual would not do so, getting an inherent pleasure from helping the community.

In fact, one might voluntarily pick up some of the existing litter. If enough people do so, the role of the state in using taxes to hire professional maintenance crews is reduced. This might imply that even someone typically inclined to free-riding would not litter, since their action would have such a cost. Public mindedness may be encouraged by non-market solutions to the economic problem, such as tradition and social norms. For example, concepts such as nationalism and patriotism have been part of most successful war efforts, complementing the roles of taxation and conscription. To some extent, public spiritedness of a more limited type is the basis for voluntary contributions that support public radio and television. Contributions to online collaborative media like Wikipedia and many other projects utilising wiki technology can also be seen to represent an example of such public spiritedness, since they provide a public good freely to all readers.

Groups relying on such social norms often have a federated structure, since collaboration emerges more readily in smaller social groups than in large ones. This explains why labour unions or charities are often organised this way.

Efficient Production Levels of Public Goods

Imagine that someone came to your door and asked you to pay twenty euros towards the cost of powering the street lamp out in the street for another year. The collector argues that the street lamp provides you with light to help you see at night when you are driving or walking home. A public good is provided efficiently at the level where the combined marginal rate of substitution of all individuals is equal to the marginal rate of transformation.

When should a public good be provided? To emphasise the basic principle, consider a community composed of just two consumers. The government is considering whether or not to provide a park. Arthur is prepared to pay up to £200 for use of the park, while Julia is willing to pay up to £100.

The total value to the two individuals of having the park is £300. If it can be produced for £225, there is a £75 gain on its production since it provides services that the community values at £300 at a cost of only £225. Regardless of the method of providing public goods, the efficient level of such provision is still being subjected to economic analysis.

For instance, the Samuelson condition calculates the efficient level of public goods production to be where the ratio of the marginal social cost of public and private goods production equals the ratio of the marginal social benefit of public and private goods production. "If the amount of a public good can be varied continuously, the optimal quantity to produce is that quantity for which the marginal cost of the last unit is just equal to the sum of the prices that all consumers would be willing to pay for that unit." This equilibrium guarantees that the last unit of the public good costs as much to produce as the value that it gives to all of its consumers.

4

Management and the Accounting Information

DEFINITION OF MANAGEMENT

Management in all business areas and organizational activities are the acts of getting people together to accomplish desired goals and objectives. Management comprises planning, organizing, staffing, leading or directing, and controlling an organization or effort for the purpose of accomplishing a goal. Resourcing encompasses the deployment and manipulation of human resources, financial resources, technological resources, and natural resources.

Because organizations can be viewed as systems, management can also be defined as human action, including design, to facilitate the production of useful outcomes from a system. This view opens the opportunity to 'manage' oneself, a pre-requisite to attempting to manage others

Management can also refer to the person or people who perform the act(s) of management.

The verb manage comes from the Italian maneggiare, which in turn derives from the Latin manus. The French word mesnagement influenced the development in meaning of the English word management in the 17th and 18th centuries.

Some definitions of management are:

- Organisation and coordination of the activities of an enterprise in accordance with certain policies and in achievement of clearly defined objectives. Management is often included as a factor of production along with machines, materials, and money.
- Directors and managers who have the power and responsibility to make decisions to manage an enterprise. As a discipline, management comprises the interlocking functions of formulating corporate policy and organizing, planning, controlling, and directing the firm's resources to achieve the policy's objectives. The size of management can range from one person in a small firm to hundreds or thousands of managers in multinational companies.

In large firms the board of directors formulates the policy which is implemented by the chief executive officer.

Mary Parker Follett, who wrote on the topic in the early twentieth century, defined management as "the art of getting things done through people". She also described management as philosophy. One can also think of management functionally, as the action of measuring a quantity on a regular basis and of adjusting some initial plan; or as the actions taken to reach one's intended goal. This applies even in situations where planning does not take place.

From this perspective, Frenchman Henri Fayol considers management to consist of seven functions:

- Planning
- Organizing
- Leading
- Coordinating
- Controlling
- Staffing
- Motivating

Some people, however, find this definition, while useful, far too narrow. The phrase "management is what managers do" occurs widely, suggesting the difficulty of defining management, the shifting nature of definitions, and the connection of managerial practices with the existence of a managerial cadre or class.

One habit of thought regards management as equivalent to "business administration" and thus excludes management in places outside commerce, as for example in charities and in the public sector. More realistically, however, every organization must manage its work, people, processes, technology, etc. in order to maximize its effectiveness. Nonetheless, many people refer to university departments which teach management as "business schools." Some institutions use that name while others employ the more inclusive term "management."

English speakers may also use the term"management" or"the management" as a collective word describing the managers of an organization, for example of a corporation. Historically this use of the term was often contrasted with the term"Labour" referring to those being managed.

In for-profit work, management has as its primary function the satisfaction of a range of stakeholders. This typically involves making a profit, creating valued products at a reasonable cost, and providing rewarding employment opportunities. In nonprofit management, add the importance of keeping the faith of donors. In most models of management/governance, shareholders vote for the board of directors, and the board then hires senior management. Some organizations have experimented with other methods of selecting or reviewing managers; but this occurs only very rarely.

In the public sector of countries constituted as representative democracies, voters elect politicians to public office. Such politicians hire many managers and administrators, and in some countries like the United States political appointees lose their jobs on the election of a new president/governor/mayor. Difficulties arise in tracing the history of management.

Some see it as a late modern conceptualization. On those terms it cannot have a pre-modern history, only harbingers. Others, however, detect management-like-thought back to Sumerian traders and to the builders of the pyramids of ancient Egypt. Slave-owners through the centuries faced the problems of exploiting/motivating a dependent but sometimes unenthusiastic or recalcitrant workforce, but many pre-industrial enterprises, given their small scale, did not feel compelled to face the issues of management systematically.

However, innovations such as the spread of Arabic numerals and the codification of double-entry book-keeping provided tools for management assessment, planning and control.

Given the scale of most commercial operations and the lack of mechanized record-keeping and recording before the industrial revolution, it made sense for most owners of enterprises in those times to carry out management functions by and for themselves. But with growing size and complexity of organizations, the split between owners and day-to-day managers gradually became more common.

MANAGEMENT AS A PROCESS

As a process, management refers to a series of inter – related functions. It is the process by which management creates, operates and directs purposive organization through systematic, coordinated and co-operated human efforts, George R. Terry, "Management is a distinct process consisting of planning, organizing, actuating and controlling, performed to determine and accomplish stated objective by the use of human beings and other resources".

As a process, management consists of three aspects:

- Management is a social process – Since human factor is most important among the other factors, therefore management is concerned with developing relationship among people. It is the duty of management to make interaction between people – productive and useful for obtaining organizational goals.
- Management is an integrating process – Management undertakes the job of bringing together human physical and financial resources so as to achieve organizational purpose. Therefore, is an important function to bring harmony between various factors.
- Management is a continuous process – It is a never ending process. It is concerned with constantly identifying the problem and solving them by taking adequate steps. It is an on-going process.

MANAGEMENT AS AN ACTIVITY

Like various other activities performed by human beings such as writing, playing, eating, cooking etc, management is also an activity because a manager is one who accomplishes the objectives by directing the efforts of others. Koontz, *"Management is what a manager does"*.

Management as an activity includes:

- *Informational activities*: In the functioning of business enterprise, the manager constantly has to receive and give information orally or in written. A communication link has to be maintained with subordinates as well as superiors for effective functioning of an enterprise.
- *Decisional activities*: Practically all types of managerial activities are based on one or the other types of decisions. Therefore, managers are continuously involved in decisions of different kinds since the decision made by one manager becomes the basis of action to be taken by other managers..
- *Inter-personal activities*: Management involves achieving goals through people. Therefore, managers have to interact with superiors as well as the sub-ordinates. They must maintain good relations with them. The inter-personal activities include with the sub-ordinates and taking care of the problem.

MANAGEMENT AS A DISCIPLINE

Management as a discipline refers to that branch of knowledge which is connected to study of principles and practices of basic administration.

It specifies certain code of conduct to be followed by the manager and also various methods for managing resources efficiently. Management as a discipline specifies certain code of conduct for managers and indicates various methods of managing an enterprise. Management is a course of study which is now formally being taught in the institutes and universities after completing a prescribed course or by obtaining degree or diploma in management, a person can get employment as a manager.

Any branch of knowledge that fulfils following two requirements is known as discipline:

- There must be scholars and thinkers who communicate relevant knowledge through research and publications.
- The knowledge should be formally imparted by education and training programmes.

Since management satisfies both these problems, therefore it qualifies to be a discipline. Though it is comparatively a new discipline but it is growing at a faster pace.

ACCOUNTING FACILITATES CORPORATE AND INVESTMENT DECISIONS

Accounting, the standard language by which such financial information can be assessed and compared, is fundamental to making these decisions.

USES OF ACCOUNTING

Accounting is used by a variety of organizations, from the federal government to nonprofit organizations to small businesses to corporations. As suggested, be discussing accounting rules as they pertain to publicly traded companies.

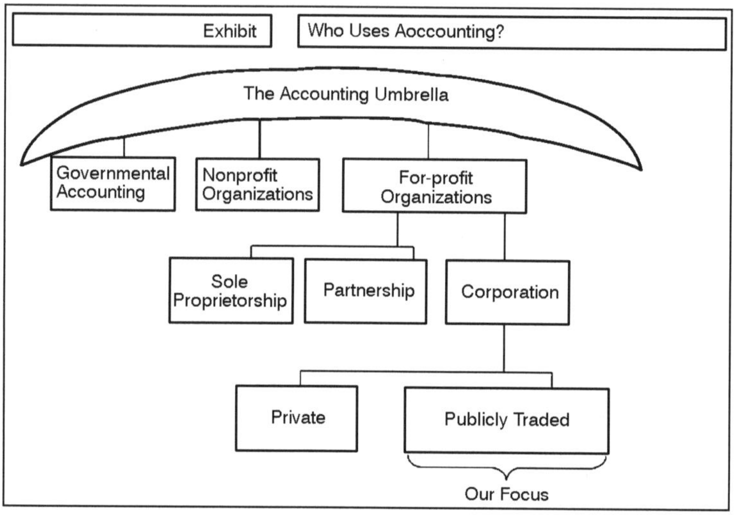

U.S. ACCOUNTING REGULATIONS

Accounting attempts to standardize financial information, and like any language, follows rules and regulations. What are these accounting rules, how are they established, and by whom?

GENERALLY ACCEPTED ACCOUNTING PRINCIPLES

In the United States, a governmental agency called the Securities and Exchange Commission authorizes the Financial Accounting Standards Board to determine U.S. accounting rules. FASB communicates these rules through the issuance of Statements of Financial Accounting Standards. These statements make up the body of U.S. accounting rules known as the Generally Accepted Accounting Principles. These rules have been developed to provide guidelines for financial accounting in order to ensure that businesses present their financial information on a fair, consistent, and straightforward basis. Financial statements of U.S. companies must be prepared according to U.S. GAAP.

INTERNATIONAL ACCOUNTING REGULATIONS

Up to now, we have discussed accounting regulations and the bodies that oversee them in the United States. But what about companies that must answer to the accounting regulations of other countries? Fortunately, there has been unprecedented convergence between the accounting standards for the United States and other countries over the last 30 years. Here is a brief recap of the history of this convergence.

In 1973, the International Accounting Standards Committee was founded by accountancy bodies in Australia, Canada, France, Germany, Ireland, Japan, Mexico, the Netherlands, the United Kingdom, and the United States, with the goal of developing global accounting standards.

In 2001, the IASC was replaced by the International Accounting Standards Board, an independent entity based in London, in order to oversee the continued convergence of global accounting standards. IASB comprises 14 board members appointed by the Trustees of the IASC Foundation, a parent organization. IASB has the sole responsibility of developing International Financial Reporting Standards.

In 2005, all EU countries adopted IFRS. In addition, accounting standards for many countries outside of Europe, including Japan, are largely equivalent to IFRS.

INDEPENDENCE AND PUBLIC ACCOUNTING

Independence is a more fundamental and pervasive concept in accounting than in the other professions. Indeed, former Chief Justice Burger stated that independence is a critical concept that sets CPAs apart from other professions. This is true because the core mission of the CPA is as auditor, one who certifies the public reports that describe a corporation's financial status. This is the only exclusive function that the CPA performs for society.

In rendering an opinion the independent auditor assumes a public duty. Moreover, this public duty must transcend any employment relationship or other duty towards the client. The CPA has what Burger calls a "public watchdog" function that demands that the auditor subordinate responsibility towards the client in order to maintain complete fidelity to the public trust.

So important and ingrained is independence in the public accounting profession that it may be regarded as a cornerstone upon which much of the ethics peculiar to the profession is built. Note the radical change in focus when the accounting profession speaks of independence. The perceived peril in lack of independence is not to the client but to an outside third party. This third party may be any person who reads and relies upon the financial statements upon which the auditor has rendered an opinion.

We find that to serve the third party the auditor must take an unbiased viewpoint when he performs audit tests, evaluates the results of those tests, and then issues an audit report and opinion with respect to the financial statements. Traditionally accountants have viewed independence on three ethical planes. First, in order to take an unbiased viewpoint, an auditor must possess the virtues of honesty, objectivity, and responsibility. In other words, on this plane we are concerned with the character of the auditor. We may regard this as the highest form of independence.

At the second level independence refers to the relationship of the CPA and the client. Here independence means avoiding any relationship that would likely, even subconsciously, tend to impair the CPA's ability to take the unbiased viewpoint. The public accountant must avoid personal and business relationships with clients that could cause even the most well-meaning person to slip or compromise in professional judgment.

On the final level, independence means the CPA should avoid any relationship that might suggest to a reasonable observer that a conflict of interest exists. Even when the professional is completely satisfied that no relationship impairs her judgment as a professional, she has not gone far enough. She must concern herself with the jaundiced eye of the beholder. So, even is she is completely satisfied that she can render an impartial judgment or opinion for a client with whom she has a particular business relationship, the standards of the profession still might prohibit her from acting as independent auditor. In this respect we can compare the accounting profession with the legal profession, which demands of the judiciary that no appearance of impropriety exists.

We thus see that on two levels independence is a condition of the mind and character of the professional. On the third level the issue is not about the professional herself but the way others view her. The common expressions used in professional circles to describe these phenomena are independence in fact and independence in appearance.

INDEPENDENCE IN FACT

Independence in fact is one of the most elusive aspects of ethics in the accounting profession. Most public accountants are ready to assert that for the most part independence in fact is the norm in daily professional life. Yet they are at a loss to provide evidence for this assertion or even to explain why they believe it is true.

After all, it is difficult to discern the virtues necessary for independence in fact. Moreover, we have little basis to doubt the existence of independence in fact in a particular circumstance until the most dramatic of events, the audit failure, comes to light. An audit failure is said to occur when a CPA opines to third parties that a client's financial statements are fairly presented in accordance with generally accepted accounting principles when in fact they are not. Often the root of the audit failure is found to be a lack of independence in fact.

Some frequently cited examples of a lack of independence in fact include lacking objectivity and skepticism, accepting the work of management for something that normally requires independent verification, agreeing to a significant client-imposed restriction on the scope of the audit, or knowingly neglecting the critical evaluation of a significant client transaction. Failure to test the accounts receivable by independent confirmation would be a concrete example. Some people also believe incompetence is a manifestation of a lack of independence in fact. In each of these cases, the virtues required to render an unbiased opinion are missing. Independence is thus violated on its highest plane. Another dimension of independence in fact originates in relationships with clients.

The Securities and Exchange Commission, in Accounting Series Release 234, has tightened the restrictions here."The application of an independent viewpoint is particularly important with respect to judgements exercised in the determination of appropriate principles and methods applied to the recording, classification and presentation of financial data. By their nature such judgements cannot subsequently be evaluated on an impartial and objective basis by the same accountant who made them."

In other words, the CPA cannot serve two masters: he cannot hold himself out to the public in a traditional auditor-client mode while at the same time serving that client as a controller, treasurer, or internal auditor. Neither can the CPA hold a direct financial or a material indirect financial interest in a client about whom he is rendering an opinion.

INDEPENDENCE IN APPEARANCE

Independence in fact exists when an auditor is actually able to maintain an unbiased attitude in the conduct of the audit. By contrast, independence in appearance refers to the interpretation or perception of others about the auditor's independence. Most of the value of the audit report stems from the independent status of the auditor.

Therefore, if auditors are independent in fact, but readers of the financial statements or members of the public at large believe them to be advocates for the client, most of the value of the audit function would be lost. These users of financial information can have faith in an auditor's representations only when they are confident that the auditor has acted as an impartial judge.

The entire reason for a profession of public accounting rests upon the foundation of independence in appearance. Otherwise the audit function could be performed by internal auditors who work for the company. These men and women are honourable people who possess requisite virtue for performing audits. Moreover, organizational systems could be devised to protect them from management retaliation. It is therefore at least possible that they could be independent in fact.

Nevertheless, users would almost always have a lingering doubt about the statements' impartiality and freedom from bias. Readers might suspect that the auditors were really serving the best interests of the company for which they worked. In other words, the internal auditor would not appear independent. Hence her representations would not have value to the user. An analogous phenomenon may be found in our government, where an independent prosecutor is appointed when a federal official, especially one in the Justice Department, is accused of a crime.

Concern about lack of independence in fact not only lowers the value of a particular audit report but also can have an adverse effect on the profession.

Certified public accounts are given special status in society-the status of"professional"-because of the perceived role that they play in that society. The role of the auditor is to give an unbiased opinion on reported financial information based upon professional judgment. If CPAs on the whole are not viewed as independent, the validity of the auditors' role in society is threatened. The very credibility of the profession, public accounting, depends ultimately upon society's perception about independence rather than the fact of independence.

AREAS OF CONCERN

Four areas in particular are significant with respect to independence in appearance:

- The competition that now exists among audit firms;
- The increasing role of management advisory services offered by auditors;
- The large and growing size of audit firms; and
- The length of time an audit firm has been filling the audit needs of a given client. Each of these areas has the potential of weakening public perception about certified public accountants' independence.

The competition we observe today among auditors was brought about because of action of the Federal Trade Commission and a Supreme Court decision. Before these events CPAs kept themselves above the fray, so to speak. They seemed content with their existing client base and were constrained by the then existing code of ethics from doing much to change that base. This way of doing business, despite being declared illegal, at least gave the illusion of being "professional."

Today auditors conduct business in a more capitalistic fashion utilizing advertising, personal selling, and other advanced marketing techniques to capture as much of the audit market as they can. It is all perfectly legal and legitimate business activity, but somehow it does not seem as "professional." The lingering question in the mind of the outside observer is whether a professional might not be willing to sacrifice independence in order to gain business advantage in an unrestrained competitive environment. Notice that the primary problem here is the appearance rather than the fact of independence.

The role of CPAs as business consultants through their management advisory services creates a similar problem. This role of the auditor is admittedly an old one. Yet today it is increasingly important to the practice of public accounting because competition for audit clients has made audit service less profitable. Moreover, the profitability of these services has been followed by increased publicity concerning the activities of CPAs in the consulting area. This is compounded by the fact that CPA firms have expanded into more and more diverse areas of consulting.

The problem once again is how the public perceives all of this. Can a person play this increasingly important role as an advisor to clients on how to conduct their businesses and at the same time give an unbiased opinion about the reported financial information? The profession strongly defends the position that by keeping auditing and consulting activities separate, independence is in fact maintained. Perhaps this is true. Yet the very fact that the question is raised means that independence in appearance is threatened.

A third problem with respect to independence in appearance arises due to the sheer size of the firms in which many certified public accountants practice. Increasingly the profession is being dominated by huge, multinational firms known as the Big Six. Ethically, there is nothing wrong here. But to the public these large firms are beginning to look more and more like big business. Therefore, these firms must be especially careful to guard against perceptions of a lack of independence.

A final factor that can erode independence in appearance is the length of time a particular client is served by a single auditor. In many cases an auditor-client relationship has stretched across decades. As time passes the client and the firm are increasingly identified with one another in the public eye. Again, the danger here is in appearance. The organizations may seem to be too close in the eye of the beholder even if the strictest measure of independence in fact is maintained. Problems of credibility in each of the above cases almost always arise outside the profession. Therefore accountants must be constantly aware of the perception issue, which can have an adverse impact upon auditing firms and the direct and indirect users of their services. The issue is rarely concerned with the validity of negative perceptions, but rather the belief that users and society hold with respect to objectivity and freedom from bias.

SOCIAL RESPONSIBILITY ACCOUNTING

THE PURSUIT 0F JUSTICE

Francis de Sales, controller of the Genesee Cable Company, was not pleased with the way the meeting of the management group had gone. At the meeting, the sales manager Teresa Avila had given a brilliant presentation, at the end of which she had recommended that cable service from the Casual Network be offered as part of their regular package in order to boost cable subscriptions. What disturbed Francis was that Casual's fare was widely regarded as soft pornography, a type of television to which Francis was opposed on moral grounds.

At first, John Cross, the president, had seemed to object. John recalled that when Genesee had been competing for the franchise in this community he had stated at a public hearing that Genesee had no intention of offering pornographic material of any type over the cable service. He wondered aloud whether taking on the Casual station wouldn't be breaking a promise to the community.

Yet Teresa had persisted. She noted that a statement made at a public hearing was not legally binding. She also cited her market research, which showed demand for Casual from many people in the community who were not currently subscribers. What galled Francis most was the fact that Teresa was able to use accounting numbers properly developed in his department to show that by adopting her recommendation Genesee would improve its profits dramatically. At the end of the meeting John seemed to be swayed by the profitability argument, although he did say he wanted to reflect on the recommendation a bit further.

After returning to his office, Francis mused: "Surely there must be more to business than just the bottom line. It seems so irresponsible to break our promise to the community for the sake of making more money. I wonder if accounting, as an information system, might not assign some sort of value to the old-fashioned notion of keeping a promise."

INFORMATION ABOUT RESPONSIBILITY

During the 1970s substantial discussion was available in accounting literature about social responsibility accounting. In recent years this topic has been placed on the back burner. Yet, with increasing attention being given to business ethics, we can expect social responsibility accounting to re-emerge as a "hot" topic.

After all, once society decides that ethical behaviour is a desired trait to be expected of businesses and business personnel, the logical question will follow: Who is and who is not acting ethically or responsibly? This question creates a demand for information, and accounting is one place to which we turn for information about business enterprise.

ETHICS AND ACCOUNTING REPORTS

A leading proponent of social responsibility accounting, defines it as "the process of selecting firm-level social performance variables, measures, and measurement procedures; systematically developing information useful for evaluating the firm's social performance; and communicating such information to concerned social groups, both within and outside the firm." A key accounting role seems apparent here. Accounting, as the language of business, is a primary provider of information. Traditional accounting concerns itself with financial information. In expanding the purview of providing information, we may be going beyond data and interpretation that are clearly financial. Yet ethical process and content may also be "accounted for."

Social responsibility accounting must somehow transform ethical information, which accountants may find "squishy," into financial information, or at least information in financial terms, so that accountants preparing and interpreting the reports are within their professional sphere.

The task here is a formidable one. Accountants must work with identified users of information to ascertain what sort of information is required. Then management must decide whether such information should be reported and, if so, in what form. Once these two barriers are surmounted, the accounting profession will be better able to satisfy the need by coming up with the "how" of reporting.

Much debate has occurred about the desirability of even having social responsibility accounting. Its proponents have suggested several models as starting points for developing this kind of accounting. Our intention is to examine the notion of social responsibility from the point of view of ethics.

Two major ethical theories, utilitarianism and deontologism. Utilitarianism can and has been used to create a good case for accountants not to engage in social responsibility accounting. Following that as suggested, present a deontological case in favour of social responsibility accounting.

UTILITARIAN ARGUMENTS

Opponents of social responsibility accounting argue in an analytical rather than descriptive fashion. That is, they approach the entire issue from the standpoint of cost/benefit analysis. Most accountants are quite comfortable with this type of analysis. Cost/benefit analysis is a concept that is deeply rooted in utilitarian ethics. In this analysis the utility defined—that is, the good we maximize—is material wealth expressed in terms of dollars. Simply stated, we sum the cost of an action and compare it with the sum of the economic benefits expressed in financial terms. Under a utilitarian criterion we should undertake a project where the economic benefits exceed the costs.

As an example of this kind of utilitarian reasoning, let's return to the Genesee Cable Company. As part of her research concerning the Casual Network, Teresa asked Francis to provide her a differential cost schedule. This kind of managerial report is a common one in accounting.

The differential cost schedule clearly points to the decision to accept Casual Network programming. The operating income with this option exceeds operating income without it by $162,000. Using the terminology of cost/ benefit analysis, we can say that the benefits exceed the costs. This is a straightforward case, since both the benefits and the costs may be clearly identified when the utility that we seek to maximize is monetary wealth measured in dollars.

A careful analysis of the social responsibility accounting issue on this utilitarian ground provides disappointing results for its proponents. From the standpoint of the corporation, the costs of placing any new accounting system into place are substantial. Here the company must consider more than the immediate costs of designing and implementing such an accounting system. Also included should be the possible consequences (costs) of publicly reporting the company's actions in the social responsibility arena.

An honest reporting of these matters could bring consequences that are not in the best interests of the owners or managers of the corporation. These might come in the form of possible calls for increased government action in the affairs of the company, possible action against the company from special interest groups, or lawsuits from parties who believe they have sustained injury from the company's actions. Moreover, these costs of implementing social responsibility accounting are fairly easy to measure using conventional business forecasting methods. We may thus be fairly certain about the magnitude of the costs.

Against these costs we should weigh the benefits of social responsibility accounting. Here we run into problems, particularly as far as the accountant is concerned. Accounting tends to deal with information that is specific in nature. Within accounting certain types of information are sanctioned as real and true. Accountants therefore focus their attention upon this type of information to the exclusion of other kinds.

The benefits of reporting social responsibility information fall into a category of information that is not currently sanctioned by accounting. Much of the benefit of ethical behaviour is not obviously financial in nature. Accountants are therefore understandably uncomfortable with attempts to measure this information, let alone report upon it. The benefits of going through this effort are therefore elusive and difficult to express in financial terms. By way of example, let's return to the Genesee Cable Company. Certainly utilitarian arguments may be made to reject Teresa's plan to schedule Casual's programming. In the long run the public, in perceiving that Genesee is a company that keeps its promises and is concerned with community values, will be anxious to have increased business contact with Genesee. In accounting terms we might be tempted to call this goodwill. Yet accountants have recognized the problems associated with measuring goodwill for years.

Today this task is not even attempted unless the goodwill is demonstrated by a purchase transaction on the open market. The economically rational manger would be hard pressed not to offer Casual's programming, especially if he attempted to use cost/benefit analysis in arriving at a decision. The possible benefits of a future good name in the community seem somewhat smaller than the prospect of an increase in profit of $162,000 when we take the cost/benefit point of view. Thus the use of cost/benefit analysis as a criterion for the desirability of social responsibility accounting usually leaves us with heavy, easy-to-measure costs on one hand balanced against vague and seemingly small benefits on the other.

Many accounting writers who have looked at the issue of social responsibility accounting from this utilitarian perspective have been quite pessimistic about its future in accounting. Indeed, the practical application of socially responsible actions themselves finds nearly insurmountable hurdles from a cost/benefit point of view. Yet there are underlying weaknesses in attempts to use cost/benefit analysis or any other utilitarian system in a practical way. These have been identified by Alasdair MacIntyre:

Utilitarian tests must presuppose the application of some prior non-utilitarian principle that sets limits on the range of activities to be considered. Utilitarian tests must presuppose some method of rank ordering the values of good and evil. This method must be non-utilitarian. Different agents will make different assessments of harms and benefits. The question of what is to count as a consequence of a given action must be answered. Boundaries must be placed upon responsibility for consequences.

A time scale must be used in assessing consequences. The question of how far the present should be sacrificed for the future requires a non-utilitarian answer.

These weaknesses of the practical application of utilitarianism readily appear in the use of cost/benefit analysis to assess the usefulness of social responsibility accounting. As we have discussed, the weakness of a non-utilitarian principle is encountered in the fact that accounting has traditionally dealt solely with financial information. The ethical benefits in cost/benefit analysis are often difficult to translate into financial terms. Thus, many accountants are uncomfortable entering into this realm.

Cost/benefit analysis presupposes that material wealth is the sole good to be considered. Thus an arbitrary, non-utilitarian method is assumed at the beginning of the utilitarian reasoning process. Yet reasonable people do not really believe that the accumulation of wealth is the only criterion to look at with respect to good and evil.

The final three weaknesses of practical utilitarianism are particularly evident in examining the benefit side of cost/benefit analysis. Hence the frustration with social responsibility accounting among so many accountants. Different agents translate the benefits into financial terms at different amounts. To many accountants this appears to violate the principle of verifiability. Which consequence of an action is the subject of measurement for the accountant also arises. Finally, the entire matter of comparing the present value of probable future benefits with the costs incurred now is a particularly sticky one in cost/benefit analysis.

We see that the deck seems stacked against not only social responsibility accounting but also socially responsible action when we attempt to apply utilitarian arguments. Yet the economic system in which corporations and their managers operate motivates them to take a utilitarian perspective.

Compounding this are forces in the business community that encourage managers to look to short-term rather than long-term results.

A change in the underlying way we view the role of the corporation in society can enable us to more realistically assess not only the need for socially responsible action but also the ways accounting can assist managers and outside readers of accounting reports in the tough choices with respect to these actions. This change is to move towards a deontological perspective.

THE DEONTOLOGICAL VIEW

The use of deontologism for the professions in general and for accounting in particular is not new. Lawyers who defend clients' interests irrespective of the general consequences use deontological reasons to justify this behaviour. Scientists frequently make inquiry into areas where an answer may lead to bad consequences (atomic power, for example). In medicine the doctrine of informed consent, whereby a patient is not subjected to an experiment without his full knowledge and approval, is well entrenched.

Many accountants agree that the Financial Accounting Standards Board should use representative faithfulness (a deontological perspective) over economic consequences (a utilitarian perspective) as a criterion for standard setting. Moreover, the accounting profession in general and certified public accountants in particular have taken great pains to present their field to society as a profession.

Among them are that each is governed by ethical principles that emphasize the virtues of self-subordination, honesty, probity, and devotion to the welfare of those served. CPAs have obligations not only to those served but also to third parties. In fact, the obligations to third parties may supersede the obligation to the party about which the CPA issues a report.

DEONTOLOGICAL FRAMEWORK

Deontological ethics can be applied to situations only if an obligation can be satisfied. The ideas of W. D. Ross, a prominent philosopher of the twentieth century. He provided specific criteria to be used as tests for the existence of an obligation and suggested a set of prima facie duties that represent the main moral convictions of the "plain man."

- Fidelity
- Reparation
- Gratitude
- Justice
- Beneficence
- Self-improvement
- Non-maleficence

We suggest that this list may serve as a starting point for discussion about whether corporations have reporting responsibilities with respect to social responsibility. Two questions must be addressed at the outset. First, do organizations such as corporations have duties that apply to the "plain man?" Second, how shall we know whether a specific duty applies to a particular organization?

Some modern ethicists argue that corporations are moral persons. This is true because people are behind the corporate veil and these people make decisions with moral implications. Society therefore cannot condone as amoral corporate actions that would be considered immoral for the individuals who actually make decisions for the corporation. Portions of the Foreign Corrupt Practices Act that hold corporate officers personally responsible for corporate actions serve as an example of this premise. P. H. Werhane convincingly takes the issue of corporate social responsibility a step farther in Persons, Rights, and Corporations. She argues that corporations have responsibilities apart from the individual responsibilities of persons behind the corporate veil.

She demonstrates that corporations argue for legal rights that must have a moral basis if they are justified. An example of this is the enforcement of contracts, which depends upon the moral duty of fidelity. Moreover, "If corporations have moral rights, then they have the obligations connected with such rights, and they can be held accountable, morally accountable."

If the prima facie duties apply correctly to individuals, including individuals who manage corporations, then they apply to corporations themselves. We may therefore turn to the second question of how to ascertain whether a specific duty applies to a corporation. S. E. Toulmin has provided a test that may be applied to the prima facie duties: In any particular community, certain principles are current-that is to say, attention is paid to certain types of argument as appealing to accepted criteria of "real goodness," "real rightness," "real obligation," etc. From these the members of the community are expected to regulate their lives and judgements. And such a set of principles of "prima facie obligations" of "categorical imperatives" is what we call the "moral code" of the community.

As citizens, readers of financial reports should be concerned about the actions a company is taking or failing to take in the realm of social responsibility. The socially responsible corporation should therefore report upon how it is meeting or failing to meet its duties to the public. Research among investors and other stakeholders indicates that they are in fact interested in corporate activities that fall within the scope of the prima facie duties. We now explain each of these in terms of the business and accounting community.

Fidelity

Fidelity is the first of two duties that rest upon previous acts. Fidelity is simply the keeping of promises. The promises to be kept may be explicit or implicit.

Many explicit promises are already recognized and reported by corporations. Warranties, for example, are accounted for as contingency liabilities with a corresponding expense. Duties stemming from explicit promises may also raise ethical questions that are not so easily recognized in financial terms.

Let us return to the cable television company case. Management here is faced with a hard choice between its often-stated duty to maximize return for stockholders and the moral duty to keep the corporation's promise. We have demonstrated how the accounting system through the commonly used differential cost schedule uses utilitarian reasoning to report upon future consequences of managerial action. We have shown that such purely utilitarian reasoning, when used alone, would rarely motivate a manager to choose the socially responsible course of action. Yet Francis, and perhaps John, believe that a duty exists here because of the statements made at the public hearing. The duty that they recognize is fidelity.

From the accountant's viewpoint, can a report be developed to assist the decision-making process from a deontological perspective? Moreover, once the choice is made, can it be reported to interested stakeholders in an accounting context?

Reparation

Duties of reparation rest upon a previous wrongful act of the one who has the duty. Examples of duties of reparation in business are quite common and well publicized. The poison gas leak at the Union Carbide plant in Bhopal, India, and Manville's asbestos-related problems provide recent examples. In both cases the victims of actions taken by the company have received monetary compensation.

A clear reporting problem appears to exist in both the Union Carbide and Manville cases; yet, the wrongful act need not be so dramatic for a duty to arise. Suppose our cable television enterprise decides to proceed with the soft pornography offering. Later Francis learns that a father accused of sexually abusing his four-year-old daughter claims that he was motivated to do so after watching a show on Genesee Cable.

Clearly no legal liability exists here under current law. Yet, ethics are usually considered to be on a higher plane than the law. Therefore a duty with corresponding social responsibility accounting implications may arise when no legal liability is present.

Suppose John, Teresa, and Francis are struck with conscience in this matter and therefore are considering paying for the treatment of the little girl. Their consideration might arise from a sense of duty of reparation. Should they later decide to have Genesee make these payments, a social responsibility accounting implication may have been created.

The management of a particular corporation would have the responsibility of deciding the corporation's ethical standards with respect to reparation. The accountant's role would be to report upon the financial implications of meeting those standards. Such reporting might be internal or external. A corporate decision not to accept a reparation duty could also be a reportable event under social responsibility accounting.

Gratitude

Duties of gratitude arise from services done by others for the one who has the duty of gratitude. At first the notion of corporate gratitude may seem questionable, yet official communication from corporations often express gratitude. Annual reports of companies frequently express corporate appreciation for a job well done by employees. Gratitude can be more specific. When Frank Cary retired as the chairman of the board of International Business Machines, the new chairman stated that the company was "indebted" to him "for the wisdom and skill with which he led the company."

The duty of gratitude is not only owed employees. A company might have reason to be grateful to a community, to suppliers, to customers, or to others who interact with it. The duty arises because of the previous actions of the other entities.

A question of interest with respect to social responsibility accounting is whether the gratitude expressed by corporations has an associated duty, and whether there is a future cost associated with the duty. If a corporation appreciates efforts by its loyal employees, has a duty been created for the corporation to those employees when economic times are not so good? Does indebtedness of IBM imply that a duty exists? Moreover, if the answers to these questions are yes, what are the costs of fulfilling these duties or not fulfilling them?

On the other hand, a company need not express gratitude for the duty to exist. From the standpoint of ethics an unrecognized duty might exist. Social responsibility accounting may be one vehicle that could assist managers and others in recognizing this duty.

Justice

Duties of justice rest on the fact or possibility of a distribution of pleasure or happiness (or the means thereto) that is not in accordance with the merit of the persons concerned. A duty may arise in such cases to upset or prevent such a distribution. Corporations are frequently confronted with duties that arise from justice. Such duties would create reporting implications under social responsibility accounting.

Suppose that a large corporation is headquartered in a maturing city that contains a ghetto. The youth of the ghetto are unable to attain employment at the corporation because, due to circumstances beyond their control, they are unqualified. In such circumstances enlightened management may believe that it is their duty, and by connection the corporation's, to overturn this state of affairs by providing job training programmes. Such a sense of duty would arise from a concern for justice.

Notice that in this case the sense of duty did not arise from any previous action or promise of the corporation or its management. Duties of justice arise simply because an observed situation is wrong per se. If the corporation recognizes such a duty, a cost may ensue in the future should the corporation create a training programme, for example.

Of interest here is that the corporation does not internalize an externality that it created, an often heard reason for socially responsible action, nor does the corporation take action because it believes that the training programme will benefit it in the long run (a utilitarian argument). Rather the action is undertaken due to a sense of duty.

The duty arises from a concept of justice, perhaps best stated by John Rawls. "Justice is the virtue of practices where there are assumed to be competing interests and conflicting claims and where it is supposed that persons will press their rights on each other. That persons are mutually self-interested in certain situations and for certain purposes is what gives rise to the questioning of justice in practices couching those circumstances." Rawls argues that every person may be supposed to have a concept of justice. This proposition is true because each person is involved in some relationships with others. In the context of these relationships each person forms a concept of justice for herself as well as for others. Corporate persons would be among those under this societal umbrella.

Beneficence

Like duties of justice, duties of beneficence do not arise because of any culpability on the part of the corporation. Duties of beneficence rest upon the mere fact that there are other beings in the world whose condition can be made better. If the corporation recognizes these beings and is able to improve their condition, then a duty of beneficence arises.

The fact that duties of beneficence are recognized by managers of corporations is demonstrated by the fact that they cause the corporations to make charitable contributions. One is hard pressed to swallow utilitarian reasoning that such contributions may in the long run improve profitability by the creation of goodwill. In fact, the best arguments against such action are utilitarian in nature. Milton Friedman represents perhaps the best-known proponent of this utilitarian point of view.

The Philip Morris Company is well known in some circles as a supporter of the arts. Yet this company does not have a great deal of goodwill in general. Contributions to the ballet are not made in the hope of generating cigarette sales. They are made because people who work for this company believe that society will benefit from having the arts more widely available to the public. In other words, the donations are made because of a sense of duty, the duty of beneficence.

Duties of beneficence on the part of corporations are recognized in the tax laws, in that amounts spent for charity are deductible for tax purposes. They provide an interesting twist in that the duty recognized by the corporation is externalized. Persons who may not recognize the duty become partners in fulfilling the duty in the sense that the government receives less revenue from the corporate source.

Self-Improvement

Duties of self-improvement are the most difficult of Ross's duties of individuals to translate to a corporation. Duties of self-improvement rest on the fact that one can improve her own condition with respect to virtue or intelligence. Interestingly, Ross includes pleasure in the improvement of another's condition but omits it in the improvement of one's own condition. The difficulty with respect to duties of self-improvement lies in defining the corporation when viewing it as something where virtue or knowledge warrant improvement. However, if we accept the notion a priori that a corporation improves itself when it improves its management, duties of self-improvement may be found.

An example is the practice of companies paying the cost of sending managers to universities to improve their education. Utilitarians would undoubtedly argue that such action is taken to improve profits through lower costs generated from the better management the corporation expects to receive from better-educated managers. Corporations would undeniably justify this practice on such utilitarian grounds.

However, the imagination must truly be stretched to translate an individual manager's education to the bottom line. A more plausible explanation for such things as classes in human relations might be found in the desire to fulfill a duty for self-improvement. If this is true, does the public bear costs when a corporation does not recognize such a duty? For example, one could argue that by failure to improve managers' knowledge of business ethics, a corporation has caused the public to incur greater risk of unethical conduct by the corporation.

The duty of self-improvement becomes one we may more easily associate with business enterprise if we expand upon Ross's definition a bit. A commonly held and frequently cited belief is that business corporations have the duty to make profits. We may easily accept this notion by stating that the company has the duty to improve itself by improving its financial position. As we do this we agree with Ross that the duty of self-improvement should be subordinated to the other duties.

Non-Maleficence

This is the only duty that is stated in a negative way. Non-maleficence is the duty not to injure others. Duties of non-maleficence are clearly the most compelling; violations of these duties create debate about corporate irresponsibility.

Pollution can serve as an example of how deontological ethics is superior to utilitarian ethics in solving dilemmas. A utilitarian argument for pollution may be made on the basis that those who pollute will generate more profit than those who incur costs to avoid pollution. Yet, reasonable men and women view pollution as undesirable. The utilitarian solution to this dilemma is to argue that the externalities created by the pollution involve more bad than the good created by the profits. The logical conclusion to the utilitarian view is that the responsible corporation should pollute just up to the point where the pollution will not exceed the good generated by the profit and no further. These arguments do not represent the attitudes of plain-thinking people. Indeed, most reasonable people could agree that pollution of the air and water is a prima facie wrong. It is wrong because it is injurious to others irrespective of utility. Because pollution is wrong, members of society, including corporate members, have a duty not to engage in the practice. This is the duty of non-maleficence.

The implications for social responsibility accounting are perhaps most clear under duties of non-maleficence. In the pollution example, those companies that internalize the cost of pollution by purchasing anti-pollution equipment have done their duty and would so report. Those who do not incur these costs will make higher profits, but should be required to report as a social cost the damage the pollution has done or will do.

The duty of non-maleficence could also apply in the Genesee Cable case. As part of his consideration of Teresa's proposal, John might recall an article that asserts that men who watch pornographic material on television develop an attitude towards women that views them as objects to be exploited rather than persons to be respected. John may decide against accepting Teresa's proposal on the grounds that he does not desire Genesee to be a party to fostering such attitudes in the community. In this case he would be acting out of the duty of non-maleficence.

EFFICIENT CAPITAL MARKETS

At its core, the theory of efficient capital markets states that prices of assets always completely reflects all existing relevant information. Due to this, there is also ultimately no possibility for property investors to develop strategies which systematically lead to an excess return over the total market. The only way to develop strategies which systematically lead to the generation of higher returns than the total market, also for tourism and leisure property, is, according to the theory, to take on a higher risk – represented as Beta Ö in financial theory – and thereby expose oneself to a disproportionately increased risk of loss.

While these theoretic assumptions are unreservedly held to be adequate on the stock market, even in business practice, the authority and application of the theory of efficient capital markets clearly showed itself to be "surmountable" for the institutions and individuals acting on the non-transparent continental European hotel investment markets, judging by their market behaviour.

Hotel properties, in particular, display a wide range of distinctive features in this regard: Hotels are transferred ready to use, feature a pre-opening phase and achieve stable results, as a rule, only after a warm-up period of two to four years. Furthermore, there is always an operation aspect as well as a property aspect to hotels. The success – and therefore also the value – of a hotel is also very much dependent on the competency of the operator. In this regard, tourism and leisure properties are fundamentally different to commercial, residential and industrial properties, whose value generally results exclusively from the level of rent which can be attained. These rents are largely, and with regard to their level, independent of the commercial success of the tenant.

Conversely, attractive potential for future increases in value in the case of hotel properties is based primarily on the success of the operator, as the value of a hotel is derived primarily from the surplus revenue associated with its management. This can be compared to the way in which the owner of a racehorse profits financially from the skills of "his" jockey. Worldwide, an estimated 98 percent of all hotels not managed by their owner are operated within the framework of a relevant management contract, which regulates the running of the hotel by the hotel operator for account of the owner.

Consequently, in the case of hotels operated according to management contracts, the investor feels the full impact of negative as well as positive business developments and if an improvement in profitability is anticipated due to a change of management or equivalent Performance and Asset Management by the owner, the subsequently improved operation results are fully incorporated into the value assessment of the hotel property. In this respect, entrepreneurial chances, but also risks, for hotel investors or owners are by far the greatest in the case of hotel management contracts, and it is possible for hotel investors to achieve the value increase ("upside") necessary to generate their high equity returns primarily with such a contract model.

Furthermore, there was no relevant market for tourism and leisure properties up until the middle of this decade due to the traditionally low transaction volume, particularly in continental Europe. This characteristic, in combination with the introduction of the Euro, reinforced the assumption of financial investors, particularly US investors, that the prices for such properties did not always reflect all available relevant information, but rather offered wide-ranging investment opportunities, which promised fewer risks or higher returns than the market price would suggest.

Thus, promising investment opportunities present themselves, particularly for those market players who recognise this type of potential sooner than the rest of the market due to better information, can make quick decisions because of flat hierarchies and flexible structures, and have access to the necessary material, human and particularly financial resources.

These types of opportunities, in turn, make up the core business activity of real estate opportunity and private equity funds, which are differentiated from conventional funds by their high expected return on equity. This differentiation is also clear by means of the classification of property investment strategies into the categories "core", "core plus/value added" and "opportunistic", demonstrate.

As early as in the mid-nineties, this risk/return spectrum posed the question, in theory and in practice, of whether it is even possible to achieve internal rate of returns of 25 percent. In the past, however, even international rating agencies supported the myth that high debt ratios in investing were safe. For many market players, this is the premise which allowed financial investors to tap the global capital markets on an unprecedented scale for the funding of property portfolios and to disperse the risks resulting from this all over the world up until the onset of the crisis.

Many compare the property and financial crisis, which is also currently afflicting tourism, to the world economic crisis of 1929 in its scale and dangers. The dyna-misation of the crisis is particularly surprising. Because of the aforementioned wide dispersion of the risks, all of the relevant countries and markets are simultaneously affected, for the first time since the depression of 1929.

The cause of the crisis, based on the US property market and the weak credit borrowers segment (subprime segment) has, at this stage, been exhaustively discussed in both economic and tourism literature. Against this background, a summary of the development of the property and financial crisis is included in this chapter only within the framework of the following recapitulatory. Two main factors made a crucial contribution to the fact that the above-displayed interdependencies, as well as individual interdependencies initially limited to specific regions and countries, would lead to a global crisis which now shows a significant impact on tourism:

The first factor has long been known and applies to a fundamental, financial theoretical construct: Both investment banks and opportunity and private equity funds attempt to capitalise on the leverage effect by increasing the debt ratio, because excess returns can be generated under certain conditions (especially through the attainment of an early resale/exit) only on the correspondingly low volume of equity. In this respect, the impressively high returns on equity effectively earned by companies like Blackstone, Whitehall, Colony Capital or Fortress, and then initially also in the tourism industry, in the years before the onset of the crisis can, to a large extent, be traced primarily back to the high leverage.

To this end, loopholes in the state equity regulation of credit institutes were consequently exploited and "levered" on a hitherto unprecedented scale *i.e.* with only an extremely small equity ratio put down.

Secondly, financial instruments have been developed since the mid-nineties to pass credit risks from the banks' accounts on to the global financial markets. For this, a large number of outstanding debts were bundled and securities were issued in several tranches on the thus-created pool. This so-called Asset Backed Securities (ABS) were given the seal of approval by internationally recognised rating agencies and could then be sold worldwide as an alternative investment form with a risk-opportunity profile which seemed very attractive. The way in which the risk from these tranches should be dispersed was even the topic of various economic studies with the aim that, despite the risk transfer, it would continue to be possible to allocate credits in a prudent manner and to adequately monitor credits which had already been allocated. Unfortunately, these abstract considerations did not seem to interest the designers of these types of financial products, or the rating agencies who evaluated them, at least as long as equity returns of over 25 percent could actually be generated, against the warning signs of the theory of efficient capital markets.

FACTS, FIGURES AND LEGACIES OF SPECULATION IN TOURISM

These high returns which were effectively achieved in the beginning certainly contributed to the fact that real estate private equity and opportunity funds, in particular, became increasingly active on the European property market from approximately 1997 and recorded enormous influxes of funds.

Declining returns in the USA, the accustomisation to EU jurisdictions and taxation laws and reasonable room rates as compared to international standards were also important factors in bringing the financial investors to Europe. In addition, cross-border transactions were significantly easier and more transparent after the introduction of the Euro.

With regard to the European hotel investment market, it is very clear, in retrospect that the – initially primarily Anglo-American – opportunity and private equity funds did not reckon with consistently low occupancy and room rates. In addition, according to the acting staff members, many of these hotels did not fully exploit their economic potential. Simultaneously, European tourism companies were still experiencing a shortage of own capital and outside capital, so that institutions from the hotel real estate private equity and opportunity funds sector, in particular, saw wide-ranging opportunities to also invest in Europe – under the banner of "Recovery" – in a tourist property category with which they had long been familiar in terms of their domestic markets.

International hotel chains, in particular, responded accordingly to this trend in their role as hotel property owners. While a large proportion of hotels had been purchased by hotel chains up to just a few years previously, in order to also secure the hotel business alongside the rising value of property, almost all international hotel companies separated management and ownership of hotel properties during the investment boom. Operating instead of owning was the order of the day in the European hotel industry. On the one hand, property sales for international hotel chains were almost forced, because of the extreme amounts of capital which streamed into the European market, as described above; on the other hand, hotel companies as sellers had the big advantage that returns were low and prices were, consequently, astronomically high.

As a consequence, hotel companies also engaged in price rigging and persistently sold large hotel portfolios, focusing at the same time on closing long-term management contracts as growth options, whereby they no longer considered themselves obliged to point out either the operational or the investment overall risk. After all, the urge for expansion among large international providers was heavily restricted time and again precisely by direct investments and fixed-lease contracts with comprehensive security deposits and guarantees, especially in continental Europe, which was traditionally more security-orientated.

Furthermore, listed hotel companies, in particular, are still facing the dilemma of having to fully balance previously received contingent liabilities from fixed-lease contracts, due to the international accounting standards which are also applicable in Europe for the foreseeable future.

Through their aggressive selling activities, hotel companies revised their balance sheets, on the one hand, and liberated an abundance of resources for their ambitious growth strategies, on the other hand. They were also called on to do this by analysts, who consider the value of hotel companies to no longer be in the property business, but rather in the operational business.

The European markets for hotel investment also boomed correspondingly, before they heavily plunged due to the crisis in 2008; in 2009 the market is continuing its downward slide. Even in comparison to the same quarter last year, which was already very weak, single asset transactions fell by a further 72 percent and portfolio transactions by a further 90 percent. Experts in the industry predict that the market level for the total year 2009 will not reach a level higher than that of 2002 – not even if the performance in the hotels improves again.

However, there is no question of an emerging improvement in performance in view of the sharp decline in demand which was evident at the outset and is currently still continuing. Correspondingly, both hotel developers and hotel operators are trying to postpone or completely back out of new construction projects to a hitherto unprecedented degree. The granting of loans, which has now become a problem, and the continuingly uncertain economic outlook is further dampening spirits.

An analysis of articles and commentaries recently published in the tourism trade press shows a basic increasing tendency to forget that, in the short term, it is more likely to come to a further intensification of competition with fewer and fewer travellers than to a recovery. After all, those projects which were signed in the times of the economic boom and which are currently under construction are highly likely to open, even with the risk that they will no longer be able to avail of external finance.

During the boom times, however, the willingness of market players to take higher risks for equity returns of over 25 percent also rose, as we know. As this went well for at least a certain time, new investors continuously entered the market, which consequently led to an increase in demand also for new hotel projects.

The legacies of the speculation and of such a herd instinct are now visible to their full extent, makes clear using selected tourist destinations. Because of such undesirable developments, a market recovery will doubtless not materialise until 2012 and 2013. However, this may only last until the next speculation and project wave.

Outlook

It is clear that the property and financial crisis has grave consequences for tourism. Some hotels also reported massive slumps, for which, in retrospect, the hotel concerns themselves have been shown to be partly responsible. They willingly created more and more new brands, in order to sell property equipped with a brand name which was as "strong" as possible at massively inflated prices.

Irrespective of this, the past offers a reason for hope in the midst of the crisis. International tourism has namely always succeeded thus far in withstanding the various crises, documents using the example of the two key hotel markets in Europe, London and Paris. The UNTWO is also maintaining the expectation that tourism will, in the long run, hold its ground as one of the main driving forces of the world economy. Furthermore, according to certain results of a recent study by the respected consulting firm Deloitte, which deals with current developments and prospects of European tourism, the outlook is not altogether negative.

However, the property and financial crisis also offers cause to critically scrutinise opinions and preconceptions which are prevalent in the economic sciences about the efficiency of a globalised capital and financial market as the crisis makes clear, above all, the actual value of a large variety of institutions within a financial system, as well as the co-existence of very diverse financial systems in a healthy competitive environment.

System errors in certain forms would then no longer be able to spread with such momentum. In addition, the regions less badly affected could support the institutions and brands which had been hit by the crisis and, ultimately, the existence of valid alternative forms would allow for creative exploration of possible solutions for a crisis.

5

Financial Management

INTRODUCTION

Management of funds is an important aspect of financial management. Management of funds act as the primary concern whether it may be in a business undertaking or in an educational institution. Financial management, which is simply meant dealing with management of money matters. A financial institution acts as an agent that provides financial services for its clients. Financial institutions generally fall under financial regulation from a government authority. Common types of financial institutions include banks, building societies, credit unions, stock brokerages, asset management firms, and similar businesses. Financial institutions provide a service as intermediaries of the capital and debt markets.

They are responsible for transferring funds from investors to companies, in need of those funds. The presences of financial institutions facilitate the flow of monies through the economy. To do so, savings accounts are pooled to mitigate the risk brought by individual account holders in order to provide funds for loans. Such is the primary means for depository institutions to develop revenue. Should the yield curve become inverse, firms in this arena will offer additional fee-generating services including securities underwriting, sales and trading, and prime brokerage.

FINANCIAL MANAGEMENT GOALS AND POLICIES

Financial management goals and policies provide the framework for financial planning and decision making by the school board, budget committee, and district staff. They are designed to help ensure the financial integrity of the district which, along with prudent management of its financial resources, is necessary if the district is to provide the educational services, support services and facilities that address the needs and desires of our students, their parents, and the community.

The following goals and policies for the school district are intended to guide the district in its financial matters. The goals are broad statements of board philosophy for financial management of the district. The policies provide more specific direction for consistent financial management decisions.

Financial Management Goals

1. The district will establish a financial base sufficient to support high quality and innovative educational programs which meet community needs.
2. The district will follow prudent and professional financial management practices in order to achieve and maintain long-term financial stability.
3. The district will demonstrate to the taxpayers of the district and the financial community that its schools are well managed.
4. The district will provide cost-effective services to citizens by cooperating with other educational, government, and nonprofit agencies.
5. The district will have an adequate capital improvement Programme that maintains existing district assets, provides for student and employee safety, maintains a quality instructional environment, and allows for enhancements that are necessary to meet changes in enrollment.
6. The district will continually review and improve its formal budget document and other financial information so that it clearly and openly communicates its resources, expenditures, and financial position.
7. The district will communicate, as permitted by law, with its employees and the community so that they understand the district's Programme requirements and financial status.

Valuing diversity is a core value of Financial Management. Financial Management uses a very broad definition of diversity. In addition to the categories identified by the steering committee (race, gender, disability, class, sexual identity/orientation, religion, age, ethnicity, culture, region/geography and indigenous statue), Financial Management also values variety in work styles, personality types and education levels.

Approximately one third of the Financial Management (FM) staff members are immigrants and non-native English speakers. Specific efforts are made to address issues of diversity within the division in order to maximize employee performance and customer satisfaction. Our diversity initiative complements other work being done on campus to support the UW's mission of creating a comfortable educational environment that will attract and retain the best and the brightest from all backgrounds.

Current Financial Management Efforts in the Interest of Diversity:

- Biennial employee surveys to gauge satisfaction in the workplace and answer specific questions about diversity
- Measure on the Operational Performance Dashboard that gauges "% of staff who agree that making FM more diverse will make the

organization better overall (top two ratings on the 7 point scale). Current measure is 72%; target is 90%.

- Formal on-going diversity initiative
- Two teams focus specifically on diversity; one has created a mentoring Programme with an emphasis on diversity, and the other helps to educate and make the division more aware and appreciative of diversity
- Development and presentation of mandatory diversity training
- Additional training for supervisors and managers
- Ongoing Programme for diversity-related presentations
- A diversity calendar on the web
- A roster of internal interpreters
- A roster of conversation coaches for improving English skills
- A set of measurements that reflect the importance of cultural competence
- Accountability to cultural competence
- An ongoing English Skills in the Workplace Programme for non-native speakers, offered through UW English Skills Programs
- Educational outreach Programme to students, parents, prospective students and campus staff, many of which are in partnership with or by request from Office of Minority Affairs
- Employee development plans for all staff that include financial support and release time for training and other developmental activities

THE NATURE OF FINANCIAL MANAGEMENT

Financial management is that part of total management which is concerned primarily with the financial affairs of an organization and the translation of actions, both past and proposed, into meaningful and relevant information for use in the management process. It includes the functions of budgeting, accounting, reporting, and the analysis and interpretation of the financial significance of past events and future plans. It sometimes also includes other related functions such as internal auditing, management analysis, and others. It is not primarily concerned with the technical procedures and methodology of those individual functions. Rather, it is characterized by the coordination and correlation of those functions into an effective and broad system of financial control that will assure that they, collectively more than individually, become an integral part of the management of the organization.

Financial management involves the art of interrelating data to obtain a perspective of the total financial situation that will assist managers in Programme planning and decision-making. A very simple operating Programme may require only a minimum of financial management, and this, in some cases, can be provided by the manager himself. However, many Federal agencies with complex programs have a need for broad financial advice and know-how — advice that can only be furnished following a synthesis, analysis, and interrelating of meaningful financial data with programming and planning information by an organization and officials particularly adept and capable in financial matters.

More fully, financial management may be described as—

Designing, establishing, and maintaining an integrated financial management system, including at least budgeting, accounting, and managerial-financial reporting, which will furnish timely data that are used in the direction, evaluation, and control of operations at the various levels of management. Such a system must be compatible with the requirements of the Bureau of the Budget, the General Accounting Office, and the Treasury Department, and should provide accountability for agency funds and assets and full disclosure of the financial results of agency operations.

This involves responsibility for proper and economic management of all financial resources under jurisdiction of the agency, in accordance with a wide variety of laws and regulations. To accomplish this, a suitable financial management organization must be established and maintained, and must be staffed with appropriate, competent personnel. Rather than being limited to supervision of separate entities such as the budgetary system, the accounting system, the financial reporting system, etc., financial management consists of the integration and coordination of those operations into a comprehensive financial system that is compatible with management needs.

Such an Integrated System Necessarily Includes:

(a) Developing an integrated financial planning and reporting process that involves both long-range plans and the annual budget as a segment of those plans. Such a planning and reporting process must be designed to provide both broad and specific financial policies that will facilitate achievement of the Programme goals and objectives of the agency, form an effective basis for formulation and justification of budget requests, and provide reliable financial and managerial data for management and control in execution of the budget and long-range plans;

(b) Using the end-products of the budgeting, accounting, and managerial-financial reporting organizations (by analyzing, evaluating, and synthesizing the data) to compare actual performance with planned objectives; interpreting and interrelating Programme plans, budget proposals, costs of operations, and Programme accomplishments; and accepting responsibility for the financial soundness of the agency — not only in terms of current year financial operations, but in terms of the soundness of financial planning for future operations. This requires the chief financial officer's involvement, on an advisory basis, in the fundamental elements of Programme development, Programme execution, and

Programme review and evaluation. It also involves furnishing integrated advice to the responsible Programme manager on the financial aspects of managing the agency's resources — so that the manager can maintain a balance between requirements and available resources that will permit the attainment of Programme objectives with minimum costs and maximum efficiency.

MANAGERIAL FINANCE

Managerial finance is the branch of the finance that concerns itself with the managerial significance of finance techniques. It is focused on assessment rather than technique.

The difference between a managerial and a technical approach can be seen in the questions one might ask of annual reports. One concerned with technique would be primarily interested in measurement. They would ask: are moneys being assigned to the right categories? Were generally accepted accounting principles GAAP followed? One concerned with management though would want to know what the figures mean.

- They might compare the returns to other businesses in their industry and ask: are we performing better or worse than our peers? If so, what is the source of the problem? Do we have the same profit margins? If not why? Do we have the same expenses? Are we paying more for something than our peers?
- They may look at changes in asset balances looking for red flags that indicate problems with bill collection or bad debt.
- They will analyse working capital to anticipate future cash flow problems.

Managerial finance is an interdisciplinary approach that borrows from both managerial accounting and corporate finance.

Sound financial management creates value and organisational agility through the allocation of scarce resources amongst competing business opportunities. It is an aid to the implementation and monitoring of business strategies and helps achieve business objectives.

MANAGERIAL ACCOUNTING ROLE

Managers also need to look at how resources are allocated within an organization. They need to know what each activity costs and why. These questions require managerial accounting techniques such as activity based costing.

Managers also need to anticipate future expenses. To get a better understanding of the accuracy of the budgeting process, they may use variable budgeting.

ROLE OF CORPORATE FINANCE

Managerial finance is also interested in determining the best way to use money to improve future opportunities to earn money and minimize the impact of financial shocks.

To accomplish these goals managerial finance uses the following techniques borrowed from Corporate finance:

- Valuation
- Portfolio theory
- Hedging
- Capital structure

CORPORATE FINANCE

Corporate finance is an area of finance dealing with financial decisions business enterprises make and the tools and analysis used to make these decisions. The primary goal of corporate finance is to maximize corporate value while managing the firm's financial risks. Although it is in principle different from managerial finance which studies the financial decisions of all firms, rather than corporations alone, the main concepts in the study of corporate finance are applicable to the financial problems of all kinds of firms.

The discipline can be divided into long-term and short-term decisions and techniques. Capital investment decisions are long-term choices about which projects receive investment, whether to finance that investment with equity or debt, and when or whether to pay dividends to shareholders. On the other hand, the short term decisions can be grouped under the heading "Working capital management". This subject deals with the short-term balance of current assets and current liabilities; the focus here is on managing cash, inventories, and short-term borrowing and lending.

The terms corporate finance and corporate financier are also associated with investment banking. The typical role of an investment bank is to evaluate the company's financial needs and raise the appropriate type of capital that best fits those needs.

CAPITAL INVESTMENT DECISIONS

Capital investment decisions are long-term corporate finance decisions relating to fixed assets and capital structure. Decisions are based on several inter-related criteria.

- Corporate management seeks to maximize the value of the firm by investing in projects which yield a positive net present value when valued using an appropriate discount rate.
- These projects must also be financed appropriately.
- If no such opportunities exist, maximizing shareholder value dictates that management must return excess cash to shareholders.

Capital investment decisions thus comprise an investment decision, a financing decision, and a dividend decision.

The Investment Decision

Management must allocate limited resources between competing opportunities in a process known as capital budgeting. Making this capital allocation decision requires estimating the value of each opportunity or project, which is a function of the size, timing and predictability of future cash flows.

Project Valuation

In general, each project's value will be estimated using a discounted cash flow valuation, and the opportunity with the highest value, as measured by the resultant net present value will be selected. This requires estimating the size and timing of all of the incremental cash flows resulting from the project. Such future cash flows are then discounted to determine their *present value*. These present values are then summed, and this sum net of the initial investment outlay is the NPV. The NPV is greatly affected by the discount rate. Thus, identifying the proper discount rate - often termed, the project "hurdle rate" - is critical to making an appropriate decision. The hurdle rate is the minimum acceptable return on an investment—i.e. the project appropriate discount rate.

The hurdle rate should reflect the riskiness of the investment, typically measured by volatility of cash flows, and must take into account the financing mix. Managers use models such as the CAPM or the APT to estimate a discount rate appropriate for a particular project, and use the weighted average cost of capital to reflect the financing mix selected.

In conjunction with NPV, there are several other measures used as selection criteria in corporate finance. These are visible from the DCF and include discounted payback period, IRR, Modified IRR, equivalent annuity, capital efficiency, and ROI. Alternatives to NPV include MVA/EVA and APV.

Valuing Flexibility

In many cases, for example RandD projects, a project may open paths of action to the company, but this reality will not typically be captured in a strict NPV approach. Management will therefore employ tools which place an explicit value on these options. So, whereas in a DCF valuation the most likely or average or scenario specific cash flows are discounted, here the"flexibile and staged nature" of the investment is modelled, and hence"all" potential payoffs are considered. The difference between the two valuations is the"value of flexibility" inherent in the project.

The two most common tools are Decision Tree Analysis and Real options analysis; they may often be used interchangeably:

- DTA values flexibility by incorporating possible events and consequent management decisions. In the decision tree, each management decision in response to an"event" generates a"branch" or"path" which the company could follow; the probabilities of each event are determined or specified by management.

Once the tree is constructed:

- "All" possible events and their resultant paths are visible to management;
- Given this"knowledge" of the events that could follow, management chooses the actions corresponding to the highest value path probability weighted;
- Then, assuming rational decision making, this path is taken as representative of project value.

• ROA is usually used when the value of a project is contingent on the value of some other asset or underlying variable.

Here:

- Using financial option theory as a framework, the decision to be taken is identified as corresponding to either a call option or a put option;
- An appropriate valuation technique is then employed - usually a variant on the Binomial options model or a bespoke simulation model, while Black Scholes type formulae are used less often.
- The"true" value of the project is then the NPV of the"most likely" scenario plus the option value.

Quantifying Uncertainty

Given the uncertainty inherent in project forecasting and valuation, analysts will wish to assess the sensitivity of project NPV to the various inputs to the DCF model. In a typical sensitivity analysis the analyst will vary one key factor while holding all other inputs constant, ceteris paribus.

The sensitivity of NPV to a change in that factor is then observed, and is calculated as a"slope": DNPV/Dfactor. For example, the analyst will determine NPV at various growth rates in annual revenue as specified, and then determine the sensitivity using this formula. Often, several variables may be of interest, and their various combinations produce a"value-surface", where NPV is then a function of several variables.

Using a related technique, analysts also run scenario based forecasts of NPV. Here, a scenario comprises a particular outcome for economy-wide,"global" factors as well as for company-specific factors. As an example, the analyst may specify specific growth scenarios, where all key inputs are adjusted so as to be consistent with the growth assumptions, and calculate the NPV for each.

Note that for scenario based analysis, the various combinations of inputs must be internally consistent, whereas for the sensitivity approach these need not be so. An application of this methodology is to determine an"unbiased" NPV, where management determines a probability for each scenario - the

NPV for the project is then the probability-weighted average of the various scenarios.

A further advancement is to construct stochastic or probabilistic financial models - as opposed to the traditional static and deterministic models. For this purpose, the most common method is to use Monte Carlo simulation to analyse the project's NPV. This method was introduced to finance by David B.

Hertz in 1964, although has only recently become common: today analysts are even able to run simulations in spreadsheet based DCF models, typically using an add-in, such as Crystal Ball. Using simulation, the cash flow components that are impacted by uncertainty are simulated, mathematically reflecting their"random characteristics". Here, in contrast to the scenario approach, the simulation produces several thousand random but possible outcomes, or"trials".

The output is then a histogram of project NPV, and the average NPV of the potential investment - as well as its volatility and other sensitivities - is then observed. This histogram provides information not visible from the static DCF: for example, it allows for an estimate of the probability that a project has a net present value greater than zero.

Continuing the example: instead of assigning three discrete values to revenue growth, and to the other relevant variables, the analyst would assign an appropriate probability distribution to each variable, and, where possible, specify the observed or supposed correlation between the variables.

These distributions would then be"sampled" repeatedly - incorporating this correlation - so as to generate several thousand scenarios, with corresponding valuations, which are then used to generate the NPV histogram.

The resultant statistics will be a more accurate mirror of the project's"randomness" than the variance observed under the scenario based approach.

The Financing Decision

Achieving the goals of corporate finance requires that any corporate investment be financed appropriately. Since both hurdle rate and cash flows will be affected, the financing mix can impact the valuation. Management must therefore identify the "optimal mix" of financing—the capital structure that results in maximum value.

The sources of financing will, generically, comprise some combination of debt and equity financing. Financing a project through debt results in a liability or obligation that must be serviced, thus entailing cash flow implications independent of the project's degree of success.

Equity financing is less risky with respect to cash flow commitments, but results in a dilution of ownership, control and earnings. The *cost of equity* is also typically higher than the *cost of debt* and so equity financing may result in an increased hurdle rate which may offset any reduction in cash flow risk.

Management must also attempt to match the financing mix to the asset being financed as closely as possible, in terms of both timing and cash flows.

One of the main theories of how firms make their financing decisions is the Pecking Order Theory, which suggests that firms avoid external financing while they have internal financing available and avoid new equity financing while they can engage in new debt financing at reasonably low interest rates. Another major theory is the Trade-Off Theory in which firms are assumed to trade-off the tax benefits of debt with the bankruptcy costs of debt when making their decisions. An emerging area in finance theory is right-financing whereby investment banks and corporations can enhance investment return and company value over time by determining the right investment objectives, policy framework, institutional structure, source of financing and expenditure framework within a given economy and under given market conditions.

One last theory about this decision is the Market timing hypothesis which states that firms look for the cheaper type of financing regardless of their current levels of internal resources, debt and equity.

The Dividend Decision

Whether to issue dividends, and what amount, is calculated mainly on the basis of the company's unappropriated profit and its earning prospects for the coming year. If there are no NPV positive opportunities, i.e. projects where returns exceed the hurdle rate, then management must return excess cash to investors. These *free cash flows* comprise cash remaining after all business expenses have been met.

This is the general case, however there are exceptions. For example, investors in a "Growth stock", expect that the company will, almost by definition, retain earnings so as to fund growth internally.

In other cases, even though an opportunity is currently NPV negative, management may consider "investment flexibility"/potential payoffs and decide to retain cash flows.Management must also decide on the form of the dividend distribution, generally as cash dividends or via a share buyback.

Various factors may be taken into consideration: where shareholders must pay tax on dividends, firms may elect to retain earnings or to perform a stock buyback, in both cases increasing the value of shares outstanding. Alternatively, some companies will pay "dividends" from stock rather than in cash. Today, it is generally accepted that dividend policy is value neutral.

Decision Criteria

Working capital is the amount of capital which is readily available to an organization. That is, working capital is the difference between resources in cash or readily convertible into cash and cash requirements. As a result, the decisions relating to working capital are always current, i.e. short term, decisions.

In addition to time horizon, working capital decisions differ from capital investment decisions in terms of discounting and profitability considerations; they are also "reversible" to some extent..

Working capital management decisions are therefore not taken on the same basis as long term decisions, and working capital management applies different criteria in decision making: the main considerations are:

- Cash flow/liquidity and
- Profitability/return on capital.
- The most widely used measure of cash flow is the net operating cycle, or cash conversion cycle. This represents the time difference between cash payment for raw materials and cash collection for sales. The cash conversion cycle indicates the firm's ability to convert its resources into cash. Because this number effectively corresponds to the time that the firm's cash is tied up in operations and unavailable for other activities, management generally aims at a low net count.
- In this context, the most useful measure of profitability is Return on capital. The result is shown as a percentage, determined by dividing relevant income for the 12 months by capital employed; Return on equity shows this result for the firm's shareholders. Firm value is enhanced when, and if, the return on capital, exceeds the cost of capital. ROC measures are therefore useful as a management tool, in that they link short-term policy with long-term decision making.

Management of Working Capital

Management will use a combination of policies and techniques for the management of working capital. These policies aim at managing the *current assets* and the short term financing, such that cash flows and returns are acceptable.

- Cash management. Identify the cash balance which allows for the business to meet day to day expenses, but reduces cash holding costs.
- Inventory management. Identify the level of inventory which allows for uninterrupted production but reduces the investment in raw materials - and minimizes reordering costs - and hence increases cash flow; Just In Time; Economic order quantity; Economic production quantity.
- Debtors management. Identify the appropriate credit policy, i.e. credit terms which will attract customers, such that any impact on cash flows and the cash conversion cycle will be offset by increased revenue and hence Return on Capital.

- Short term financing. Identify the appropriate source of financing, given the cash conversion cycle: the inventory is ideally financed by credit granted by the supplier; however, it may be necessary to utilize a bank loan or to "convert debtors to cash" through "factoring".

THE COMPONENTS OF THE WORK OF FINANCIAL MANAGERS

In general, the work of the financial manager may be divided into two categories; viz., that which must be included to meet the minimum requirements for this series and that which may be included in addition. These are as follows:

A. Functions which must be included:

1. Accounting — typically includes:
   (a) Planning the Programme within delegated limits;
   (b) Developing, revising, and/or adapting accounting systems;
   (c) Executing day-to-day ledger maintenance and related operations for the classification and other recording of financial transactions;
   (d) Analyzing the results and interpreting the effects of transactions upon the financial resources of the organization;
   (e) Applying accounting concepts to solve problems, render advice, or to meet other needs of management; and
   (f) Managing the total accounting Programme, including supervision of subordinate accountants, accounting technicians, voucher examiners, payroll clerks, and other similar supporting personnel.
2. Budgeting — typically includes:
   (a) The formulation — developing instructions, calls for estimates, preparing estimates, reviewing and consolidating estimates;
   (b) The presentation either within the organization or at hearings (within the agency, at the budget bureau, or subcommittee); and
   (c) The execution — funds control, Programme adjustments, review of reports and preparation of reports.
3. Managerial-Financial Reporting — typically includes not only the recurring budget, accounting, and financial reports but also Programme operation evaluation and statistical reports and other work performance type reports, both regular and one-time in nature. Managerial-financial reporting is the process of providing appropriate data to key officials at all levels of management for the purpose of helping to achieve the most effective Programme and financial management. Stress is placed on aiding in the making of management decisions. Normally, much of such data will be of a

financial character, developed from the accounting and the budget systems; however, frequently data will be a combination of both financial and non-financial information and, in some cases, the data may be entirely non-financial in nature. In its ideal form, the data are so integrated as to represent a single total data system. Since in good managerial-financial reporting, concern is given to the development of the systems that will provide the essential data, one of the normal responsibilities of the Financial Manager is the development, revision and/or adaptation of the managerial-financial reporting system.

4. Advice to Management — typically includes: advising from a financial point of view and serving as the technical expert on the financial aspects of all matters.

B. Functions directly related to the management of Financial Resources and Which* may *be Included:

1. Management Analysis
   —Typically includes: administering, supervising, or performing study, analysis, evaluation, development or improvement of managerial policies, practices, methods, and procedures;
2. Records or Paperwork Management
   — Typically includes: operating, maintaining, or administering one or more administrative control systems, services, processes or functions such as those for forms control, the handling of correspondence, directives control, the disposition of records;
3. Auditing
   — Typically includes: the establishment and improvement of audit policies, programs, methods, and procedures, and the achievement of a high standard of auditing; the proper timing and coverage of audits; the disposition of technical accounting questions developed in audits, including disposition through negotiations and conferences with affected business establishments or other interested organizations; responsibility for all auditing and related activities in connection with payments and cost analyses; and shaping, directing, and administering the audit activities;
4. Statistics
   — Typically includes: administering or performing professional work, or providing professional consultation in the application of statistical theories, techniques, and methods to the gathering and/or interpretation of quantified information; or advising on, administering, supervising, or performing work involved in collecting, editing, computing, compiling, analyzing; and presenting statistical data, where the work requires knowledge

and application of statistical methods and procedures, and techniques, but does not require professional knowledge of the mathematical or statistical theories, assumptions, or principles upon which they are based;

5. Digital Computer, Electric Accounting Machines, and Other Machine Systems
   — Typically includes: supervising or administering overall digital computer systems activities, including combined digital computer-tabulating equipment organizations; performing staff planning and administrative work in administering a machine system organization, whether EAM, ADP, or other.

MEANING OF FINANCIAL MANAGEMENT

By Financial Management we mean efficient use of economic resources namely capital funds. According to Phillippatus, "Financial management is concerned with the managerial decisions that result in the acquisition and financing of short term and long term credits for the firm". Here it deals with the situations that require selection of specific assets (or combination of assets), the selection of specific problem of size and growth of an enterprise.

Here the analysis deals with the expected inflows and outflows of funds and their effect on managerial objectives. Most acceptable definition was given by S.C. Kuchhal is that;"Financial Management deals with Procurement of funds and their effective utilization in the business". So the analysis simply states two main aspects of financial management like procurement of funds and an effective use of funds to achieve business objectives.

Procurement of Funds

As funds can be obtained from different sources so procurement of funds is considered as an important problem of business concerns. Funds procured from different sources have different characteristics in terms of risk, cost and control. Funds issued by the issue of equity shares are the best from risk point of view for the company as there is no question of repayment of equity capital except when the company is under liquidation. From the cost point of view equity capital is most expensive source of funds as dividend expectations of shareholders are normally higher than prevalent interest rates.

Financial management constitutes risk, cost and control. The cost of funds should be at minimum for a proper balancing of risk and control. In the globalised competitive scenario mobilization of funds plays a very significant role. Funds can be raised either through domestic market or from abroad. Foreign Direct Investment (FDI) as well as Foreign Institutional Investors (FII) are two major sources of raising funds. The mechanism of procurement of funds has to be modified in the light of requirements of foreign investors. From time to time it is seen that many firms have been liquidated not because their technology was obsolete or because their products were not in demand or their labour was not skilled and motivated but there was a complete mismanagement of financial affairs.

Even in a boom period, when a company make high profits there is also a fear of liquidation because of bad financial management. Financial management optimizes the output from the given input of funds. In the country like India where resources are scarce and the demand for funds are many, the need of proper financial management is required. In case of newly started companies with a high growth rate it is more important to have sound financial management since finance alone guarantees their survival. Financial management is very important in case of non-profit organizations, which do not pay adequate attentions to financial management. How ever a sound system of financial management has to be cultivated among bureaucrats, administrators, engineers, educationalists and public at a large.

Utilization of Funds

Effective utilization of funds as an important aspect of financial management avoids the situations where funds are either kept idle or proper uses are not being made. Funds procured involve a certain cost and risk. If the funds are not used properly then running business will be too difficult. In case of dividend decisions we also consider this. So it is crucial to employ the funds properly and profitably.

SCOPE OF FINANCIAL MANAGEMENT

A sound financial management is essential in all types of organizations whether it may be profit or non-profit. Financial management is essential in a planned Economy as well as in a capitalist set-up as it involves efficient use of the resources.

OBJECTIVES OF FINANCIAL MANAGEMENT

Efficient Financial management requires the existence of some objectives, which are as follows:

Wealth Maximization

It is commonly agreed that the objective of a firm is to maximize value or wealth. Value of a firm is represented by the market price of the company's common stock. The market price of a firm's stock represents the focal judgement of all market participants as to what the value of the particular firm is. It takes in to account present and prospective future earnings per share, the timing and risk of these earning, the dividend policy of the firm and many other factors that bear upon the market price of the stock. Market price acts as the performance index or report card of the firm's progress.

Prices in the share markets are largely affected by many factors like general economic outlook, outlook of particular company, technical factors and even mass psychology. Normally this value is a function of two factors as given below,

- The anticipated rate of earnings per share of the company
- The capitalization rate.

The likely rate of earnings per shares (EPS) depends upon the assessment as to how profitably a company is growing to operate in the future. The capitalization rate reflects the liking of the investors for the company.

Profit Maximization

Objective of financial management is same as the objective of a company that is to earn profit. But profit maximization cannot the sole objective of a company. It is a limited objective. If profits are given undue Importance then problems may arise as discussed below.

- The term profit is vague and it involves much more contradictions.
- Profit maximization has to be attempted with a realization of risks involved. A positive relationship exists between risk and profits. So both risk and profit objectives should be balanced.
- Profit Maximization does not take into account the time pattern of returns.
- Profit maximization fails to take into account the social considerations

METHODS OF FINANCIAL MANAGEMENT

In the field of financing there are various methods to procure funds. Funds may be obtained from long-term sources as well as from short-term sources. Long-term funds may be availed by owners that are shareholders, lenders by issuing debentures, from financial institutions, banks and public at large. Short-term funds may be availed from commercial banks, public deposits, etc. Financial leverage or trading on equity is an important method by which a finance manager may increase the return to common shareholders.

At the time of evaluating capital expenditure projects methods like average rate of return, pay back, internal rate of returns, net present value and profitability index are used. A firm can increase its profitability without affecting its liquidity by an efficient utilization of the current resources at the disposal of the firm. A firm can increase its profitability without affecting its liquidity by an efficient management of working capital. Similarly for the evaluation of a firm's performance there are different methods. Ratio analysis is a popular technique to evaluate different aspects of a firm. An investor takes in to account various ratios to know wheather investment in a particular company will be profitable or not. These ratios enable him to judge the profitability, solvency, liquidity and growth aspect of the firm.

FINANCIAL MANAGEMENT IN INDIA

In the country like India there is a changing scenario of financial management. As the economy is opening up and global participation is increasing very fast, the opportunities have no limits. Presently financial management passes through an era of experimentation as a larger part of finance activities are carried out.

A few highlights in this context:

- Interest rates are free from regulations.
- Rupee is fully convertible in current account.
- Optimum debt equity mix is possible.
- Maintaining share prices are also crucial. In liberalized scenario the capital market is an important avenue of funds for business.
- Ensuring management control is vital especially in the light of foreign participation.

CORPORATE VALUATION

Use Equity Multiples (as opposed to Enterprise Multiples). In order to consider how valuing a Financial Institution's balance sheet is different from a non-Financial firm. Consider how an industrials firm wields capital machinery (asset) and the loans it used to finance that asset (liabilities). The line is blurred in Financial Institutions, which must hold deposit accounts (assets) to fuel the issuance of loans. The same accounts are considered loans as they are held in ownership not of the bank, but of the individual client.

Discounted Cash Flow (DCF) Model

You'll need the FCFE (Free Cash Flow for Equity), which is the amount of money that is returned to shareholders. Calculate a FCFF (Free Cash Flow to the Firm): EBIT(1-tax rate)-Capital Expenditures+(Depreciation & Amortization) - (Net increase in working capital)= FCFF

FCFF-Debt+Cash=FCFE

Use the Capital Asset Pricing Model, not the Weighted Average Cost of Capital (for the same reasons one uses Equity Multiples in relative valuation) to determine the cost of equity (the return required by shareholders in order to make the decision to invest in a financial institutions)

Bank

The First Provincial Bank of Taiwan in Taipei, Republic of China was formerly the central bank of the Republic of China and issued the New Taiwan dollar. A bank is a business that provides banking services for profit. Traditional banking services include receiving deposits of money, lending money and processing transactions. Some banks (called Banks of Issue) issue banknotes as legal tender. Many banks offer ancillary financial services to make additional profit; for example: selling insurance products, investment products or stock broking.

Currently in most jurisdictions the business of banking is regulated and banks require permission to trade. Authorisation to trade is granted by bank regulatory authorities and provide rights to conduct the most fundamental banking services such as accepting deposits and making loans. There are also financial institutions that provide banking services without meeting the legal definition of a bank . Banks have a long history, and have influenced economies and politics for centuries.

The word bank comes from the early modern English banke, from French banque, an adaptation of Italian banca feminine, "used side by side," and in same sense, with banco masculine; adaptation of Teutonic bank, banc, "bench." The double form and gender in Romanic, cf. Italian, Spanish, Portuguese banco, banca, Provençal banc, banca, French banc, banche, are apparently original (cf. medieval Latin bancus, banca), and due to the double gender of the German: Old High German der, diu banch, Middle High German der, die banc, early modern and dialect German der, die bank. The original meaning "shelf, bench" was extended in Italian to that of "tradesman's stall, counter, money-changer's table, mensa argentaria, whence "money-shop, bank," a use of the word which passed, with the trade of banking, from Italy into other countries. In this sense, Italian uses both banco and banca, Spanish and Portuguese the masculine banco; but in French the Italian feminine banca was adapted as banque, whence English banke, bank. The word is thus ultimately identical with Bench and Bank.

Italian, monte "mount, heap, amount, stock," was used in some of the senses of "bank," the notion that the name banco, banca, originated in a German rendering of monte is erroneous: German bank had no such sense as "mount, heap," only that of "bench, shelf." Rather is it the fact, that in the development of banking, the banco of the money-changer, and the monte or "joint-stock capital" were at length combined, and bank applied in English to both. The terms bankrupt and "broke" are similarly derived from banca rotta, which refers to an out-of-business bank, having its bench physically broken. Money lenders in Northern Italy originally did business in open areas, or big open rooms, with each lender working from his own bench or table.

Traditionally, a bank generates profits from transaction fees on financial services and from the interest it charges for lending. In recent history, with historically low interest rates limiting banks' ability to earn money by lending deposited funds, much of a bank's income is provided by overdraft fees and riskier investments.

BANKS IN THE ECONOMY

ROLE IN THE MONEY SUPPLY

A bank raises funds by attracting deposits, borrowing money in the inter-bank market, or issuing financial instruments in the money market or a capital market. The bank then lends out most of these funds to borrowers. However, it would not be prudent for a bank to lend out all of its balance sheet. It must keep a certain proportion of its funds in reserve so that it can repay depositors who withdraw their deposits. Bank reserves are typically kept in the form of a deposit with a central bank. This behaviour is called fractional-reserve banking and it is a central issue of monetary policy. Some governments (or their central banks) restrict the proportion of a bank's balance sheet that can be lent out, and use this as a tool for controlling the money supply. Even where the reserve ratio is not controlled by the government, a minimum figure will still be set by regulatory authorities as part of bank regulation.

Size of Global Banking Industry

Worldwide assets of the largest 1,000 banks grew 15.5% in 2005 to reach a record $60.5 trillion. This follows a 19.3% increase in the previous year. EU banks held the largest share, 50% at the end of 2005, up from 38% a decade earlier. The growth in Europe's share was mostly at the expense of Japanese banks whose share more than halved during this period from 33% to 13%. The share of US banks also rose, from 10% to 14%. Most of the remainder was from other Asian and European countries.

The US had by far the most banks (7,540 at end-2005) and branches (75,000) in the world. The large number of banks in the US is an indicator of its geographical dispersity and regulatory structure resulting in a large number of small to medium sized institutions in its banking system. Japan had 129 banks and 12,000 branches. In 2004, Germany, France, and Italy had more than 30,000 branches each—more than double the 15,000 branches in the UK.

Bank Crises

Banks are susceptible to many forms of risk which have triggered occasional systemic crises. Risks include liquidity risk (the risk that many depositors will request withdrawals beyond available funds), credit risk (the risk that those that owe money to the bank will not repay), and interest rate risk (the risk that the bank will become unprofitable if rising interest rates force it to pay relatively more on its deposits than it receives on its loans), among others.

Banking crises have developed many times throughout history when one or more risks materialize for a banking sector as a whole. Prominent examples include the U.S. Savings and Loan crisis in 1980s and early 1990s, the Japanese banking crisis during the 1990s, the bank run that occurred during the Great Depression, and the recent liquidation by the central Bank of Nigeria, where about 25 banks were liquidated.

Regulation

The combination of the instability of banks as well as their important facilitating role in the economy led to banking being thoroughly regulated.

The amount of capital a bank is required to hold is a function of the amount and quality of its assets. Major banks are subject to the Basel Capital Accord promulgated by the Bank for International Settlements. In addition, banks are usually required to purchase deposit insurance to make sure smaller investors are not wiped out in the event of a bank failure.

Another reason banks are thoroughly regulated is that ultimately, no government can allow the banking system to fail. There is almost always a lender of last resort—in the event of a liquidity crisis (where short term obligations exceed short term assets) some element of government will step in to lend banks enough money to avoid bankruptcy.

Public Perceptions of Banks

In United States history, the National Bank was a major political issue during the presidency of Andrew Jackson. Jackson fought against the bank as a symbol of greed and profit-mongering, antithetical to the democratic ideals of the United States. Currently, many people consider that various banking policies take advantage of customers. Specific concerns are policies that permit banks to hold deposited funds for several days, to apply withdrawals before deposits or from greatest to least, which is most likely to cause the greatest overdraft, that allow backdating funds transfers and fee assessments, and that authorize electronic funds transfers despite an overdraft.

In response to the perceived greed and socially-irresponsible all-for-the-profit attitude of banks, in the last few decades a new type of banks called ethical banks have emerged, which only make social-responsible investments (for instance, no investment in the arms industry) and are transparent in all its operations. In the US, Credit unions have also gained popularity as an alternative financial resource for many consumers. Also, in various European countries, cooperative banks are regularly gaining market share in retail banking.

Profitability

Large banks in the United States are some of the most profitable corporations, especially relative to the small market shares they have. This amount is even higher if one counts the credit divisions of companies like Ford, which are responsible for a large proportion of those companies' profits. For example, the largest bank, Citigroup, which for the past 3 years has made more profit than any other company in the world, has only a 5% market share. If Citigroup were to be as dominant in its industry as a Home Depot, Starbucks, or Wal Mart in their respective industries, with a 30% market share — and if its profit margins scaled up proportionally — it would make more money than the top ten non-banking U.S. industries combined.

In the past 10 years in the United States, banks have taken many measures to ensure that they remain profitable while responding to ever-changing market conditions. First, this includes the Gramm-Leach-Bliley Act, which allows banks again to merge with investment and insurance houses. Merging banking, investment, and insurance functions allows traditional banks to respond to increasing consumer demands for "one stop shopping" by enabling cross-selling of products (which, the banks hope, will also increase profitability). Second, they have moved toward risk-based pricing on loans, which means charging higher interest rates for those people who they deem more risky to default on loans.

This dramatically helps to offset the losses from bad loans, lowers the price of loans to those who have better credit histories, and extends credit products to high risk customers who would have been denied credit under the previous system. Third, they have sought to increase the methods of payment processing available to the general public and business clients. These products include debit cards, pre-paid cards, smart-cards, and credit cards. These products make it easier for consumers to conveniently make transactions and smooth their consumption over time (in some countries with under-developed financial systems, it is still common to deal strictly in cash, including carrying suitcases filled with cash to purchase a home). However, with convenience there is also increased risk that consumers will mismanage their financial resources and accumulate excessive debt. Banks make money from card products through interest payments and fees charged to consumers and companies that accept the cards. The banks' main obstacles to increasing profits are existing regulatory burdens, new government regulation, and increasing competition from non-traditional financial institutions.

ROLE OF THE ACCOUNTANT

Financial reporting is a crucial element necessary for the corporate governance system to function effectively. Accountants and auditors are the primary providers of information to capital market participants. The directors of the company should be entitled to expect that management prepare the financial information in compliance with statutory and ethical obligations, and rely on auditors' competence.

Current accounting practice allows a degree of choice of method in determining the method of measurement, criteria for recognition, and even the definition of the accounting entity. The exercise of this choice to improve apparent performance (popularly known as creative accounting) imposes extra information costs on users. In the extreme, it can involve non-disclosure of information.

One area of concern is whether the accounting firm acts as both independent auditor and management consultant to the firm they are auditing. This may result in a conflict of interest which places the integrity of financial reports in doubt due to client pressure to appease management. The power of the corporate client to initiate and terminate management consulting services and, more fundamentally, to select and dismiss accounting firms contradicts the concept of an independent auditor.

The Enron collapse is an example of misleading financial reporting. Enron concealed huge losses by creating illusions that a third party was contractually obliged to pay the amount of any losses. However, the third party was an entity in which Enron had a substantial economic stake. In discussions of accounting practices with Arthur Andersen, the partner in charge of auditing, views inevitably led to the client prevailing.

However, good financial reporting is not a sufficient condition for the effectiveness of corporate governance if users don't process it, or if the informed user is unable to exercise a monitoring role due to high costs.

Regulation

Rules Versus Principles

Rules are typically thought to be simpler to follow than principles, demarcating a clear line between acceptable and unacceptable behaviour. Rules also reduce discretion on the part of individual managers or auditors.

In practice rules can be more complex than principles. They may be ill-equipped to deal with new types of transactions not covered by the code. Moreover, even if clear rules are followed, one can still find a way to circumvent their underlying purpose - this is harder to achieve if one is bound by a broader principle.

Enforcement

Enforcement can affect the overall credibility of a regulatory system. They both deter bad actors and level the competitive playing field. Nevertheless, greater enforcement is not always better, for taken too far it can dampen valuable risk-taking. In practice, however, this is largely a theoretical, as opposed to a real, risk.

BOARD COMPOSITION

Some researchers have found support for the relationship between frequency of meetings and profitability. Others have found a negative relationship between the proportion of external directors and firm performance, while others found no relationship between external board membership and performance. In a recent paper Bagahat and Black found that companies with more independent boards do not perform better than other companies. It is unlikely that board composition has a direct impact on firm performance.

Remuneration/Compensation

The results of previous research on the relationship between firm performance and executive compensation have failed to find consistent and significant relationships between executives' remuneration and firm performance. Low average levels of pay-performance alignment do not necessarily imply that this form of governance control is inefficient. Not all firms experience the same levels of agency conflict, and external and internal monitoring devices may be more effective for some than for others.

Some researchers have found that the largest CEO performance incentives came from ownership of the firm's shares, while other researchers found that the relationship between share ownership and firm performance was dependent on the level of ownership. The results suggest that increases in ownership above 20% cause management to become more entrenched, and less interested in the welfare of their shareholders.

Firm performance has been found to be positively associated with share option plans. These plans direct managers' energies and extend their decision horizons toward the long-term, rather than the short-term, performance of the company.

Attention to Corporate Governance

Corporate governance issues are receiving greater attention in both developed and developing countries as a result of the increasing recognition that a firm's corporate governance affects both its economic performance and its ability to access long-term, low-cost investment capital. In response to calls by OECD ministers, a revised version of its "Principles of Corporate Governance" was produced in 2004.

Numerous high-profile cases of corporate governance failure have focused the minds of governments, companies and the general public on the threat posed to the integrity of financial markets, although it is not clear that any system will or should prevent business failures, or that it is possible to provide a guarantee against fraud.

Corporate Governance concerns have been widely studied. For the United States, an analysis of these concerns has been published by the New York Society of Securities Analysts in their 2003 Corporate Governance Handbook. What constitutes good and bad corporate governance is an on-going debate in politics, civil society, and academia. For an international survey of the scientific literature see Becht, Bolton and Roell 2002.

The OECD publishes an annual paper on corporate governance. First issued in 1999, this chapter has provided the framework for regional corporate governance roundtables in cooperation with the World Bank around the world. It has been endorsed as one of the Financial Stability Forum's 12 key standards, and form the basis for the World Bank's Review of Observance of Standards and Codes.

Principal-agent Problem

In economics, the principal-agent problem treats the difficulties that arise under conditions of incomplete and asymmetric information when a principal hires an agent. Various mechanisms may be used to try to align the interests of the agent with those of the principal, such as piece rates/commissions, profit sharing, efficiency wages, the agent posting a bond, or fear of firing. The principal-agent problem is found in most employer/employee relationships, for example, when stockholders hire top executives of corporations.

Overview

In economics, the problem of motivating one party to act on behalf of another is known as 'the principal-agent problem'. The principal-agent problem arises when a principal compensates an agency for performing certain acts that are useful to the principal and costly to the agent, and where there are elements of the performance that are costly to observe. This is the case to some extent for all contracts that are written in a world of information asymmetry, uncertainty and risk. Here, principals do not know enough about whether (or to what extent) a contract is or has been satisfied. The solution to this information problem – closely related to the moral hazard problem – is to ensure (as far as possible) the provision of appropriate incentives so that agents act in the way principals wish. In terms of game theory, it involves changing the rules of the game so that the self-interested rational choices that the principal predicts the agent will make coincide with the choices the principal desires. Even in the limited arena of employment contracts, the difficulty of doing this in practice is reflected in a multitude of compensation mechanisms ('the carrot') and supervisory schemes ('the stick'), as well as in critique of such mechanisms as e.g. Deming expresses in his Seven Deadly Diseases of management.

Employment Contract

In the context of the employment contract, individual contracts form a major method of restructuring incentives, by connecting as closely as is optimal the information available about employee performance, and the compensation for that performance. Because of differences in the quantity and quality of information available about the performance of individual employees, the ability of employees to bear risk, and the ability of employees to manipulate evaluation methods, the structural details of individual contracts vary widely, including such mechanisms as "piece rates, options, discretionary bonuses, promotions, profit sharing, efficiency wages, deferred compensation, and so on." Typically, these mechanisms are used in the context of different types of employment: salespeople often receive some or all of their remuneration as commission, production workers are usually paid an hourly wage, while office workers are typically paid monthly or semimonthly (and if paid overtime, typically at a higher rate than the hourly rate implied by the salary). The way in which these mechanisms are used is different in the two parts of the economy which Doeringer and Piore called the "primary" and "secondary" sectors. The secondary sector is characterised by short-term employment relationships, little or no prospect of internal promotion, and the determination of wages primarily by market forces. In terms of occupations, it consists primarily of low or unskilled jobs, whether they are blue-collar (manual-labour), white-collar (e.g. filing clerks), or service jobs (e.g. waiters). These jobs are linked by the fact that they are characterized by "low skill levels, low earnings, easy entry, job impermanence, and low returns to education or experience."

Non-financial Compensation

Part of this variation in incentive structures and supervisory mechanisms may be attributable to variation in the level of intrinsic psychological satisfaction to be had from different types of work. Sociologists and psychologists frequently argue that individuals take a certain degree of pride in their work, and that introducing performance-related pay can destroy this "psycho-social compensation", because the exchange relation between employer and employee becomes much more narrowly economic, destroying most or all of the potential for social exchange. Evidence for this is inconclusive – Deci, and Lepper, Greene and Nisbett find support for this argument; Staw suggests other interpretations of the findings.

Team Production

On a related note, Drago and Garvey use Australian survey data to show that when agents are placed on individual pay-for-performance schemes, they are less likely to help their coworkers. This negative effect is particularly important in those jobs that involve strong elements of 'team production', where output reflects the contribution of many individuals, and individual contributions cannot be easily identified, and compensation is therefore based largely on the output of the team. In other words, pay-for-performance increases the incentives to free-ride, as there are large positive externalities to the efforts of an individual team member, and low returns to the individual. The negative incentive effects implied are confirmed by some empirical studies, eg Newhouse for shared medical practices (costs rise and doctors work fewer hours as more revenue is shared), and Leibowitz and Tollison find that larger law partnerships typically result in worse cost containment. As a counter, peer pressure can potentially solve the problem, but this depends on peer monitoring being relatively costless to the individuals doing the monitoring/ censuring in any particular instance (unless one brings in social considerations of norms and group identity and so on). Studies suggest that profit-sharing, for example, typically raises productivity by 3-5%, although there are some selection issues (Prendergast).

Empirical Evidence

There is however considerable empirical evidence of a positive effect of compensation on performance (although the studies usually involve "simple" jobs where aggregate measures of performance are available, which is where piece rates should be most effective). In one study, Lazear saw productivity rising by 35% (and wages by 12%) in a change from salary to piece rates, with a third of the productivity gain due to worker selection effects. Paarsch and Shearer also find evidence supportive of incentive and productivity effects from piece rates, as do Banker, Lee, and Potter , although the latter do not distinguish between incentive and worker selection effects. Fernie and Metcalf find that British jockeys perform significantly better when offered prizes for winning races compared to being on fixed retainers. McMillan, Whalley and Zhu and Groves et al look at Chinese agricultural and industrial data respectively and find significant incentive effects. Kahn and Sherer find that better evaluations of white-collar office workers were achieved by those employees who had a steeper relation between evaluations and pay. Nikkinen and Sahlstrom find empirical evidence that agency theory can be used, at least to some extent, to explain financial audit fees internationally.

Four principles of Contract Design

Milgrom and Roberts identify four basic principles of contract design:

- The Informativeness Principle,
- The Incentive-Intensity Principle,
- The Monitoring Intensity Principle, and
- The Equal Compensation Principle.

Informativeness Principle

In the absence of a world of perfect information, Holmstrom developed what became known as the Informativeness Principle. This essentially states that any measure of performance that (on the margin) reveals information about the effort level chosen by the agent should be included in the compensation contract. This includes, for example, Relative Performance Evaluation – measurement relative to other, similar agents, so as to filter out some common background noise factors, such as fluctuations in demand. By removing some exogenous sources of randomness in the agent's income, a greater proportion of the fluctuation in the agent's income falls under his control, increasing his ability to bear risk. If taken advantage of, by greater use of piece rates, this should improve incentives.

Incentive-Intensity Principle

However, setting incentives as intense as possible is not necessarily optimal from the point of view of the employer. The Incentive-Intensity Principle states that the optimal intensity of incentives depends on four factors: the incremental profits created by additional effort, the precision with which the desired activities are assessed, the agent's risk tolerance, and the agent's responsiveness to incentives. According to Prendergast, "the primary constraint on performance-related pay is that provision imposes additional risk on workers."

A typical result of the early principal-agent literature was that piece rates tend to 100% (of the compensation package) as the worker becomes more able to handle risk, as this ensures that workers fully internalize the consequences of their costly actions. In incentive terms, where we conceive of workers as self-interested rational individuals who provide costly effort (in the most general sense of the worker's input to the firm's production function), the more compensation varies with effort, the better the incentives for the worker to produce.

Monitoring Intensity Principle

The third principle – the Monitoring Intensity Principle – is complementary to the second, in that situations in which the optimal intensity of incentives is high correspond to situations in which the optimal level of monitoring is also high. Thus employers effectively choose from a "menu" of monitoring/incentive intensities. This is because monitoring is a costly means of reducing the variance of employee performance, which makes more difference to profits in the kinds of situations where it is also optimal to make incentives intense.

Equal Compensation Principle

The final principle is the Equal Compensation Principle, which essentially states that activities equally valued by the employer should be equally valuable (in terms of compensation, including non-financial things such as pleasantness) to the employee. This relates to the problem that employees may be engaged in several activities, and if some of these are not monitored or are monitored less heavily, these will be neglected, as activities with higher marginal returns to the employee are favoured. This can be thought of as a kind of "disintermediation" – targeting certain measurable variables may cause others to suffer. For example, teachers being rewarded by test scores of their students are likely to tend more towards teaching 'for the test', and de-emphasise less relevant but perhaps equally or more important aspects of education; while AT&T's practice at one time of rewarding programmers by the number of lines of code written resulted in programs that were longer than necessary – i.e. Programme efficiency suffering.

Following Holmstom and Milgrom (1990) and Baker (1992), this has become known as "multi-tasking" (where a subset of relevant tasks is rewarded, non-rewarded tasks suffer relative neglect). Because of this, the more difficult it is to completely specify and measure the variables on which reward is to be conditioned, the less likely that performance-related pay will be used: "in essence, complex jobs will typically not be evaluated through explicit contracts." Where explicit measures are used, they are more likely to be some kind of aggregate measure, for example, baseball and American Football players are rarely rewarded on the many specific measures available, but frequently receive bonuses for aggregate performance measures such as Most Valuable Player.

The alternative to objective measures is subjective performance evaluation, typically by supervisors. However, there is here a similar effect to "multi-tasking", as workers shift effort from that subset of tasks which they consider useful and constructive, to that subset which they think gives the greatest appearance of being useful and constructive, and more generally to try to curry personal favour with supervisors. (One can interpret this as a destruction of organizational social capital – workers identifying with, and actively working for the benefit of, the firm – in favour of the creation of personal social capital – the individual-level social relations which enable workers to get ahead.

A linear model

The four principles can be summarised in terms of the simplest (linear) model of incentive compensation:

$$w = a + b(e + x + g \times y)$$

where w stands for the wage, e for (unobserved) effort, x for unobserved exogenous effects on outcomes, and y for observed exogenous effects; while g and a represent the weight given to y, and the base salary, respectively. The interpretation of b is as the intensity of incentives provided to the employee.

Nonlinearities

The above discussion on explicit measures assumed that contracts would create the linear incentive structures summarised in the model above. But while the combination of normal errors and the absence of income effects yields linear contracts, many observed contracts are nonlinear. To some extent this is due to income effects as workers rise up a tournament/hierarchy: "Quite simply, it may take more money to induce effort from the rich than from the less well off." In addition, the marginal return to effort may increase: it is more important for a CEO to work hard than for a shop floor worker (eg Murphy 1998 highlights the importance of bonuses for executives). Similarly, the threat of being fired creates a nonlinearity in wages earned versus performance.

Moreover, many empirical studies illustrate inefficient behaviour arising from nonlinear objective performance measures, or measures over the course of a long period (eg a year), which create nonlinearities in time due to discounting behaviour. This inefficient behaviour arises because incentive structures are varying: for example, when a worker has already exceeded a quota or has no hope of reaching it, versus being close to reaching it – eg Healy (1985), Oyer (1997), Leventis (1997). Leventis shows that New York surgeons, penalised for exceeding a certain mortality rate, take less risky cases as they approach the threshold. Courty and Marshke (1997) provide evidence on incentive contracts offered to agencies, which receive bonuses on reaching a quota of graduated trainees within a year. This causes them to 'rush-graduate' trainees in order to make the quota.

OBJECTIVE AND SUBJECTIVE PERFORMANCE EVALUATION

The major problem in measuring employee performance in cases where it is difficult to draw a straightforward connection between performance and profitability is the setting of a standard by which to judge the performance. One method of setting an absolute objective performance standard - rarely used because it is costly and only appropriate for simple repetitive tasks - is time-and-motion studies, which study in detail how fast it is possible to do a certain task. These have been used constructively in the past, particularly in manufacturing. More generally, however, even within the field of objective performance evaluation, some form of relative performance evaluation must be used. Typically this takes the form of comparing the performance of a worker to that of his peers in the firm or industry, perhaps taking account of different exogenous circumstances affecting that

Subjective Performance Evaluation

Subjective performance evaluation allows the use of a subtler, more balanced assessment of employee performance, and is typically used for more complex jobs where comprehensive objective measures are difficult to specify and/or measure. Whilst often the only feasible method, the attendant problems with subjective performance evaluation have resulted in a variety of incentive structures and supervisory schemes.

One problem, for example, is that supervisors may under-report performance in order to save on wages, if they are in some way residual claimants, or perhaps rewarded on the basis of cost savings. This tendency is of course to some extent offset by the danger of retaliation and/or demotivation of the employee, if the supervisor is responsible for that employee's output. As an example, there have been numerous cases where net profits were apparently underreported on successful Hollywood films, where actors or writers had been promised a percentage of net profits – Cheatham, David, and Cheatham.

Another problem relates to what is known as the "compression of ratings". Two related influences – centrality bias, and leniency bias - have been documented (Landy and Farr 1980, Murphy and Cleveland 1991). The former results from supervisors being reluctant to distinguish critically between workers (perhaps for fear of destroying team spirit), while the latter derives from supervisors being averse to offering poor ratings to subordinates, especially where these ratings are used to determine pay, not least because bad evaluations may be demotivating rather than motivating. However, these biases introduce noise into the relationship between pay and effort, reducing the incentive effect of performance-related pay. Milkovich and Wigdor (1991) suggest that this is the reason for the common separation of evaluations and pay, with evaluations primarily used to allocate training.

PROCESSES, CUSTOMS, POLICIES, LAWS OF CORPORATE GOVERNANCE

Corporate governance is the set of processes, customs, policies, laws and institutions affecting the way a corporation is directed, administered or controlled. Corporate governance also includes the relationships among the many players involved (the stakeholders) and the goals for which the corporation is governed. The principal players are the shareholders, management and the board of directors. Other stakeholders include employees, suppliers, customers, banks and other lenders, regulators, the environment and the community at large.

Corporate governance is a multi-faceted subject. An important theme of corporate governance deals with issues of accountability and fiduciary duty, essentially advocating the implementation of guidelines and mechanisms to ensure good behaviour and protect shareholders. Another key focus is the economic efficiency view, through which the corporate governance system should aim to optimize economic results, with a strong emphasis on shareholders welfare. There are yet other sides to the corporate governance subject, such as the stakeholder view, which calls for more attention and accountability to players other than the shareholders (e.g.: the employees or the environment). Recently there has been considerable interest in the corporate governance practices of modern corporations, particularly since the high-profile collapses of large US firms such as Enron Corporation and Worldcom.

Definition

The term corporate governance has come to mean two things.

- The processes by which companies are directed and controlled.
- A field in economics, which studies the many issues arising from the separation of ownership and control.

Relevant rules include applicable laws of the land as well as internal rules of a corporation. Relationships include those between all related parties, the most important of which are the owners, managers, directors of the board, regulatory authorities and to a lesser extent employees and the community at large. Systems and processes deal with matters such as delegation of authority. The corporate governance structure spells out the rules and procedures for making decisions on corporate affairs. It also provides the structure through which the company objectives are set, as well as the means of attaining and monitoring the performance of those objectives.

Corporate governance is used to monitor whether outcomes are in accordance with plans and to motivate the organisation to be more fully informed in order to maintain or alter organisational activity. Corporate governance is the mechanism by which individuals are motivated to align their actual behaviours with the overall participants.

History

In the 19th century, state corporation law enhanced the rights of corporate boards to govern without unanimous consent of shareholders in exchange for statutory benefits like appraisal rights, in order to make corporate governance more efficient. Since that time, and because most large publicly traded corporations in America are incorporated under corporate administration friendly Delaware law, and because America's wealth has been increasingly securitized into various corporate entities and institutions, the rights of individual owners and shareholders have become increasingly derivative and dissipated. The concerns of shareholders over administration pay and stock losses periodically has led to more frequent calls for Corporate Governance reforms.

In the 20th century in the immediate aftermath of the Wall Street Crash of 1929 legal scholars such as Adolf Augustus Berle, Edwin Dodd, and Gardiner C. Means pondered on the changing role of the modern corporation in society. Berle and Means' monograph "The Modern Corporation and Private Property" continues to have a profound influence on the conception of corporate governance in scholarly debates today.

From the Chicago school of economics, Ronald Coase's "Nature of the Firm" introduced the notion of transaction costs into the understanding of why firms are founded and how they continue to behave. Fifty years later, Eugene Fama and Michael Jensen's "The Separation of Ownership and Control" (1983, Journal of Law and Economics) firmly established agency theory as a way of understanding corporate governance: the firm is seen as a series of contracts. Agency theory's dominance was highlighted in a 1989 article by Kathleen Eisenhardt.

American expansion after World War II through the emergence of multinational corporations saw the establishment of the managerial class. Accordingly, the following Harvard Business School management professors published influential monographs studying their prominence: Myles Mace (entrepreneurship), Alfred D. Chandler, Jr. (business history), Jay Lorsch (organizational behaviour) and Elizabeth MacIver (organizational behaviour). According to Lorsch and MacIver "many large corporations have dominant control over business affairs without sufficient accountability or monitoring by their board of directors."

Current preoccupation with corporate governance can be pinpointed at two events: The East Asian Crisis of 1997 saw the economies of Thailand, Indonesia, South Korea, Malaysia and The Philippines severely affected by the exit of foreign capital after property assets collapsed. The lack of corporate governance mechanisms in these countries highlighted the weaknesses of the institutions in their economies. The second event was the American corporate crises of 2001-2002 which saw the collapse of two big corporations: Enron and WorldCom, and the ensuing scandals and collapses in other corporations such as Arthur Andersen, Global Crossing and Tyco.

Role of Institutional Investors

Many years ago, worldwide, buyers and sellers of corporation stocks were *individual* investors, such as wealthy businessmen. Over time, markets have become more *institutionalized*; buyers and sellers are largely institutions (e.g., pension funds, insurance companies, mutual funds, hedge funds, investor groups, and banks). The rise of the institutional investor has brought with it some increase of professional diligence which has tended to improve regulation of the stock market (but not necessarily in the interest of the small investor or even of the naïve institutions, of which there are many). Note that this process occurred simultaneously with the direct growth of individuals investing in the market (for example individuals have twice as much money in mutual funds as they do in bank accounts). However this growth occurred primarily in individuals turning over their funds to professionals to manage, such as in mutual funds. In this way, the majority of investment now is described as "institutional investment" even though the vast majority of the funds are for the benefit of individual investors.

Unfortunately, there has been a concurrent lapse in the oversight of large corporations, which are now almost all owned by large institutions. The Board of Directors of large corporations used to be chosen by the principal shareholders, who usually had an emotional as well as monetary investment in the company (think Ford), and the Board diligently kept an eye on the company and its principal executives (they usually hired and fired the President, or Chief executive officer— CEO). Nowadays, if the owning institutions don't like what the President/CEO is doing and they feel that firing him will be costly (think "golden handshake") and/or time consuming, they will simply sell out their interest. Also, nowadays, the Board is mostly chosen by the President/CEO, and may be made up primarily of his cronies (or, at least, officers of the corporation, who owe their jobs to him, or fellow CEOs from other corporations). Since the (institutional) shareholders rarely object, the President/CEO generally takes the Chairman of the Board position for himself (which makes it much more difficult for the institutional owners to "fire" him). Finally, the largest pools of invested money (such as the mutual fund 'Vanguard 500', or the largest investment management firm for corporations, State Street) are designed simply to invest in a very large number of companies with sufficient liquidity, based on the idea that this strategy will largely eliminate individual company or financial risk and, therefore, these investors have even less interest in what a particular company is doing.

Since the marked rise in the use of Internet transactions in the 1990s, both individual and professional stock investors around the world have emerged as a potential new kind of major (short term) force in the ownership of corporations and in the markets: the casual participant. Even as the purchase of individual shares in any one corporation by individual investors diminishes, the sale of derivatives (e.g., exchange-traded funds (ETFs), Stock market index options, etc.) has soared. So, the interests of most investors are now increasingly rarely tied to the fortunes of individual corporations.

But, the ownership of stocks in markets around the world varies; for example, the majority of the shares in the Japanese market are held by financial companies and industrial corporations (there is a large amount of cross-holding among Japanese keiretsu corporations and within S. Korean chaebol 'groups'), whereas stock in the USA or the UK and Europe are much more broadly owned, often still by large individual investors. In the latter half of the 1990s, during the Asian financial crisis, a lot of the attention fell upon the corporate governance systems of the developing world, which tend to be heavily into cronyism and nepotism.

In the first half of the 1990s, the issue of corporate governance in the U.S. received considerable press attention due to the wave of (belated?) CEO dismissals (e.g.: IBM, Kodak, Honeywell) by their boards. Calpers led a wave of institutional shareholder activism (something only very rarely seen before), as a way of ensuring that corporate value would not be destroyed by the now traditionally cozy relationships between the CEO and the board of directors. In the early 2000s, the massive bankruptcies (and criminal malfeasance) of Enron and Worldcom, as well as lesser corporate debacles, such as Adelphia Communications, AOL, Arthur Andersen, Global Crossing, Tyco, and, more recently, Freddie Mac and Fannie Mae, led to increased shareholder and governmental interest in corporate governance, culminating in the passage of the Sarbanes-Oxley Act of 2002. Since then, the stock market has greatly recovered, and shareholder zeal has waned accordingly.

PARTIES TO CORPORATE GOVERNANCE

Parties involved in corporate governance include the regulatory body (e.g. the Chief Executive Officer, the board of directors, management and shareholders. Other stakeholders who take part include suppliers, employees, creditors, customers and the community at large. In corporations, the shareholder delegates decision rights to the manager to act in the principal's best interests. This separation of ownership from control implies a loss of effective control by shareholders over managerial decisions. Partly as a result of this separation between the two parties, a system of corporate governance controls is implemented to assist in aligning the incentives of managers with those of shareholders. With the significant increase in equity holdings of investors, there has been an opportunity for a reversal of the separation of ownership and control problems because ownership is not so diffuse.

A board of directors often plays a key role in corporate governance. It is their responsibility to endorse the organisation's strategy, develop directional policy, appoint, supervise and remunerate senior executives and to ensure accountability of the organisation to its owners and authorities. All parties to corporate governance have an interest, whether direct or indirect, in the effective performance of the organisation. Directors, workers and management receive salaries, benefits and reputation, while shareholders receive capital return. Customers receive goods and services; suppliers receive compensation for their goods or services. In return these individuals provide value in the form of natural, human, social and other forms of capital.

A key factor in an individual's decision to participate in an organisation e.g. through providing financial capital and trust that they will receive a fair share of the organisational returns. If some parties are receiving more than their fair return then participants may choose to not continue participating leading to organisational collapse.

Principles

Key elements of good corporate governance principles include honesty, trust and integrity, openness, performance orientation, responsibility and accountability, mutual respect, and commitment to the organisation. Of importance is how directors and management develop a model of governance that aligns the values of the corporate participants and then evaluate this model periodically for its effectiveness. In particular, senior executives should conduct themselves honestly and ethically, especially concerning actual or apparent conflicts of interest, and disclosure in financial reports.

Commonly accepted principles of corporate governance include:

- Rights and equitable treatment of shareholders: Organisations should respect the rights of shareholders and help shareholders to exercise those rights. They can help shareholders exercise their rights by effectively communicating information that is understandable and accessible and encouraging shareholders to participate in general meetings.
- Interests of other stakeholders: Organisations should recognise that they have legal and other obligations to all legitimate stakeholders.
- Role and responsibilities of the board: The board needs a range of skills and understanding to be able to deal with various business issues and have the ability to review and challenge management performance. It needs to be of sufficient size and have an appropriate level of commitment to fulfill its responsibilities and duties. There are issues about the appropriate mix of executive and non-executive directors. The key roles of chairperson and CEO should not be held by the same person.
- Integrity and ethical behaviour: Organisations should develop a code of conduct for their directors and executives that promotes ethical and responsible decision making. It is important to understand, though, that systemic reliance on integrity and ethics is bound to eventual failure.
- Disclosure and transparency: Organisations should clarify and make publicly known the roles and responsibilities of board and management to provide shareholders with a level of accountability.

They should also implement procedures to independently verify and safeguard the integrity of the company's financial reporting. Disclosure of material matters concerning the organisation should be timely and balanced to ensure that all investors have access to clear, factual information.

Issues involving corporate governance principles include:

- Oversight of the preparation of the entity's financial statements
- Internal controls and the independence of the entity's auditors
- Review of the compensation arrangements for the chief executive officer and other senior executives
- The way in which individuals are nominated for positions on the board
- The resources made available to directors in carrying out their duties
- Oversight and management of risk
- Dividend policy

Mechanisms and Controls

Corporate governance mechanisms and controls are designed to reduce the inefficiencies that arise from moral hazard and adverse selection. For example, to monitor managers' behaviour, an independent third party (the auditor) attests the accuracy of information provided by management to investors. An ideal control system should regulate both motivation and ability.

Internal Corporate Governance Controls

Internal corporate governance controls monitor activities and then take corrective action to accomplish organisational goals. Examples include:

- Monitoring by the board of directors: The board of directors, with its legal authority to hire, fire and compensate top management, safeguards invested capital. Regular board meetings allow potential problems to be identified, discussed and avoided. Whilst non-executive directors are thought to be more independent, they may not always result in more effective corporate governance and may not increase performance. Different board structures are optimal for different firms. Moreover, the ability of the board to monitor the firm's executives is a function of its access to information. Executive directors possess superior knowledge of the decision-making process and therefore evaluate top management on the basis of the quality of its decisions that lead to financial performance outcomes, *ex ante*. It could be argued, therefore, that executive directors look beyond the financial criteria.
- Remuneration: Performance-based remuneration is designed to relate some proportion of salary to individual performance. It may be in the form of cash or non-cash payments such as shares and share

options, superannuation or other benefits. Such incentive schemes, however, are reactive in the sense that they provide no mechanism for preventing mistakes or opportunistic behaviour, and can elicit myopic behaviour.

- Audit committees

External Corporate Governance Controls

External corporate governance controls encompass the controls external stakeholders exercise over the organisation.

Examples include:

- Debt covenants
- External auditors
- Government regulations
- Media pressure
- Takeovers
- Competition
- Managerial labour market

Systemic Problems of Corporate Governance

- Supply of accounting information: Financial accounts form a crucial link in enabling providers of finance to monitor directors. Imperfections in the financial reporting process will cause imperfections in the effectiveness of corporate governance. This should, ideally, be corrected by the working of the external auditing process.
- Demand for information: A barrier to shareholders using good information is the cost of processing it, especially to a small shareholder. The traditional answer to this problem is the efficient market hypothesis (in finance, the efficient market hypothesis (EMH) asserts that financial markets are efficient), which suggests that the shareholder will free ride on the judgements of larger professional investors.
- Monitoring costs: In order to influence the directors, the shareholders must combine with others to form a significant voting group which can pose a real threat of carrying resolutions or appointing directors at a general meeting.

CORPORATE GOVERNANCE MODELS AROUND THE WORLD

Anglo-American Model

There are many different models of corporate governance around the world. These differ according to the variety of capitalism in which they are embedded. The liberal model that is common in Anglo-American countries tends to give priority to the interests of shareholders. The coordinated model that one finds in Continental Europe and Japan also recognizes the interests of workers, managers, suppliers, customers, and the community. Both models have distinct competitive advantages, but in different ways. The liberal model of corporate governance encourages radical innovation and cost competition, whereas the coordinated model of corporate governance facilitates incremental innovation and quality competition.

In the United States, a corporation is governed by a board of directors, which has the power to choose an executive officer, usually known as the chief executive officer. The CEO has broad power to manage the corporation on a daily basis, but needs to get board approval for certain major actions, such as hiring his/her immediate subordinates, raising money, acquiring another company, major capital expansions, or other expensive projects. Other duties of the board may include policy setting, decision making, monitoring management's performance, or corporate control.

The board of directors is nominally selected by and responsible to the shareholders, but the bylaws of many companies make it difficult for all but the largest shareholders to have any influence over the makeup of the board; normally, individual shareholders are not offered a choice of board nominees among which to choose, but are merely asked to rubberstamp the nominees of the sitting board. Perverse incentives have pervaded many corporate boards in the developed world, with board members beholden to the chief executive whose actions they are intended to oversee. Frequently, members of the boards of directors are CEOs of other corporations, which some see as a conflict of interest.

Non Anglo-American Model

In East Asian countries, family-owned companies dominate. A study by Claessens, Djankov and Lang (2000) investigated the top 15 families in East Asian countries and found that they dominated listed corporate assets. In countries such as Pakistan, Indonesia and the Philippines, the top 15 families controlled over 50% of publicly owned corporations through a system of family cross-holdings, thus dominating the capital markets. Family-owned companies also dominate the Latin model of corporate governance, that is companies in Italy, Spain, France (to a certain extent), Brazil, Mexico and other countries in South America.

Codes and Guidelines

Corporate governance principles and codes have been developed in different countries and issued from stock exchanges, corporations, institutional investors, or associations (institutes) of directors and managers with the support of governments and international organizations. As a rule, compliance with these governance recommendations is not mandated by law, although the codes linked to stock exchange listing requirements may have a coercive effect.

For example, companies quoted on the London and Toronto Stock Exchanges formally need not follow the recommendations of their respective national codes. However, they must disclose whether they follow the recommendations in those documents and, where not, they should provide explanations concerning divergent practices. Such disclosure requirements exert a significant pressure on listed companies for compliance.

In the United States, companies are primarily regulated by the state in which they incorporate though they are also regulated by the federal government and, if they are public, by their stock exchange. The highest number of companies are incorporated in Delaware, including more than half of the Fortune 500. This is due to Delaware's generally business-friendly corporate legal environment and the existence of a state court dedicated solely to business issues (Delaware Court of Chancery). Most states' corporate law generally follow the American Bar Association's Model Business Corporation Act. While Delaware does not follow the Act, it still considers its provisions and several prominent Delaware justices, including former Delaware Supreme Court Chief Justice E. Norman Veasey, participate on ABA committees.

One issue that has been raised since the Disney decision in 2005 is the degree to which companies manage their governance responsibilities; in other words, do they merely try to supersede the legal threashold or should they create governance guidelines that ascend to the level of best practice. For example, the guidelines issued by associations of directors, corporate managers and individual companies tend to be wholly voluntary. For example, The GM Board Guidelines reflect the company's efforts to improve its own governance capacity. Such documents, however, may have a wider multiplying effect prompting other companies to adopt similar documents and standards of best practice.

One of the most influential guidelines has been the 1999 OECD Principles of Corporate Governance. This was revised in 2004. The OECD remains a proponent of corporate governance principles throughout the world. The World Business Council for Sustainable Development WBCSD has also done substantial work on corporate governance, particularly on accountability and reporting, and in 2004 created an Issue Management Tool: Strategic challenges for business in the use of corporate responsibility codes, standards, and frameworks.This document aims to provide general information, a "snap-shot" of the landscape and a perspective from a think-tank/professional association on a few key codes, standards and frameworks relevant to the sustainability agenda.

Corporate Governance and Firm Performance

In its 'Global Investor Opinion Survey' of over 200 institutional investors first undertaken in 2000 and updated in 2002, McKinsey found that 80% of the respondents would pay a premium for well-governed companies. They defined a well-governed company as one that had mostly out-side directors, who had no management ties, undertook formal evaluation of its directors, and was responsive to investors' requests for information on governance issues. The size of the premium varied by market, from 11% for Canadian companies to around 40% for companies where the regulatory backdrop was least certain (those in Morocco, Egypt and Russia).

Other studies have linked broad perceptions of the quality of companies to superior share price performance. In a study of five year cumulative returns of Fortune Magazine's survey of 'most admired firms', Antunovich et al found that those "most admired" had an average return of 125%, whilst the 'least admired' firms returned 80%. In a separate study Business Week enlisted institutional investors and 'experts' to assist in differentiating between boards with good and bad governance and found that companies with the highest rankings had the highest financial returns. On the other hand, research into the relationship between specific corporate governance controls and firm performance has been mixed and often weak. The following examples are illustrative.

FINANCIAL RATIO ANALYSIS

Financial ratio analysis is the calculation and comparison of ratios which are derived from the information in a company's financial statements. The level and historical trends of these ratios can be used to make inferences about a company's financial condition, its operations and attractiveness as an investment.

Financial ratios are calculated from one or more pieces of information from a company's financial statements. For example, the "gross margin" is the gross profit from operations divided by the total sales or revenues of a company, expressed in percentage terms. In isolation, a financial ratio is a useless piece of information. In context, however, a financial ratio can give a financial analyst an excellent picture of a company's situation and the trends that are developing.

A ratio gains utility by comparison to other data and standards. Taking our example, a gross profit margin for a company of 25% is meaningless by itself. If we know that this company's competitors have profit margins of 10%, we know that it is more profitable than its industry peers which is quite favourable.

If we also know that the historical trend is upwards, for example has been increasing steadily for the last few years, this would also be a favourable sign that management is implementing effective business policies and strategies.

Financial ratio analysis groups the ratios into categories which tell us about different facets of a company's finances and operations. An overview of some of the categories of ratios is given below.

- Leverage Ratios which show the extent that debt is used in a company's capital structure.
- Liquidity Ratios which give a picture of a company's short term financial situation or solvency.

- Operational Ratios which use turnover measures to show how efficient a company is in its operations and use of assets.
- Profitability Ratios which use margin analysis and show the return on sales and capital employed.
- Solvency Ratios which give a picture of a company's ability to generate cashflow and pay it financial obligations.

It is imperative to note the importance of the proper context for ratio analysis. Like computer programming, financial ratio is governed by the GIGO law of *"Garbage In...Garbage Out!"* A cross industry comparison of the leverage of stable utility companies and cyclical mining companies would be worse than useless.

Examining a cyclical company's profitability ratios over less than a full commodity or business cycle would fail to give an accurate long-term measure of profitability. Using historical data independent of fundamental changes in a company's situation or prospects would predict very little about future trends. For example, the historical ratios of a company that has undergone a merger or had a substantive change in its technology or market position would tell very little about the prospects for this company.

Credit analysts, those interpreting the financial ratios from the prospects of a lender, focus on the "downside" risk since they gain none of the upside from an improvement in operations.

They pay great attention to liquidity and leverage ratios to ascertain a company's financial risk. Equity analysts look more to the operational and profitability ratios, to determine the future profits that will accrue to the shareholder.Although financial ratio analysis is well-developed and the actual ratios are well-known, practicing financial analysts often develop their own measures for particular industries and even individual companies. Analysts will often differ drastically in their conclusions from the same ratio analysis.

Profitability Ratios

These ratios tell us whether a business is making profits - and if so whether at an acceptable rate.

The key ratios are:

Ratio	Calculation	Comments
Gross Profit Margin	[Gross Profit / Revenue] x 100 (expressed as a percentage	This ratio tells us something about the business's ability consistently to control its production costs or to manage the margins its makes on products its buys and sells. Whilst sales value and volumes may move up and down significantly, the gross profit margin is usually quite stable (in percentage terms). However, a small increase (or decrease) in profit margin, however caused can produce a substantial change in overall profits.
Operating Profit Margin	[Operating Profit / Revenue] x 100 (expressed as a percentage)	Assuming a constant gross profit margin, the operating profit margin tells us something about a company's ability to control its other operating costs or overheads.
Return on capital employed ("ROCE")	Net profit before tax, interest and dividends ("EBIT") / total assets (or total assets less current liabilities	ROCE is sometimes referred to as the "primary ratio"; it tells us what returns management has made on the resources made available to them before making any distribution of those returns.

Efficiency ratios

These ratios give us an insight into how efficiently the business is employing those resources invested in fixed assets and working capital.

Ratio	Calculation	Comments
Sales /Capital Employed	Sales / Capital employed	A measure of total asset utilisation. Helps to answer the question - what sales are being generated by each pound's worth of assets invested in the business. Note, when combined with the return on sales it generates the primary ratio - ROCE.
Sales or Profit / Fixed Assets	Sales or profit / Fixed Assets	This ratio is about fixed asset capacity. A reducing sales or profit being generated from each pound invested in fixed assets may indicate overcapacity or poorer-performing equipment.
Stock Turnover	Cost of Sales / Average Stock Value	Stock turnover helps answer questions such as "have we got too much money tied up in inventory"?. An increasing stock turnover figure or one which is much larger than the "average" for an industry, may indicate poor stock management.
Credit Given / "Debtor Days"	(Trade debtors (average, if possible) / (Sales)) x 365	The "debtor days" ratio indicates whether debtors are being allowed excessive credit. A high figure (more than the industry average) may suggest general problems with debt collection or the financial position of major customers.
Credit taken / "Creditor Days"	((Trade creditors + accruals) / (cost Of sales + Other purchases)) x 365	A similar calculation to that for debtors, giving an insight into whether a business i taking full advantage of trade credit available to it.

Liquidity Ratios

Liquidity ratios indicate how capable a business is of meeting its short-term obligations as they fall due:

Ratio	Calculation	Comments
Current Ratio	Current Assets / Current Liabilities	A simple measure that estimates whether the business can pay debts due within one year from assets that it expects to turn into cash within that year. A ratio of less than one is often a cause for concern, particularly if it persists for any length of time.
Quick Ratio (or "Acid Test"	Cash and near cash (short-term investments + trade debtors)	Not all assets can be turned into cash quickly or easily. Some - notably raw materials and other stocks - must first be turned into final product, then sold and the cash collected from debtors. The Quick Ratio therefore adjusts the Current Ratio to eliminate all assets that are not already in cash (or "near-cash") form. Once again, a ratio of less than one would start to send out danger signals.

Stability Ratios

These ratios concentrate on the long-term health of a business - particularly the effect of the capital/finance structure on the business:

Ratio	Calculation	Comments
Gearing	Borrowing (all long-term debts + normal overdraft) / Net Assets (or Shareholders' Funds)	Gearing (otherwise known as "leverage") measures the proportion of assets invested in a business that are financed by borrowing. In theory, the higher the level of borrowing (gearing) the higher are the risks to a business, since the payment of interest and repayment of debts are not "optional" in the same way as dividends. However, gearing can be a financially sound part of a business's capital structure particularly if the business has strong, predictable cash flows.
Interest cover	Operating profit before interest / Interest	This measures the ability of the business to "service" its debt. Are profits sufficient to be able to pay interest and other finance costs?

Investor Ratios

There are several ratios commonly used by investors to assess the performance of a business as an investment:

Ratio	Calculation	Comments
Earnings per share ("EPS")	Earnings (profits) attributable to rdinary shareholders / Weighted average ordinary shares in issue during the year	A requirement of the London Stock Exchange - an important ratio. EPS measures the overall profit generated for each share in existence over a particular period.
Price-Earnings Ratio ("P/E Ratio")	Market price of share / Earnings per Share	At any time, the P/E ratio is an indication of how highly the market "rates" or "values" a business. A P/E ratio is best viewed in the context of a sector or market average to get a feel for relative value and stock market pricing.
Dividend Yield	(Latest dividend per ordinary share / current market price of share) x 100	This is known as the "payout ratio". It provides a guide as to the ability of a business to maintain a dividend payment. It also measures the proportion of earnings that are being retained by the business rather than distributed as dividends.

ADVANTAGE AND DISADVANTAGES OF FINANCIAL STATEMENT ANALYSIS

There are three main financial statements investors analyse. They are the balance sheet, income statement and the cash flow statement. The balance sheet is a snapshot in time. It shows all the assets owned and liabilities owed for a company. It also shows the amount of equity or ownership that is paid for by investors. The income statement looks at the entire year.

It starts with revenues and then deducts expenses for net income. The cash flow statement shows where the cash is really coming by breaking down cash flow into cash from operations, investing and financing. There are advantages and disadvantages to analyzing financial statements for investment decisions.

FULL DISCLOSURE

Full disclosure is one of the main advantages of, and one of the main purposes for, financial statements. The Securities and Exchange Commission made the 10K report a requirement for all public companies. This 10K includes full disclosure of all financial statements as well as notes explaining all assumptions contained with the notes.

INTRINSIC VALUE VS. MARKET VALUE

While financial statements are good for the data needed to conduct a thorough ratio analysis, they are based on the accrual system of accounting, which is not market based. This is both an advantage and a disadvantage. It's good to have a basis for comparing book value to market value.

All it helps to pinpoint bargains in the market. However, value discrepancies can also work to the disadvantage of financial statement analysis. It can make it difficult to know the real value of assets, which translates into unreliable ratios.

TRANSPARENCY

Unfortunately, since financial statements are easy for everyone to understand, it's also very easy for people to hide information. For instance, an analyst has to look at the cash flow statement to know if cash flow is coming from operations or additional financing activities. There are also certain conventions like depreciation and inventory accounting that can increase or decrease net income, depending on the convention used.

INTERPRETATION OF FINANCIAL STATEMENTS

The Interpretation of Financial Statements is a wonderful reference guide for those who want to understand published financial statements and reports. Although some of the information is slightly out of date, you can be sure this book will still be useful in twenty years.

- Offers an explanation of the most common terms found on financial statements
- Gives ratios and formulas for investors to calculate
- Includes many examples

CONS

- Some of the information is dated due to changes in accounting rules
- The reader should have a working knowledge of stocks

DESCRIPTION

- Small, easy to carry edition with classic typeface.
- Makes an excellent business gift for clients and colleagues.
- Published by Harper Collins.

6

Investment Management in Hospitality Industry

INTRODUCTION

Investment management, the professional management of various securities (shares, bonds etc) and other assets (e.g. real estate), to meet specified investment goals for the benefit of the investors. Investors may be institutions (insurance companies, pension funds, corporations etc.) or private investors (both directly via investment contracts and more commonly via collective investment schemes eg. mutual funds). The term asset management is often used to refer to the investment management of collective investments, whilst the more generic fund management may refer to all forms of institutional investment as well as investment management for private investors.

Investment managers who specialize in advisory or discretionary management on behalf of (normally wealthy) private investors may often refer to their services as wealth management or portfolio management often within the context of so-called "private banking". The provision of 'investment management services' includes elements of financial analysis, asset selection, stock selection, plan implementation and ongoing monitoring of investments.

Investment management is a large and important global industry in its own right responsible for caretaking of trillions of dollars, euros, pounds and yen. Coming under the remit of financial services many of the worlds largest companies are at least in part investment managers and employ millions of staff and create billions in revenue. Fund manager (or investment advisor in the U.S.) refers to both a firm that provides investment management services and an individual(s) who directs 'fund management' decisions.

HOTEL INVESTMENT

Real estate investment trusts (REITs) provide an investment opportunity for hoteliers. In the Spring 2000 Virginia Hospitality and Leisure Executive Report, P. Anthony Brown of Arthur Andersen wrote the following about the U.S. Tax Relief Extension Act of 1999. This information will be useful as you plan your career. The most significant provision, however, is creation of a new type of corporation—a "Taxable REIT Subsidiary"—which will allow REITs to create new incremental income streams. With new growth opportunities, shareholders should be rewarded with higher stock prices since companies with increased growth rates typically trade in the market at higher earnings multiples.

Under the terms of the 1999 legislation, Taxable REIT Subsidiaries can provide non-customary services to tenants through their subsidiaries. This legislation should enable REITs to provide better customer service, create stronger customer loyalty and sell new, non-customary services to tenants. In addition these new subsidiaries can lease lodging facilities from REITs. However, the lodging facilities must be managed by an independent contractor that is actively engaged in the trade or business of operating lodging facilities for any person other than the REIT.

With these changes, hotel REITs will be able to reorganize their structure in order to retain more of the income generated by their hotels. For example, FelCor Lodging Trust Inc., a hotel REIT based in Irving, Texas, currently leases its hotels to two tenants: 1) a company owned by its executives and directors; and 2) Bristol Hotels and Resorts, a publicly traded company. With the new legislation, FelCor will be able to form a new Taxable REIT Subsidiary and transfer the leases of its hotels to this new subsidiary. Accordingly, the net income of the existing lessee would be transferred to the new Taxable REIT Subsidiary. However, a management company (not owned by FelCor) must manage the hotels and must be actively engaged in the trade or business of operating lodging facilities for any person other than the REIT.

The terrorist events of September 11, 2001, will have a lasting effect on how a hotel markets its products and services and delivers hospitality. The immediate impact of the terrorist attacks was a decrease in the number of people willing to fly and, thus, a decrease in demand for hotel rooms. Hotels (as well as restaurateurs, tourist attractions, government agencies, and the like) and the federal, regional, and state tourism associations continue to cooperate to address the issue of fear as it relates to travel and tourism. Hoteliers reviewed their marketing plans and determined how to attract the post-9/11 corporate traveller.

The huge corporate guest market can no longer be taken for granted. Corporate executives, travel planners, and traffic managers now must be greeted personally by hotel staff and asked when business might be expected. New methods of attracting markets such as local and regional residents are being developed. These efforts include special packages emphasizing local history and culture, businesses, sporting events, and natural attractions and are combined with the products and services of an individual hotel. Is this an easy challenge? Indeed no, yet it is one that hoteliers had to grasp with eagerness and enthusiasm in order to succeed.

R. Mark Woodworth reports that this effort is indeed a formidable task in light of the data revealed in Trends in the Hotel Industry—USA, published by PKF Consulting and the Hospitality Research Group (HRG). The 2003 edition reported that "the operating profit for the average U.S. hotel dropped 9.6 per cent in 2002, this after a 19.4 per cent decline in profits in 2001."

Rick Swig of RSBA and Associates notes that although hotel revenues increased by 2 per cent from 2003 to 2004, "other issues such as supply of hotel rooms of 4.4% since June 2001 versus average number of rooms sold increasing only by 3.3%." He urges, "Hotel operators should focus on pricing power for the next 24 months until occupancy returns to pre-2001 levels and compression begins to build. National consortium and high volume travel contracts are being finalized for 2005. Hotels will have to be successful in achieving significant rate hikes through these conduits, since the past two years of negotiations have yielded little or no rate increase as operating expense inflated." Further insight into the challenge facing hoteliers is expressed by Tom Belden of The Philadelphia Inquirer, who relates that 94 per cent of the 112 corporations surveyed by the Business Travel Coalition of Radnor, Pennsylvania, cut their travel spending over a three-year period. He reports that one participant increased its use of web-based meeting software by 50 per cent in one particular year.

The delivery of hospitality in hotels has also come under review. For example, hoteliers are reviewing security plans to include the front-line employee who must take immediate action based on observations at the front desk, in the dining room and recreational areas, and on guest and public floors. The front-line employee who sees uncommon activities has to know the importance of reporting concerns to supervisors. Special training in what to look for in guest interactions in public areas and on guest floors assists the front-line person in becoming proactive. Hoteliers must also be concerned with how to support hospitality as part of responsible community citizenship. Hotel general managers should develop emergency plans that allow immediately offering public space to medical personnel and disaster victims. Short term concerns such as feeding disaster victims and emergency personnel and long-term commitments such as housing displaced members of the community are among the many issues faced by the hotel industry.

Liability implications for the owner, management contractor, or lessee with respect to repair of facilities have arisen in addition to concerns for the safety of guests resulting from terrorism. Andrew MacGeoch, reporting in Hotel, notes: The obligation of an owner to repair the hotel under a management agreement usually depends on the extent of the damage. In general, if the costs of repair do not exceed a certain threshold specified in the management agreement [which is usually a certain percentage of the replacement costs of the hotel], the owner will be obliged to repair the hotel to its condition prior to the destruction. However, if the costs of repair exceed the specified threshold, the owner will have the right to choose not to undertake the repair and to terminate the management agreement.

MacGeoch continues with a note on liability towards guests by acts of terrorism. Generally, neither the operator nor the owner would be held liable for any injury or death caused by terrorist activities, unless the owner or operator has failed to exercise reasonable care for the safety and security of their guests. Therefore, to make sure that the reasonable-care standard is met, it is necessary and advisable for owners and operators to take reasonable and necessary steps to protect the safety of guests, including implementing appropriate security policies and measures and providing crisis management training to all employees.

These issues of marketing, delivering hospitality, and the ramifications of possible terrorism are ongoing concerns that hoteliers must continue to discuss. They must focus on goals and subsequent planning for implementation of a safe environment for guests and employees. A working knowledge of the classifications used in the hotel industry is important to understanding its organization. The various types of properties, their market orientation and location, sales indicators, occupancy, and revenues as they relate to levels of service and various types of business affiliations are all means of classifying hotel properties.

Classification of hotel facilities is not based on rigid criteria. The definitions can change depending on market forces, legal criteria, location, function, and, in some cases, personal preference, but the definitions that follow are generally accepted and are the ones intended for these classifications throughout this text. A hotel usually offers guests a full range of accommodations and services, which may include reservations, suites, public dining and banquet facilities, lounge and entertainment areas, room service, cable television, personal computers, business services, meeting rooms, specialty shops, personal services, valet, laundry, hair care, swimming pool and other recreational activities, gaming/casino operations, ground transportation to and from an airport, and concierge services.

The size of the property can range from 20 to more than 2,000 rooms. Hotels are found in centre-city, suburban, and airport locations. Guest stays can be overnight or long-term, as much as several weeks in length. Properties sometimes specialize in catering to particular markets, such as conventions or gambling. Casino hotels usually take a secondary role to the casino operation, where the emphasis is on profitable gaming operations. Marriott's hotels operated as JW Marriott Hotels and Resorts and Renaissance Hotels, as well as Hyatt Hotels and Resorts brands operated as Hyatt Regency, Grand Hyatt, and Park Hyatt Hotels, are examples in this category.

Motels offer guests a limited range of services, which may include reservations, vending machines, swimming pools, and cable television. The size of these properties averages from 10 to 50 units. Motels are usually in suburban highway and airport locations. Guests typically stay overnight or for a few days. Motels may be located near a freestanding restaurant.

The all-suites concept was developed in the 1980s as a separate marketing concept. These hotels offer guests a wide range of services that may include reservations, living room and separate bedroom, kitchenette, optional public dining room and room service, cable television, videocassette players and recorders, specialty shops, personal services, valet and laundry, swimming pool, and ground transportation to and from an airport. The size of the operation can range from 50 to more than 100 units.

This type of property is usually found in centre-city, suburban, and airport locations. The length of guest stay can be overnight, several days, or long term. Although this type of hotel may seem new, many downtown, centre-city hotels have offered accommodations with in-room kitchenette and sitting room since the early 1900s. Now with mass marketing—advertising products and services through mass communications such as television, radio, and the Internet— this type of hotel is considered "new." Examples of the all-suite concept include Hilton's Embassy Suites and InterContinental's Candlewood Suites.

Limited-service hotels appeared in the mid-1980s. Hampton Inn and Marriott were among the first organizations to offer limited-service properties. The concept of limited service was developed for a specific segment of the market: business and cost-conscious travellers. The range of accommodations and services may include reservations, minimal public dining and meeting facilities, cable television, personal computers, personal services (valet and laundry), and ground transportation to and from an airport. The size of the property can range from 100 to more than 200 rooms.

Limited-service hotels are found in centre-city, suburban, and airport locations. They are usually located near restaurants for guest convenience. Guest stays can be overnight or long term. These properties sometimes specialize in catering to the business traveller and offer special business technology centres. Limited-service hotel properties include Holiday InnExpress, operated by InterContinetal Hotels Group; Comfort Inn, by Choice Hotels International; and Marriott's Fairfield Inn.

One of only 17 hotels in North America to receive both the Mobil Five Star and AAA Five Diamond ratings, The Jefferson Hotel offers guests the highest level of products and services available, with a strong commitment to warm, genuine, and gracious service. Mr. Longo obtained B.S. degrees in business administration and communication from Saint John's University in New York. While in college, he worked at the front desk at The Saint Regis Hotel in New York City and began his professional career at the Sheraton-Carlton Hotel in Washington, D.C., as the rooms division manager. He then became general manager of The River Inn hotel in Washington, D.C., and then the regional director of operations for the Potomac Hotel Group. Prior to becoming general manager of The Jefferson Hotel, Mr. Longo was regional director of operations for the Field Hotel Association in Valley Forge, Pennsylvania.

The sales and marketing effort for this independently owned property requires aggressive sales and public relations strategies. Focus is placed not only on the guest rooms but also on the 26,000 square feet of function space and the two restaurants, one an AAA Five Diamond Award winner. Mr. Longo encourages students who are pursuing a hospitality management career to remember that, as innkeepers, the hotel is like your home, where all of your guests are made to feel welcome.

This means providing all guests with the basics of hospitality: a comfortable room, exceptional food, and a friendly staff to serve them. He adds that hospitality is a diverse business, offering a unique work experience each day.

EXTENDED-STAY HOTELS

Extended-stay properties were designed to offer guests a home-away-from-home atmosphere over long stays precipitated by business, leisure, or personal necessity. For example, a person may have to attend to a business project for several days or weeks; another may want to visit with relatives whose home does not have adequate accommodations for visitors; a third may be accompanying a relative or friend receiving an extended health treatment at a medical centre and require overnight accommodations. The patient himself may appreciate the homelike atmosphere of the extended-stay hotel in which to recover between treatments.

Leon Stafford of The *Atlanta Journal-Constitution* writes, "The big, fancy hotels... have struggled to get 60 per cent of their rooms filled since 2001. Meanwhile, extended stays... have remained at least 70 per cent filled." He adds an interesting concept for your career development consideration: "About three extended-stay lodges were built for every traditional hotel constructed between 2001 and 2004." At Hilton's Homewood Suites, the following room amenities are included: king-size bed or two double beds in the bedroom and foldout sofa in the living room; two remote controlled colour televisions; fully equipped kitchen with a microwave, refrigerator with ice maker, coffee-maker, twin-burner stove, and kitchen utensils; a spacious, well-lit dining area; and ceiling fans and iron and ironing board.

Additional hotel services include a business centre, an exercise room, and a pool. This hotel concept also structures its room rates to attract the long-term guest. Charles Gellad is the general manager of the Homewood Suites in Alexandria, Virginia. He began his career at the Hampton Inn in Alexandria as a front desk clerk and progressed to guest services manager there.

Then he took a position as sales manager at the Hampton Inn in Fairfax, Virginia, and then as director of sales at the Hampton Inn in Alexandria. He was on board as director of sales prior to the opening of the Homewood

Suites in Alexandria. Mr. Gellad said his market for guests includes people who are going to be in town for an extended period because of government contracts, special projects, training, or relocation in the military or in the private sector.

Relocation is a common characteristic with this market. Mr. Gellad's extended-stay hotel offers breakfast in the morning and a manager's reception (light foods and beverages); a fitness centre and an indoor whirlpool; a coin-operated laundry; an executive centre equipped with a fax machine, personal computer, copying machine, and other office amenities; a convenience store called the Suite Shop; free parking; and free local, credit-card, and collect calls.

Mr. Gellad's entry-level experience provided him with many opportunities to learn how to deal with different personalities. He says that when you become a supervisor, your employees want to be treated as individuals, but you must be fair in interpreting the polices to everyone. He also extends his hope that you will develop a balance between work and a personal life. This business can be very time-consuming, but you must take time to develop a life outside the hotel.

Market orientation in the hotel industry is categorized into two segments:

1. Residential hotels, which provide guest accommodations for the long term; and
2. Commercial hotels, which provide short-term accommodations for traveling guests.

Residential properties include hotels, all-suites, limited-service, and extended-stay properties. Services may include (but are not limited to) public dining, recreational facilities, social activities, and personal services. These hotels are usually located in centre-city and suburban areas where other activities (shopping, arts and entertainment, business services, public transportation) are available to round out the living experience. Barry Griffith, general manager of the Holiday Inn Express Hotel and Suites in Reading, Pennsylvania, feels that guest service is the centre of the hospitality business and that this is achieved by finding employees to deliver that service. He states, "We as managers have to be motivators and coaches to ensure that front line employees deliver that service. We must also lead by example."

The customer mix at the Holiday Inn Express Hotel and Suites changes depending on the time of the week. On weekdays, the mix is 80 per cent business and 20 per cent leisure; on the weekend it is 80 per cent leisure and 20 per cent business. Mr. Griffith noted that an old, established hospital in the area is relocating near his hotel. He expects this to reconfigure his customer mix: During the week it will be 70 per cent business and 30 per cent leisure, while on the weekend it will be 90 per cent leisure and 10 per cent business. What do all these customers want? Guests in both segments want a warm welcome and a clean room. However, the business segment wants quick, efficient service and high-speed Internet service for their computers. The leisure segment wants directions to local attractions and value (free phone calls, breakfast, and manager's reception on selected days).

The Holiday Inn Express is a franchise of Inter-Continental Hotels Group. This franchise offers reservation service, a priority club for free upgrade on rooms, *USA Today*, points on merchandise and free room-nights or air travel, high-speed Internet service, shuttle service, free continental breakfast, and a manager's reception on Mondays, Tuesdays, and Wednesdays featuring cocktails and hors d'oeuvres. Mr. Griffith graduated from Penn State Berks with an associate degree in housing and food service. His professional experience includes serving as assistant general manager at the Sheraton Reading Hotel and Sheraton Lancaster Resort. He was also in management with the Bennigan's Restaurants chain.

Commercial properties service the short-term transient guest. Services include (but are not limited to) computerized reservation systems, public dining, banquet service, lounge and entertainment areas, personal services, and shuttle transportation to airports. These hotels may be located almost anywhere. It is essential to note the gray areas where these two categories overlap. A commercial lodging establishment may have a certain percentage of permanent residents. Likewise, a residential hotel may have nightly rentals available. Owners and general managers must exhibit a great deal of flexibility in meeting the needs of the available markets.

Sales indicators, including hotel occupancy and average daily rate, are another way of describing hotels. This information is necessary for business investors to estimate the profitability of a hotel. Four factors measure a hotel's degree of financial success: occupancy percentage, average daily rate, yield percentage, and revenue per available room (RevPAR). Occupancy percentage is the number of rooms sold divided by the number of rooms available. Average daily rate (ADR) is the total room revenue divided by the number of rooms sold. Yield percentage, the effectiveness of a hotel at selling its rooms at the highest rate available to the most profitable guest, reveals a facility's success in selling its room inventory on a daily basis. RevPAR is used to indicate the ability of each guest room to produce a profit. Once the daily sales opportunity has presented itself, it cannot be repeated (excluding the opportunity to sell a room at a half-day rate).

OCCUPANCY

Occupancy percentages measure the effectiveness of the marketing and sales department as well as the external and internal marketing efforts of the front office. Occupancy percentage is also used by investors to determine the potential gross income, or the amount of sales a hotel might obtain at a given level of occupancy, average daily rate, and anticipated yield. However, it is important not to assume that occupancy is standard each night. Variations occur daily and seasonally.

AVERAGE DAILY RATE

The average daily rate (sometimes referred to as average room rate) is also used in projecting room revenues—the amount of room sales received—for a hotel. However, this figure also affects guests' expectations of their hotel experience. Guests expect higher room rates to correlate with higher levels of service; the hotel with a rate of $175 per night is expected to offer more services than a hotel in the same geographic area with a rate of $85 per night. These expectations have been extensively capitalized on by major hotel chains, which develop different properties to meet the expectations of various segments of the hotel market.

YIELD PERCENTAGE

Yield percentage measures a hotel manager's efforts in achieving maximum occupancy at the highest room rate possible. This term is discussed. It is sufficient to note here that this concept is relatively new in the hotel industry. Prior to the 1990s, hotel managers relied on occupancy and average daily rate as indicators of meeting financial goals. Yield percentage forces managers to think in more active terms.

REVENUE PER AVAILABLE ROOM

RevPAR is determined by dividing room revenue received for a specific day by the number of rooms available in the hotel for that day. The formulas for determining RevPAR are as follows: For example, RevPAR for a hotel that has $10,000 in room revenue for the night of September 15 with 200 rooms available equals $50 ($10,000 ÷ 200 = $50). This same hotel on September 15 with 200 rooms, room revenue of $10,000, 125 rooms sold at an average daily rate of $80 ($10,000 ÷ 125 = $80), and with hotel occupancy of 62.5 per cent (125 rooms sold ÷ 200 rooms available × 100 = 62.5 per cent), produces the same RevPAR (0.625 × $80 = $50).

RevPAR is used in hotels to determine the amount of dollars each hotel room produces for the overall financial success of the hotel. The profit from the sale of a hotel room is much greater than that from a similar food and beverage sale. However, the food and beverage aspect of the hotel industry is essential in attracting some categories of guests who want conference services. "Revenue Management," discusses the importance of considering the potential income from room and food and beverage sales.

Consider the following article, "January RevPAR Grows Nearly Ten Per cent at Suburban Lodge Company-Owned Hotels," which was published online. It shows how RevPAR is dependent on hotel occupancy. This article also addresses the importance of using RevPAR to present a fuller financial picture based on factors that affect room sales, such as economic conditions, weather patterns, and business travel, and ownership. NEW YORK, September 16, 2004: Price water house Coopers forecasts revenue per available room

(RevPAR) to increase by 6.3 per cent in 2004, the largest increase in 20 years.

The 3.7 forecast increase in average daily rate in 2004 will contribute almost 60 per cent of the total forecast RevPAR gain for the year.

Many factors support the favourable outlook for ADR:

- Upward revisions to inflation forecasts;
- Acceleration of business travel and the consequent increase in higher-rate lodging demand;
- Consolidation of ownership, and therefore, more properties under pricing discipline;
- Dramatic increase in control being exercised by hotel companies and owners over rate integrity and inventory, leading to less discounting on third-party distribution channels; and
- Aftermath of hurricanes in Florida, generating room demand from people involved in damage assessment, insurance, and reconstruction in otherwise low-occupancy months, with especially positive effects on room rates.

The lodging expansion that is underway will bring lodging demand to 2.71 million daily occupied rooms in 2004, or 2.1 per cent above the previous peak level recorded in the 2000. With supply expanding by only 1.3 per cent in 2004 amid 3.7 per cent demand growth, occupancy will advance to 60.6 per cent, an increase of 1.5 occupancy points from 2003.

"We were criticized for being too negative in 2002 and 2003, but our forecasts were almost exactly the actual results, and for 2004 and 2005 we have been criticized for being too positive. But this regularly scheduled quarterly update is for even more positive growth in rate; our demand forecast for 2004 is unchanged," said Dr. Bjorn Hanson, Global Practice Leader of Price water house Coopers Hospitality and Leisure Practice. Real GDP is forecast by Macroeconomic Advisers to grow by 4.4 per cent in 2004, followed by 3.9 per cent growth in 2005 and 3.6 per cent growth in 2006. Consumer prices are expected to advance by 2.7 per cent in 2004, followed by 2.2 per cent annual increases in both 2005 and 2006. These new forecasts represent slightly slower real GDP growth and an acceleration in inflationary pressures, compared to the macroeconomic forecasts underlying our June 2004 forecasts. Demand growth is expected to moderate in the next two years to the long-term annual growth rate of approximately 2.8 per cent. Occupancies will improve to 62.1 per cent by 2006, as supply growth remains moderate at 1.5 per cent in 2005 and 1.7 per cent in 2006. After achieving 3.7 per cent growth in 2004, ADR will increase by 3.5 per cent in 2005 and 3.4 per cent in 2006, making ADR increases the primary driver of the robust forecast RevPAR growth of 5.0 per cent in 2005 and 4.5 per cent in 2006.

The four commonly used market segments—identifiable groups of customers with similar needs for products and services—are full service, all-suites, limited service, and extended stay. There is a great deal of overlap among these divisions, and much confusion, some of which occurs because leaders in the hotel industry do not agree on terminology. Some industry leaders avoid the "budget" tag because of its connotations of cheapness and poor quality. Others welcome the label because it appeals to travellers looking for basic accommodations at inexpensive rates. Nevertheless, the following definitions provide some idea of what is offered at each level of service.

Full service is a level that provides a wide range of conveniences for the guest. These services include, but are not limited to, reservations, on-premises dining, banquet and meeting facilities, and recreational facilities. Examples of full-service hotels include Marriott Hotels and Resorts, Renaissance Hotels, and Holiday Inns.

As discussed earlier, the all-suites category indicates a level of service appropriate for a guest who desires an at-home atmosphere. Services include separate sleeping and living areas or working areas, kitchenette facilities, wet bars, and other amenities at the mid-price level. This concept appeals to the business traveller as well as to families. Marriott's SpringHill Suites and Embassy Suites Hotels are examples of all-suite hotels. It is interesting to note that this concept is also employed in older centre-city commercial hotels, in which rooms adjoining the bedroom and bath have been remodeled as living rooms and kitchenettes to create suites. Limited service emphasizes basic room accommodations, guest amenities, and minimal public areas.

A continental breakfast and/or an evening cocktail is often included in the price of the room. The guest has the opportunity to trade the public meeting room for free in-room movies, the dining room for free local phone calls. Hampton Inns and Holiday Inn Express Limited are examples of limited-service hotels. Extended stay is a level of service that offers a home-away-from-home atmosphere for business executives, visitors, and families who are planning to visit an area for an extended period. A fully equipped kitchenette allows international guests to prepare comforting foods in a new environment. The spacious bedrooms and living areas provide work and recreational areas. Light breakfast and evening meals included. Examples of this level of service include Hilton's Homewood Suites hotels, InterContinental's Staybridge Suites, and Choice Hotels International's MainStay Suites.

Business affiliations, which indicate either chain or independent ownership of hotels, also categorize the hotel industry. These classifications are the most easily recognizable by consumers with regard to such features as brand name, structural appearance, and ambience. Long-lasting marketing effects develop a brand loyalty and acceptance that are most important to the long-term profitability for a hotel.

CHAIN AFFILIATION

When asked to name several chain operations (a group of hotels that follow standard operating procedures such as marketing, reservations, quality of service, food and beverage operations, housekeeping, and accounting), most people would probably mention Holiday Inn, Marriott, Sheraton, Days Inn, Hyatt, Hilton, or Econo Lodge. Students should stay up to date regarding developments in the industry, such as acquisitions, restructuring, and other changes in these organizations. This information, important to know when making career decisions, can be obtained from trade journals such as Hotels, whose annual July issue includes a listing of hotel chains, addresses, and number of rooms; the Wall Street Journal; and other newspapers, magazines, and websites.

Chain affiliations, which include hotels that purchase operational and marketing services from a corporation, are further divided into franchisee, referral, company-owned properties, and management contract companies. Franchise corporations offer support to the franchisee, who is the owner of the land and building, in the form of reservation systems, advertising, operations management, and management development. In return for these services, the franchisee pays fees for items such as initial startup, rental of signs and other equipment, use of the corporation's reservation referral system, and national advertising.

Anyone wishing to enter the hotel business by investing personal funds wants to be sure of realizing a profit. Perhaps due to lack of experience in operating a hotel or motel, a lack of business acumen, a poor credit rating, or limited knowledge of real estate development, this type of entrepreneur may need to seek the guidance of others. He or she can receive direction from a corporation, such as Days Inn, Sheraton, or Hilton, concerning land, building, and management development.

REFERRAL PROPERTY

Sometimes a hotel organization chooses to become a referral property—that is, to operate as an independent in association with a certain chain. Because the property is already physically developed, the entrepreneur may want assistance only with management, marketing and advertising, or reservation referral. Likewise, the fees are based on services required. The chain's quality assurance standards must, however, be met by the referral property.

COMPANY-OWNED PROPERTY

A company-owned property, a hotel that is owned and operated by a chain organization, allows the hotel company developer to act as an independent entrepreneur. The hotel company developer operates the hotel property in competition with all other properties in the area. It uses its own expertise in site selection, property development, marketing and advertising, and operations management. The hotel company developer recruits talented professions into the organization to manage such properties. It uses the chain's reservation system. The hotel company developer may set a limit on the number of franchises so that a majority of the properties remain company-owned.

MANAGEMENT CONTRACT PROPERTY

A management contract property, a hotel operated by a consulting company that provides operational and marketing expertise and a professional staff, is similar to a referral property. Several management contract organizations develop business relationships with existing hotels and operate the hotels as their own. Their business relationship requires financial accountability and profitability. Management contract companies may choose to operate each hotel as a member of a franchise or as an independent.

BRANDS

Hotel brands are an important part of the lodging industry, especially in consumer marketing. Branding allows a hotel company to create a concept in the mind of a consumer. This mind-concept helps the consumer classify a hotel's offerings. For example, a fictitious brand such as the Hotel Flower Chain may have three distinct offerings in its portfolio of lodgings: the Tulip Extended Stay, the Rose Limited Inn, and the Violet All-Suites.

Another fictitious brand such as the Timber Chain may have seven more brands in their chain with similar facilities, such as the Pine All-Suites, the Maple All-Suites, the Sunset Extended-Stay Suites, the Timber Express, the Timber Grand Hotels, the Timber Falls, and the Pine Limited Service. Each of these brands has distinct product and service offerings such as communication via website, reservation service, reservation reward point programme, room accommodations, food service, personal fitness and business equipment, and meeting and convention facilities. Therefore, when guests have certain needs for business or pleasure traveling, they can match them up to a certain brand. The following is a list of major hotel brands. Further information can be accessed on each of the hotel companies on the Internet.

INDEPENDENT PROPERTIES

An independent hotel is one that is not associated with a franchise. It provides a greater sense of warmth and individuality than does a property associated with a chain. Independent hotel characteristics include an owner who functions as a manager, room rates similar to chain properties, rooms decorated in different styles, and inviting dining rooms. These hotels may be residential or commercial, with locations in the centre city, suburbia, along the highway, or near an airport. The number of rooms can range from 50 to 1,000. They may offer full services to the guest, including suites, dining room, room service, banquets, gift shop, beauty shop, athletic facilities, swimming pool, theaters, valet services, concierge, and airport shuttle service. Some older independent hotels have refurbished their suites to capture a share of the all-suites market. With all of these advantages, why aren't all lodging properties independent? The answer lies with the U.S. economy.

The development of large chains and of smaller properties often brings tax advantages and improved profits to investors. Millions of dollars in capital are required to develop a 2,000-room full-service property. Business, financial, and managerial expertise is more readily available in a company in which there is a pool of skilled experts. Large corporations can also offset financial losses in certain fiscal years or from certain properties against financial gains of other companies or properties in their diversified portfolios.

The independent entrepreneur operates his or her business without the advantages of consultation and assistance. This person may have worked for a large chain or gained a great deal of operations and development experience in the industry. He or she may also purchase a hotel property to balance an investment portfolio. As for any financial investment, the entrepreneur seeks a professional to manage and operate the establishment. The person chosen for this job must manage all aspects of the business: room, food and beverage, housekeeping, security, maintenance, parking, controller's office, and marketing and sales. All business decisions on expenditures must be coordinated with a profit-and loss statement and a balance sheet. Every sale of a guest room, every guest purchase of food and beverage, occurs because the management of that property has been able to market and manage the property effectively. The challenge of managing an independent property can be overwhelming. It can, however, also offer enormous satisfaction and financial independence.

Future professionals in the hotel industry must be able to analyse who their customers will be and why they will have customers. Marketing classes teach how to determine the buyers of a particular product—who the potential guests of a particular hotel property are. Such courses show how to evaluate demographic data (the size, density, distribution, and vital statistics of a population broken down into, for example, age, sex, martial status, and occupation categories) and psychographic data (emotional and motivational forces that affect a service or product) for potential markets.

The second question—why there will be customers—is an important one. Students will explore this question many times during their career in the lodging industry. A manager must plan for profitable results. This plan must take into account the reasons customers purchase a product—what trends will increase or decrease the need for hotel facilities? Factors include the growth of leisure time, the development of the me/pleasure concept, increases in discretionary income, the trend towards smaller families, changes in business travel, and expansion of the travel experience. Other economics and political trends—such as public liability, insurance costs, overbuilding, the value of the U.S. dollar overseas, gasoline prices, safety from random danger while traveling, and legislation—affect commerce; labour and the airline industry also have an impact on current sales as well as growth in the lodging industry.

LEISURE TIME

The trend towards increased leisure time—in the form of three-day weekends, paid vacations and personal days, a workweek of 40 hours or less, and early retirement—sets the stage for the growth of the lodging industry. As more people have available leisure time to explore new geographical areas, try new hobbies, sample culinary trends, participate in sporting events, and just relax, the customer base of the hotel industry expands. Workers are spending fewer years in the labour force as the concept of early retirement becomes more popular. As the population segment known as the baby boom ages, the number of retirees is projected to soar. Many of them will take on a second career, but part-time jobs will likely be more common. With the two prime ingredients for using hotel facilities—time and money—readily at hand, these people will be a primary market for the hotel industry.

ME/PLEASURE CONCEPT

The idea of deserving recreation away from the job to restore mental acuity and improve attitude has evolved over the years. The work ethic of the eighteenth and nineteenth centuries strongly influenced the way Americans played, as recreation and leisure were considered privileges reserved for the wealthy. Today, most workers enjoy vacations and the feeling of getting away from it all.

This trend towards fulfilling personal needs continues in the twenty-first century. The isolated nature of many jobs increases the need for respite. As more and more people find themselves spending more time communicating via computer and other machinery rather than face to face, social needs continue to grow. Workers need the away-from-job experience to balance their social and mental needs with their daily-life demands. Travel helps satisfy these needs, and the hotel industry benefits as a result.

DISCRETIONARY INCOME

Discretionary income, the money remaining from wages after paying for necessities such as food, clothing, and shelter, is the most important of all the trends that support the growth of the hospitality industry. One of the main reasons for the increase in discretionary income of American families is the emergence of the two-income family. An almost double-income family unit has emerged over the years as more married women join or stay in the labour force. The strong growth in this labour segment will undoubtedly continue. As more income becomes available to pay for the necessities of life, discretionary income for leisure time and corresponding goods and services also becomes available.

Discretionary income is not a constant. It is strongly affected by economic factors; an economic downturn with increased unemployment reduces discretionary income, for example. Different economic conditions tend to favour different ways of spending discretionary income; for example, low interest rates, which make the purchase of high-ticket items (such as homes, cars, boats, and aircraft) more desirable, make less discretionary income available for short vacations or quick day trips. Students of the U.S. economy need only review the effects of recessions, the energy crisis of the 1970s, and September 11, 2001, to see how quickly discretionary income formerly directed to the hospitality industry can evaporate.

BUSINESS OF INVESTMENT MANAGEMENT

Industry Scope

The business of investment management has several facets, including the employment of professional fund managers, research (of individual assets and asset classes), dealing, settlement, marketing, internal auditing, and the preparation of reports for clients. The largest financial fund managers are firms that exhibit all the complexity their size demands. Apart from the people who bring in the money (marketers) and the people who direct investment (the fund managers), there are compliance staff (to ensure accord with legislative and regulatory constraints), internal auditors of various kinds (to examine internal systems and controls), financial controllers (to account for the institutions' own money and costs), computer experts, and "back office" employees (to track and record transactions and fund valuations for up to thousands of clients per institution).

The most successful investment firms in the world have probably been those that have been separated physically and psychologically from banks and insurance companies. That is, the best performance and also the most dynamic business strategies (in this field) have generally come from independent investment management firms.

Representing the Owners of Shares

Institutions often control huge shareholdings. In most cases they are acting as agents (intermediaries between owners of the shares and the companies owned) rather than principals (direct owners). The owners of shares theoretically have great power to alter the companies they own...via the voting rights the shares carry and the consequent ability to pressure managements, and if necessary out-vote them at annual and other meetings.

In practice, the ultimate owners of shares often do not exercise the power they collectively hold (because the owners are many, each with small holdings); financial institutions (as agents) sometimes do. There is a general belief that shareholders - in this case, the institutions acting as agents - could and should exercise more active influence over the companies in which they hold shares (e.g., to hold managers to account, to ensure Boards effective functioning). Such action would add a pressure group to those (the regulators and the Board) overseeing management.

Some institutions have been more vocal and active in pursuing such matters; for instance, some firms believe that there are investment advantages to accumulating substantial minority shareholdings (i.e, 10% or more) and putting pressure on management to implement significant changes in the business. In some cases, institutions with minority holdings work together to force management change. Perhaps more frequent is the sustained pressure that large institutions bring to bear on management teams through persuasive discourse and PR. On the other hand, some of the largest investment managers - such as Barclays Global Investors and Vanguard - advocate simply owning every company, reducing the incentive to influence management teams.

The national context in which shareholder representation considerations are set is variable and important. The USA is a litigious society and shareholders use the law as a lever to pressure management teams. In Japan it is traditional for shareholders to be low in the 'pecking order,' which often allows management and labour to ignore the rights of the ultimate owners. Whereas US firms generally cater to shareholders, Japanese businesses generally exhibit a *stakeholder* mentality, in which they seek consensus amongst all interested parties (against a background of strong unions and labour legislation).

INTERNATIONAL CONVERGENCE OF CAPITAL MEASUREMENT AND CAPITAL STANDARDS

Basel II

Basel II, also called The New Accord (correct full name is the International Convergence of Capital Measurement and Capital Standards - A Revised Framework) is the second Basel Accord and represents recommendations by bank supervisors and central bankers from the 13 countries making up the Basel Committee on Banking Supervision (BCBS) to revise the international standards for measuring the adequacy of a bank's capital. It was created to promote greater consistency in the way banks and banking regulators approach risk management across national borders. The Bank for International Settlements (often confused with the BCBS) supplies the secretariat for the BCBS and is not itself the BCBS.

History

An earlier accord, Basel I, adopted in 1988, is now widely viewed as outmoded as it is risk insensitive and can easily be circumvented by regulatory arbitrage.

The Basel II deliberations began in January 2001, driven largely by concern about the arbitrage issues that develop when regulatory capital requirements diverge from accurate economic capital calculations.

With the first draft (called Consultative Paper 1) published in June 1999, further consultative papers followed together with a large quantity of other releases, Quantitative Impact Studies Nos. 2, 3 and 4, and papers. A final version was issued in June 2004, with a minor revision released in November 2005. In June 2006 a Comprehensive version was published including all Basel regulations up to this date. Implementation of the Accord is expected by 2008 in many of the over 100 countries currently using the Basel I accord.

The final version aims at:

1. Ensuring that capital allocation is more risk sensitive;
2. Separating operational risk from credit risk, and quantifying both;
3. Attempting to align economic and regulatory capital more closely to reduce the scope for regulatory arbitrage.

While the final accord has largely addressed the regulatory arbitrage issue, there are still areas where regulatory capital requirements will diverge from the economic.

Basel II has largely left unchanged the question of how to actually define bank capital, which diverges from accounting equity in important respects. The Basel I definition, as modified up to the present, remains in place.

The Accord In Operation

Basel II uses a "three pillars" concept - (1) minimum capital requirements, (2) supervisory review and (3) market discipline - to promote greater stability in the financial system. The Basel I accord only dealt with parts of each of these pillars. For example: of the key pillar one risk, credit risk, was dealt with in a simple manner and market risk was an afterthought. Operational risk was not dealt with at all.

The First Pillar

The first pillar provides improved risk sensitivity in the way that capital requirements are calculated for three major components of risk that a bank faces: credit risk, operational risk and market risk. In turn, each of these components can be calculated in two or three ways of varying sophistication. Other risks are not considered fully quantifiable at this stage.

Technical terms in the more sophisticated measures of market risk include VaR (Value at Risk), EL (Loss function) whose components are PD (Probability of Default), LGD (Loss Given Default), and EAD (Exposure At Default). Calculation of these components requires advanced data collection and sophisticated risk management techniques.

The Second Pillar

The second pillar deals with the regulatory response to the first pillar, giving regulators much improved 'tools' over those available to them under Basel I. It also provides a framework for dealing with all the other risks a bank may face, such as name risk, liquidity risk and legal risk, which the accord combines under the title of residual risk.

The Third Pillar

The third pillar greatly increases the disclosures that the bank must make. This is designed to allow the market to have a better picture of the overall risk position of the bank and to allow the counterparties of the bank to price and deal appropriately.

Criticisms

There are many criticisms that are made of Basel II. These include that the more sophisticated risk measures unfairly advantage the larger banks that are able to implement them and, from the same perspective, that the developing countries generally also do not have these banks and that Basel II will disadvantage the economically marginalized by restricting their access to credit or by making it more expensive.

The first of these is a valid point, but it is difficult to see how this can be overcome. More risk sensitive risk measures were required for the larger, more sophisticated banks and, while the less sophisticated measures are simpler to calculate, due to their lower risk sensitivity they need to be more conservative.

The second criticism has elements of truth; the better credit risks will be advantaged as banks move towards true pricing for risk. Experience with these systems in the United States and the United Kingdom, however, shows that the improved risk sensitivity means that banks are more willing to lend to higher risk borrowers, just with higher prices. Borrowers previously 'locked out' of the banking system have a chance to establish a good credit history.

A more serious criticism is that the operation of Basel II will lead to a more pronounced business cycle. This criticism arises because the credit models used for pillar 1 compliance typically use a one year time horizon. This would mean that, during a downturn in the business cycle, banks would need to reduce lending as their models forecast increased losses, increasing the magnitude of the downturn. Regulators should be aware of this risk and can be expected to include it in their assessment of the bank models used.

On September 30, 2005, the four US Federal banking agencies (the Office of the Comptroller of the Currency, the Board of Governors of the Federal Reserve System, the Federal Deposit Insurance Corporation, and the Office of Thrift Supervision) announced their revised plans for the U.S. implementation of the Basel II accord. This delays implementation of the accord for US banks by 12 months.

On November 15, 2005, the committee released a revised version of the Accord, incorporating changes to the calculations for market risk and the treatment of double default effects. These changes had been flagged well in advance, as part of a paper released in July 2005.

On July 4, 2006, the committee released a comprehensive version of the Accord, incorporating the June 2004 Basel II Framework, the elements of the 1988 Accord that were not revised during the Basel II process, the 1996 Amendment to the Capital Accord to Incorporate Market Risks, and the November 2005 paper on Basel II: International Convergence of Capital Measurement and Capital Standards: A Revised Framework. No new elements have been introduced in this compilation. This version is now the current version.

INTERNATIONAL AGREEMENT IS THE NEED TO ACCOMMODATE DIFFERING CULTURES

BASEL II AND THE REGULATORS

One of the most difficult aspects of implementing an international agreement is the need to accommodate differing cultures, varying structural models, and the complexities of public policy and existing regulation. Banks' senior management will determine corporate strategy, as well as the country in which to base a particular type of business, based in part on how Basel II is ultimately interpreted by various countries' legislatures and regulators.

To assist banks operating with multiple reporting requirements for different regulators according to geographic location, there are several software applications available. These include capital calculation engines and extend to automated reporting solutions which include the reports required under COREP/FINREP.

Implementation Progress

Regulators in most jurisdictions around the world plan to implement the new Accord, but with widely varying timelines and use of the varying methodologies being restricted. The United States of America's various regulators are yet (October 2006) to agree on a final approach - see Basel IA for a discussion. In response to a questionaire released by the Financial Stability Institute (FSI), 95 national regulators indicated they were to implement Basel II, in some form or another, by 2015.

The Future

Work is apparently already underway on Basel III, at least in a preliminary sense. The goals of this project are to refine the definition of bank capital, quantify further classes of risk and to further improve the sensitivity of the risk measures.

BUSINESS ETHICS AND ETHICAL RULES

Business ethics is a form of applied ethics that examines ethical rules and principles within a commercial context, the various moral or ethical problems that can arise in a business setting, and any special duties or obligations that apply to persons who are engaged in commerce.

Business ethics can be both a normative and a descriptive discipline. As a corporate practice and a career specialisation, the field is primarily normative. In academia descriptive approaches are also taken. The range and quantity of business ethical issues reflects the degree to which business is perceived to be at odds with non-economic social values. Historically, interest in business ethics accelerated dramatically during the 1980's and 1990's, both within major corporations and within academia. For example, today most major corporate websites lay emphasis on commitment to promoting non-economic social values under a variety of headings (e.g. ethics codes, social responsibility charters). In some cases, corporations have redefined their core values in the light of business ethical considerations.

OVERVIEW OF ISSUES IN BUSINESS ETHICS

General Business Ethics

- This part of business ethics overlaps with the philosophy of business, one of the aims of which is to determine the fundamental purposes of a company. If a company's main purpose is to maximize the returns to its shareholders, then it could be seen as unethical for a company to consider the interests and rights of anyone else.
- Corporate social responsibility or CSR: an umbrella term under which the ethical rights and duties existing between companies and society is debated.
- Issues regarding the moral rights and duties between a company and its shareholders: fiduciary responsibility, stakeholder concept v. shareholder concept.
- Ethical issues concerning relations between different companies: e.g. hostile take-overs, industrial espionage.
- Leadership issues: corporate governance.
- Political contributions made by corporations.
- Law reform, such as the ethical debate over introducing a crime of corporate manslaughter.
- The misuse of corporate ethics policies as marketing instruments.

Professional Ethics

Professional ethics covers the myriad of practical ethical problems and phenomena which arise out of specific functional areas of companies or in relation to recognized business professions.

Ethics of Finance and Accounting

Enron logo

- Creative accounting, earnings management, misleading financial analysis.

- Insider trading, securities fraud, bucket shop, forex scams: concerns (criminal) manipulation of the financial markets.
- Executive compensation: concerns excessive payments made to corporate CEO's.
- Bribery, kickbacks, facilitation payments: while these may be in the (short-term) interests of the company and its shareholders, these practices may be anti-competitive or offend against the values of society.

Ethics of Human Resource Management

The ethics of human resource management (HRM) covers those ethical issues arising around the employer-employee relationship, such as the rights and duties owed between employer and employee.

- Discrimination issues include discrimination on the bases of age (ageism), gender, race, religion, disabilities, weight and attractiveness.
- Issues surrounding the representation of employees and the democratisation of the workplace: union busting, strike breaking.
- Issues affecting the privacy of the employee: workplace surveillance, drug testing.
- Issues affecting the privacy of the *employer*: whistle-blowing.
- Issues relating to the fairness of the employment contract and the balance of power between employer and employee: slavery, indentured servitude, employment law.
- Occupational safety and health.

Ethics of Sales and Marketing

Marketing which goes beyond the mere provision of information about (and access to) a product may seek to manipulate our values and behaviour. To some extent society regards this as acceptable, but where is the ethical line to be drawn? Marketing ethics overlaps strongly with media ethics, because marketing makes heavy use of media. However media ethics is a much larger topic and extends outside business ethics.

- Pricing: price fixing, price discrimination, price skimming.
- Anti-competitive practices: these include but go beyond pricing tactics to cover issues such as manipulation of loyalty and supply chains.
- Specific marketing strategies: greenwash, bait and switch, shill, viral marketing, spam (electronic), pyramid scheme, planned obsolescence.
- Content of advertisements: attack ads, subliminal messages, sex in advertising, products regarded as immoral or harmful
- Children and marketing: marketing in schools.
- Black markets, grey markets.

INTERNATIONAL BUSINESS ETHICS

While business ethics emerged as a field in the 1970's, international business ethics did not emerge until the late 1990's, looking back on the international developments of that decade. Many new practical issues arose out of the international context of business. Theoretical issues such as cultural relativity of ethical values receive more emphasis in this field. Other, older issues can be grouped here as well. Issues and subfields include:

- The search for universal values as a basis for international commercial behaviour.
- Comparison of business ethical traditions in different countries.
- Comparison of business ethical traditions from various religious perspectives.
- Ethical issues arising out of international business transactions; e.g. bioprospecting and biopiracy in the pharmaceutical industry; the fair trade movement; transfer pricing.
- Issues such as globalisation and cultural imperialism.
- Varying global standards - e.g. the use of child labour.
- The way in which multinationals take advantage of international differences, such as outsourcing production (e.g. clothes) and services (e.g. call centres) to low-wage countries.
- The permissibility of international commerce with pariah states.

Ethics of Economic Systems

This vaguely defined area, perhaps not part of but only related to business ethics, is where business ethicists venture into the fields of political economy and political philosophy, focussing on the rights and wrongs of various systems for the distribution of economic benefits. The work of John Rawls is a notable contribution.

Theoretical Issues in Business Ethics

Conflicting Interests

Business ethics can be examined from various perspectives, including the perspective of the employee, the commercial enterprise, and society as a whole. Very often, situations arise in which there is conflict between one or more of the parties, such that serving the interest of one party is a detriment to the other(s). For example, a particular outcome might be good for the employee, whereas, it would be bad for the company, society, or vice versa. Some ethicists (e.g., Henry Sidgwick) see the principal role of ethics as the harmonization and reconciliation of conflicting interests.

Ethical Issues and Approaches

Philosophers and others disagree about the purpose of a business in society. For example, some suggest that the principal purpose of a business is to maximize returns to its owners, or in the case of a publicly-traded concern, its shareholders. Thus, under this view, only those activities that increase profitability and shareholder value should be encouraged. Some believe that the only companies that are likely to survive in a competitive marketplace are those that place profit maximization above everything else. However, some point out that self interest would still require a business to obey the law and adhere to basic moral rules, because the consequences of failing to do so could be very costly in fines, loss of licensure, or company reputation. The economist Milton Friedman was a leading proponent of this view.

Other theorists contend that a business has moral duties that extend well beyond serving the interests of its owners or stockholders, and that these duties consist of more than simply obeying the law. They believe a business has moral responsibilities to so-called stakeholders, people who have an interest in the conduct of the business, which might include employees, customers, vendors, the local community, or even society as a whole. They would say that stakeholders have certain rights with regard to how the business operates, and some would even suggest that this even includes rights of governance.

Some theorists have adapted social contract theory to business, whereby companies become quasi-democratic associations, and employees and other stakeholders are given voice over a company's operations. This approach has become especially popular subsequent to the revival of contract theory in political philosophy, which is largely due to John Rawls' *A Theory of Justice*, and the advent of the consensus-oriented approach to solving business problems, an aspect of the "quality movement" that emerged in the 1980s.

Professors Thomas Donaldson and Thomas Dunfee proposed a version of contract theory for business, which they call Integrative Social Contracts Theory. They posit that conflicting interests are best resolved by formulating a "fair agreement" between the parties, using a combination of i) macro-principles that all rational people would agree upon as universal principles, and, ii) micro-principles formulated by actual agreements among the interested parties. Critics say the proponents of contract theories miss a central point, namely, that a business is someone's property and not a mini-state or a means of distributing social justice.

Ethical issues can arise when companies must comply with multiple and sometimes conflicting legal or cultural standards, as in the case of multinational companies that operate in countries with varying practices. The question arises, for example, ought a company to obey the laws of its home country, or should it follow the less stringent laws of the developing country in which it does business? To illustrate, United States law forbids companies from paying bribes either domestically or overseas; however, in other parts of the world, bribery is a customary, accepted way of doing business. Similar problems can occur with regard to child labour, employee safety, work hours, wages, discrimination, and environmental protection laws.

It is sometimes claimed that a Gresham's law of ethics applies in which bad ethical practices drive out good ethical practices. It is claimed that in a competitive business environment, those companies that survive are the ones that recognize that their only role is to maximize profits. On this view, the competitive system fosters a downward ethical spiral.

Business Ethics in the Field

Many companies have formulated internal policies pertaining to the ethical conduct of employees. These policies can be simple exhortations in broad, highly-generalized language (typically called a corporate ethics statement), or they can be more detailed policies, containing specific behavioral requirements (typically called corporate ethics codes). They are generally meant to identify the company's expectations of workers and to offer guidance on handling some of the more common ethical problems that might arise in the course of doing business. It is hoped that having such a policy will lead to greater ethical awareness, consistency in application, and the avoidance of ethical disasters.

An increasing number of companies also requires employees to attend seminars regarding business conduct, which often include discussion of the company's policies, specific case studies, and legal requirements. Some companies even require their employees to sign agreements stating that they will abide by the company's rules of conduct. Many companies are assessing the environmental factors that can lead employees to engage in unethical conduct.

Not everyone supports corporate policies that govern ethical conduct. Some claim that ethical problems are better dealt with by depending upon employees to use their own judgment. Others believe that corporate ethics policies are primarily rooted in utilitarian concerns, and that they are mainly to limit the company's legal liability, or to curry public favour by giving the appearance of being a good corporate citizen. Ideally, the company will avoid a lawsuit because its employees will follow the rules. Should a lawsuit occur, the company can claim that the problem would not have arisen if the employee had only followed the code properly.

Sometimes there is disconnection between the company's code of ethics and the company's actual practices. Thus, whether or not such conduct is explicitly sanctioned by management, at worst, this makes the policy duplicitous, and, at best, it is merely a marketing tool.

To be successful, most ethicists would suggest that an ethics policy should be:

- Given the unequivocal support of top management, by both word and by example.
- Explained in writing and orally, with periodic reinforcement.

- Doable....something employees can both understand and perform.
- Monitored by top management, with routine inspections for compliance and improvement.
- Backed up by clearly stated consequences in the case of disobedience.
- Remain neutral and nonsexist.

Ethics of Production

This area of business ethics deals with the duties of a company to ensure that products and production processes do not cause harm. Some of the more acute dilemmas in this area arise out of the fact that there is usually a degree of danger in any product or production process and it is difficult to define a degree of permissibility, or the degree of permissibility may depend on the changing state of preventative technologies or changing social perceptions of acceptable risk.

- Defective, addictive and inherently dangerous products and services (e.g. tobacco, alcohol, weapons, motor vehicles, chemical manufacturing, bungee jumping).
- Ethical relations between the company and the environment: pollution, environmental ethics, carbon emissions trading
- Ethical problems arising out of new technologies: genetically modified food, mobile phone radiation and health.
- Product testing ethics: animal rights and animal testing, use of economically disadvantaged groups (such as students) as test objects.

Ethics of Intellectual Property, Knowledge and Skills

Knowledge and skills are valuable but not easily "ownable" objects. Nor is it obvious who has the greater rights to an idea: the company who trained the employee or the employee themselves? The country in which the plant grew, or the company which discovered and developed the plant's medicinal potential? As a result, attempts to assert ownership and ethical disputes over ownership arise.

- Patent infringement, copyright infringement, trademark infringement.
- Misuse of the intellectual property systems to stifle competition: patent misuse, copyright misuse, patent troll, submarine patent.
- Even the notion of intellectual property itself has been criticised on ethical grounds.
- Employee raiding: the practice of attracting key employees away from a competitor to take unfair advantage of the knowledge or skills they may possess.
- The practice of employing all the most talented people in a specific field, regardless of need, in order to prevent any competitors employing them.

- Bioprospecting (ethical) and biopiracy (unethical).
- Business intelligence and industrial espionage.

International Business Ethics and Ethics of Economic Systems

The issues here are grouped together because they involve a much wider, global view on business ethical matters.

ETHICS OFFICERS

Ethics officers (sometimes called "compliance" or "business conduct officers") have been appointed formally by organizations since the mid-1980s. One of the catalysts for the creation of this new role was a series of fraud, corruption and abuse scandals that afflicted the U.S. defense industry at that time. This led to the creation of the Defense Industry Initiative (DII), a pan-industry initiative to promote and ensure ethical business practices. The DII set an early benchmark for ethics management in corporations. In 1991, the Ethics and Compliance Officer Association (ECOA) — originally the Ethics Officer Association (EOA)— was founded at the Center for Business Ethics(at Bentley College, Waltham, MA) as a professional association for those responsible for managing organizations' efforts to achieve ethical best practices. The membership grew rapidly (the ECOA now has over 1,100 members) and was soon established as an independent organization.

Another critical factor in the decisions of companies to appoint ethics/ compliance officers was the passing of the Federal Sentencing Guidelines for Organizations in 1991, which set standards that organizations (large or small, commercial and non-commercial) had to follow to obtain a reduction in sentence if they should be convicted of a federal offense. Although intended to assist judges with sentencing, the influence in helping to establish best practices has been far-reaching.

In the wake of numerous corporate scandals between 2001-04 (affecting large corporations like Enron, WorldCom and Tyco), even small and medium-sized companies have begun to appoint ethics officers. They often report to the Chief Executive Officer and are responsible for assessing the ethical implications of the company's activities, making recommendations regarding the company's ethical policies, and disseminating information to employees. They are particularly interested in uncovering or preventing unethical and illegal actions. This trend is partly due to the Sarbanes-Oxley Act in the United States, which was enacted in reaction to the above scandals. A related trend is the introduction of risk assessment officers that monitor how shareholders' investments might be affected by the company's decisions.

The effectiveness of ethics officers in the marketplace is not clear. If the appointment is made primarily as a reaction to legislative requirements, one might expect the efficacy to be minimal, at least, over the short term. In part, this is because ethical business practices result from a corporate culture that consistently places value on ethical behaviour, a culture and climate that usually emanates from the top of the organization. The mere establishment of a position to oversee ethics will most likely be insufficient to inculcate ethical behaviour: a more systemic programme with consistent support from general management will be necessary.

The foundation for ethical behaviour goes well beyond corporate culture and the policies of any given company, for it also depends greatly upon an individual's early moral training, the other institutions that affect an individual, the competitive business environment the company is in and, indeed, society as a whole.

Religious Views on Business Ethics

The historical and global importance of religious views on business ethics is sometimes underestimated in standard introductions to business ethics. Particularly in Asia and the Middle East, religious and cultural perspectives have a strong influence on the conduct of business and the creation of business values.

Examples include:

- Islamic banking, associated with the avoidance of charging interest on loans.
- Traditional Confucian disapproval of the profit-seeking motive.

Related Disciplines

Business ethics should be distinguished from the philosophy of business, the branch of philosophy that deals with the philosophical, political, and ethical underpinnings of business and economics. Business ethics operates on the premise, for example, that the ethical operation of a private business is possible — those who dispute that premise, such as libertarian socialists, (who contend that "business ethics" is an oxymoron) do so by definition outside of the domain of business ethics proper.

The philosophy of business also deals with questions such as what, if any, are the social responsibilities of a business; business management theory; theories of individualism vs. collectivism; free will among participants in the marketplace; the role of self interest; invisible hand theories; the requirements of social justice; and natural rights, especially property rights, in relation to the business enterprise.

Business ethics is also related to political economy, which is economic analysis from political and historical perspectives. Political economy deals with the distributive consequences of economic actions. It asks who gains and who loses from economic activity, and is the resultant distribution fair or just, which are central ethical issues.

Corporate Behaviour

Corporate Behaviour (or corporate behaviour) is the behaviour of a corporation or corporations (or company or companies). The corporate behaviour of for-profit (capitalist) corporations and not-for-profit (non-capitalist) corporations differ due to the fundamental drive for profit in for-profit corporations, compared to the non-monetary goals often held by not-for-profit corporations.

The Characteristics of for-profit (Capitalist) Corporate Behaviour

Corporate behaviour of for-profit corporations has characteristics. These characteristics are unlikely to remain fixed for various reasons, but key characteristics are discernable from the history of for-profit corporations. Some of the key characteristics may not apply to individual for-profit corporations at a point in time and space, though some key characteristics are probably present at all times. The best example is the drive for profit. The strength or importance of a key characteristic will also vary in time and space for many reasons. For instance a for-profit corporation may be able to grow at a faster rate if it has subsidiaries in other countries.

Reasons are numerous as to why key characteristics are absent or vary in strength or importance. Some reasons could be as follows:

- Economic decline
- Poor performance
- Size of for-profit corporation
- Management decisions
- Type of for-profit corporation
- Competition

Certain individuals and groups have proposed and described the characteristics of corporate behaviour. These attempts, whilst a useful contribution, are not objective and should be read with this in mind.

Key characteristics of for-profit Corporate Behaviour

The key characteristics of corporate behaviour are as follows:

- Profit: Profitability is the ultimate driver of corporate decisions. Corporations prefer higher profits to lower profits, at least in the long-run. Profitability is not necessarily the same as community well-being, though a profitable company is more likely to, for example, employ more people than an unprofitable company. Conflicts can exist, however, between what's good for a corporation and what's good for the environment, for example, or its employees or even the good of the state. A corporation is a complex organism and there has been much debate about what drives it. There is an argument that the divorce of ownership from decision-taking means that profitability isn't the main drive - senior managers may have other imperatives like keeping their jobs and avoiding being taken-over (which might run counter to the interests of share-holders). Corporations often like to grow, if only because they fear a bigger competitor having cost advantages. This is not always true, however: there have been cases where corporations have been broken up into constituent parts.

- Amorality: Not being human, corporations as such do not have morals or altruistic goals. Neither, though, does any other organisation. Corporations are, though, run by people who are subject to law and rules of morality.
- Hierarchy: Corporations are usually hierarchical, though the structure of the hierarchy varies. Some are relatively flat with a wide layer of middle managers answerable to a few individuals while others are like a pyramid. A very few corporations have a great degree of democracy to them. Ricardo Semmler owns corporations in Brazil but allows all his staff to pick managers and decide strategy. He puts himself up for election as a chief executive.

The Characteristics of not-for-profit (non-Capitalist) Corporate Behaviour

As non-capitalist corporations such as NGO's or charities are not driven by the fundamentals of profit and economic growth, these do not show many of the characteristics of capitalist corporations. The behaviour of non-capitalist corporations is however often influenced by these characteristics of capitalist corporations, in similar ways to the influence of corporate behaviour on individuals. Due to this influence non-capitalist corporations can sometimes be seen to exhibit the characteristics of hierarchy, competition and ephemerality.

The Influence of Corporate Behaviour on Individuals and Society

Due to the dominance of capitalist corporations in Western societies the behaviour of corporations can be seen to have significant impacts on individuals and society. A person or group of people can have links to a corporation or corporations that range from weak to strong, if a person or group of people exhibit corporate behaviour that does not mean the person or group of people is employed by a corporation or corporations. A person or group of people may show corporate behaviour for different lengths of time, for some people they exhibit this behaviour at their place of work; for others it is exhibited at work, home and outside the home. Many people display corporate behaviour but do not agree with actions and outcomes that result from it.

The fact that individuals may not agree with the outcomes of corporate behaviour is central to the concept in itself, the characteristics of capitalist corporations do not reflect the characteristics of any individual or group of individuals but are the characteristics required for the survival of capitalist corporations *due to the nature of the system within which corporations operate.*

Ethics

Under the law, corporations are treated in many ways as persons. However, in other ways, they are not. One example is as follows. The thought of being put in prison acts as a powerful deterrent for most people: it prevents people from committing many crimes. But this powerful deterrent to harming people or society has no effect on a corporation, for a corporation cannot be put in prison.

Corporate Benefit

Corporate benefit (sometimes referred to as commercial benefit) is the requirement under some legal systems that the directors of a company must exercise the powers of the company for the commercial benefit of the company and its members. At common law, transactions which were not ostensibly beneficial to the company were set aside as being void as against the company.

Perhaps the best illustration of this principle is to be found in Hutton v West Cork Railway Co (1883) 23 Ch D 654, where the English Court of Appeal held that the paying of a gratuity to employees prior to their dismissal was an improper exercise of the powers of the company, because the company was no longer a going concern, and thus stood to obtain no benefit (and no furtherance of its objects) through the payment of the gratuity; as Bowen L.J. memorably remarked: "there are to be no cakes and ale except such as are required for the benefit of the company."

Any transaction which the directors enter into which is outside the powers of the company (and thus outside the scope of their authority) may nonetheless be ratified by the shareholders of the company, and will thereby be binding upon the company, see Multinational Gas and Petrochemical Co v Multinational Gas and Petrochemical Services Ltd.

Modern Developments

The rule is generally seen to be particularly harsh towards both third parties and against directors, who are regarded as being in breach of their duty only be acting with what others might regard as common human decency. Where the company's property could not be recovered from the third party, the directors would be personally liable to recompense the company.

There were also concerns that running companies ruthless for the financial benefit of the shareholders had a countervailing cost, making directors unwilling to participate in programmes that were beneficial to the community generally, or to the environment. It also meant that companies became much less willing to make donations to political parties, which may have had more impetus in bringing about legislative change than concern for communities or the environment.

Most legal systems have now abrogated by statute the rule that as against third parties the transaction may be void if it has insufficient commercial benefit to the company. In some countries, statutes now expressly provide for the directors to consider interests other than the pure financial interests of the shareholders.

However, in some jurisdictions there are proposals to make the power to act otherwise than for the financial benefit of the company even wider. For example, in the United Kingdom, the Companies Act 2006, when brought into force, will require that directors have to consider the impact of their actions on a much wider range of stakeholders. That Act would require a director "to promote the success of the company for the benefit of its members as a whole", but sets out six factors to which a director must have regards in fulfilling the duty to promote success. These are:

- the likely consequences of any decision in the long term
- the interests of the company's employees
- the need to foster the company's business relationships with suppliers, customers and others
- the impact of the company's operations on the community and the environment
- the desirability of the company maintaining a reputation for high standards of business conduct, and
- the need to act fairly as between members of a company

The proposed new duties have been subject to some criticism, both from those who argue that the new duties do not have sufficient bite, and also from those who fear that it diverts directors' focus from what it is that they are meant to be doing (viz., generating profits), and there are fears of widespread litigation, and increase in director's insurance premiums. However, because the new duties are expressed in non-imperative terms, and there is no sanction, the likelihood is that although they will empower the board of directors to take decisions that do not appear to directly financially benefit the company, they are unlikely to ever be required to do so.

Distinction from Other Legal Concepts

Conceptually, it is important to distinguish failure of a transaction for want of corporate benefit from other related legal concepts. These include:

- *Failure of consideration*: Under contract law in most common law legal systems, to be enforceable a contract requires both parties to provide consideration (ie. something of value). However, the consideration does not need to be equal, and the gratuity given in *Hutton v West Cork Railway Co* would still have failed for want of corporate benefit if, for example, the company had allowed employees to purchase company property at a discount.
- *Transactions at an undervalue*: Although most examples of failure for want of corporate benefit involve transactions which were either a gift, or were made at a substantial undervalue, the concept is different in purpose and effect from provisions of insolvency law which

prohibit undervalue transactions at a time when the company is insolvent.

Corporate Crime

In criminology, corporate crime refers to crimes either committed by a corporation, i.e. a business entity having a separate legal personality from the natural persons that manage its activities, or by individuals that may be identified with a corporation or other business entity. This type of crime therefore overlaps with:

- White-collar crime because the majority of individuals who may act as or represent the interests of the corporation will be employees or professionals of a higher social class;
- Organized crime because criminals can set up corporations either for the purposes of crime or as vehicles for laundering the proceeds of crime. Organized crime has become a branch of big business and is simply the illegal sector of capital. It has been estimated that, by the middle of the 1990s, the "gross criminal product" of organised crime made it the twentieth richest organisation in the world and richer than 150 sovereign states. The world's gross criminal product has been estimated at 20 percent of world trade; and
- State-corporate crime because, in many contexts, the opportunity to commit crime emerges from the relationship between the corporation and the state.

Definitional Issues

Legal Person

The Fourteenth Amendment to the U.S. Constitution stipulates that,

> "No State shall make or enforce any law which shall abridge the privileges or immunities of citizens of the United States; nor shall any State deprive any person of life, liberty, or property, without due process of law; nor deny to any person within its jurisdiction the equal protection of the laws."

In Santa Clara County v. Southern Pacific Railroad, 118 U.S. 394 (1886) the United States Supreme Court declared that a corporation was a "person" as interpreted by the Fourteenth Amendment. In a preface to the Court's argument, Chief Justice Morrison R. Waite stated the unanimous opinion that the Fourteenth Amendment applied equally to persons and "applied to these corporations." In English law, this was matched the decision in Salomon v Salomon & Co.

Function of Law

History shows that laws have sometimes been used as instruments of repression, exclusion, and marginalisation; and that certain criminal justice policies may sometimes be intended to serve the interests of particular groups or to undermine other groups. Thus, the definition of crime and the nature of criminal justice policies in society usually reflect the structures of power in that society. Also, while mainstream criminologists tend to focus mostly on street crimes and crimes of marginalised groups, the less obvious crimes of states, corporate organisations, and powerful groups are often ignored or under-emphasised. Lea (2001) argues that whereas crime used to be the exceptional event, disrupting the otherwise normal socio-economic processes, as crime becomes more frequent it lost its status as an exceptional event and became "a standard, background feature of our lives—a taken for granted element of late modernity."

POLICY TO ENFORCE THE LAW AGAINST CORPORATIONS

Corporate crime has become politically sensitive in some countries. For example, in the United Kingdom following a number of fatal disasters on the rail network and at sea, the term is used to refer to corporate manslaughter and to involve a more general discussion about the technological hazards posed by business enterprises and consider incidents such as the 1985 Union Carbide accident in Bhopal, India and the behaviour of the pharmaceutical industry.

The Law Reform Commission of New South Wales puts it thus:

> Corporate crime poses a significant threat to the welfare of the community. Given the pervasive presence of corporations in a wide range of activities in our society, and the impact of their actions on a much wider group of people than are affected by individual action, the potential for both economic and physical harm caused by a corporation is great.

Similarly, Mokhiber and Weismann (1999) assert:

At one level, corporations develop new technologies and economies of scale. These may serve the economic interests of mass consumers by introducing new products and more efficient methods of mass production. On another level, given the absence of political control today, corporations serve to destroy the foundations of the civic community and the lives of people who reside in them.

Discussion

What Behaviour to Criminalize

Behaviour can be regulated by the civil law (including administrative law) or the criminal law. In deciding to criminalise particular behaviour, the legislature is making the political judgment that this behaviour is sufficiently culpable to deserve the stigma of being labelled as a crime. In law, corporations can commit the same offences as natural persons. Simpson avers that this process should be straightforward because a state should simply engage in victimology to identify which behaviour causes the most loss and damage to its citizens, and then represent the majority view that justice requires the intervention of the criminal law. But states depend on the business sector to deliver a stable economy, so the politics of regulating the individuals and corporations that supply that stability become more complex. For the views of Marxist criminology, see Snider and Snider & Pearce, for Left realism, see Pearce & Tombs and Schulte-Bockholt, and for Right Realism, see Reed & Yeager. More specifically, the historical tradition of sovereign state control of prisons is ending through the process of privatisation. Corporate profitability in these areas therefore depends on building more prison facilities, managing their operations, and selling inmate labour. In turn, this requires a steady stream of prisoners able to work.

The majority of crimes are committed because the offender has the "right" opportunity, i.e. where the offender simply sees the chance and thinks that he or she will be able to commit the crime and not be detected. For the most part, greed, rather than conceit, is the motive, and the rationalisation for choosing to break the law usually arises out of a form of contempt for the victim, namely that he, she or it will be powerless to prevent it, and has it coming for some reason. For these purposes, the corporation is the vehicle for the crime. This may be a short-term crime, i.e. the corporation is set up as a shell to open credit trading accounts with manufacturers and wholesalers, trades for a short period of time and then disappears with the revenue and without paying for the inventory. Alternatively and most commonly, the primary purpose of the corporation is as a legitimate business, but criminal activity is secretly intermixed with legal activity to escape detection. To achieve a suitable level of secrecy, senior managers will usually be involved. The explanations and exculpations may therefore centre around rogue individuals who acted outside the organisational structures, or there may be a serious examination of the occupational and organisational structures that facilitated the crime. and around the socio-economic system, gender, racism and age.

While bribery and corruption are problems in the developed world, the corruption of public officials is one of the main causes of crime in developing societies because it is a precondition for much of the state, corporate, and organised crime which occurs. Peear discussing the implications for policing in Eastern Europe as it seeks to adapt its laws to match a capitalist model, pointing to the difficulty of distinguishing between lack of morality and criminality in economic crimes that tend to emerge from the structural relationships in modern commerce.

What Penalties to Impose

In part, this will be a function of the public perception of the degree of culpability involved. Weissman and Mokhiber (1999) catalogue the silence and indifference of the major media in the face of the widespread corporate corruption. Only in part is this justifiable. The news media find it difficult to respond to corporate crime both because reporting may compromise the trial by tainting the jury's perceptions, or because of the danger of defamation proceedings. Further, major corporate crime is often complicated and more difficult to explain to the lay public, as against street crime which may provide visuals of victims injured or of property damaged in spectacular fashion. But, more significantly, the news media are owned by large corporations which may also own prisons. Thus, the political decisions on the resources to allocate to investigate and prosecute will tend to match the electorate's understanding of the dangers posed by "crime". In sentencing, the fact that the convicted individuals may have had an impeccable character as presidents, CEOs, chairmen, directors and managers is likely to be a mitigating factor.

Examples of criminal behaviour in most jurisdictions include: insider trading, antitrust violations, fraud (usually involving the consumers), damage to the environment, exploitation of labour in violation of labour and health and safety laws, and the failure to maintain a fiduciary responsibility towards shareholders.

CORPORATE LAW ECONOMIC REFORM PROGRAMME ACT 2004

Corporate Law Economic Reform Programme (Audit Reform & Corporate Disclosure) Act 2004, commonly called CLERP 9, is the most recent reform to the Corporations Act 2001 (Commonwealth) which governs corporations law in Australia. It was enacted in July 2004.

It is based on the reform proposals contained in the CLERP 9 discussion paper, Corporation disclosure - strengthening the financial reporting framework, which was released by the Australian government in September 2002. The CLERP Act also contains a number of reforms flowing from the recommendations contained in the report of the HIH Insurance Royal Commission released in April 2003.

The CLERP Act proposes three bodies to represent a range of interests:

1. The Financial Reporting Council to oversee standard setting for audit and accounting;
2. The Australian Stock Exchange's Corporate Governance Council to oversee the development of best practice guidelines for corporate governance within listed companies;
3. And the Shareholders and Investors Advisory Council to provide a forum for the consideration of retail investors' concerns.

CPA Australia suggested that the legislation should build a framework that also identifies the conduct and practices of boards of directors, staff who prepare financial reports and internal and external audit functions. It also suggested including the roles of institutional investors, credit rating agencies, financial analysts and investment banks.

Corporate Social Responsibility

Corporate social responsibility (CSR) is a concept that suggests that commercial corporations have a duty of care to all of their stakeholders in all aspects of their business operations. A company's stakeholders are all those who are influenced by, or can influence, a business's decisions and actions. These can include (but are not limited to): employees, customers, suppliers, community organizations, subsidiaries and affiliates, joint venture partners, local neighborhoods, investors, and shareholders.

CSR requires that businesses account for and measure the actual or potential economic, social and environmental impacts of their decisions. In some cases the application of a strong CSR policy by a business can involve actions being taken which exceed the mere compliance with minimum legal requirements. This can sometimes give a company a competitive/reputational advantage by demonstrating that they have the interests of society at large as an integral part of their policy making. CSR goes beyond simple philanthropy and is more about corporate behaviour than it is about a company's charitable donation budget.

CSR is closely linked with the principles of Sustainable Development which argue that enterprises should be obliged to make decisions based not only on financial/economic factors (e.g. Profits, Return on Investment, dividend payments etc.) but also on the social, environmental and other consequences of their activities.

Development and Analysis

Today's heightened interest in the role of businesses in society has been promoted by increased sensitivity to, and awareness of environmental and ethical issues. Issues like environmental damage, improper treatment of workers, and faulty production leading to customers inconvenience or danger, are highlighted in the media. In some countries government regulation regarding environmental and social issues has increased, and standards and laws are also often set at a supranational level (e.g., by the European Union). Some investors and investment fund managers have begun to take account of a corporation's CSR policy in making investment decisions (so called "ethical investing"). Some consumers have become increasingly sensitive to the CSR performance of the companies from which they buy their goods and services. These trends have contributed to the pressure on companies to operate in an economically, socially and environmentally sustainable way.

It is important to distinguish CSR from charitable donations and "good works" (i.e., philanthropy, e.g., Habitat for Humanity or Ronald McDonald House). Corporations have often, in the past, spent money on community projects, the endowment of scholarships, and the establishment of foundations. They have also often encouraged their employees to volunteer to take part in community work and thereby create goodwill in the community which will directly enhance the reputation of the company and strengthen its brand. CSR goes beyond charity and requires that a responsible company take into full account their impact on all stakeholders and on the environment when making decisions. This requires them to balance the needs of all stakeholders with their need to make a profit and reward their shareholders adequately.

A widely quoted definition by the World Business Council for Sustainable Development states that "Corporate social responsibility is the continuing commitment by business to behave ethically and contribute to economic development while improving the quality of life of the workforce and their families as well as of the local community and society at large." This holistic approach to business regards organizations as (for example) being full partners in their communities, rather than seeing them more narrowly as being primarily in business to make profits and serve the needs of their shareholders.

Auditing and Reporting

To demonstrate good business citizenship, firms can report compliance with a number of CSR standards, including:

- AccountAbility's AA1000 standard, based on John Elkington's triple bottom line (3BL) reporting
- Global Reporting Initiative's Sustainability Reporting Guidelines
- Social Accountability International's SA8000 standard
- The ISO 14000 environmental management standard

Some nations require CSR reporting, though agreement on meaningful measurements of social and environmental performance is difficult. Many companies now produce externally audited annual reports that cover Sustainable Development and CSR issues, but the reports vary widely in format, style, and evaluation methodology (even within the same industry). Critics dismiss these reports as lip service, a charge that carries some weight given notable examples: Enron's yearly "Corporate Responsibility Annual Report" and tobacco corporations' social reports. CSR reporting draws much inspiration from its much older cousin, environmental and sustainability reporting.

The Business Case for CSR

The benefits of CSR to businesses vary depending on the nature of the enterprise, and are difficult to quantify, though there is a large body of literature exhorting business to adopt measures beyond financial ones (e.g., Deming's Fourteen Points, balanced scorecards). Orlizty, Schmidt, and Rynes found a correlation between social/environmental performance and financial performance. However, businesses may not be looking at short-run financial returns when developing their CSR strategy.

The definition of CSR used within business can vary from the strict "stakeholder impacts" definition used in this article and will often include charitable efforts and volunteering. CSR may be based within the human resources, business development or PR departments of a company, or may be given a separate unit reporting to the CEO or in some cases directly to the board. Progressive companies do not have a CSR department or function at all — the concept is so ingrained in the company itself that employees implement the company's values directly. The business case for CSR within a company will likely rest on one or more of these arguments:

Human Resources

Corporate Social Responsibility can be an important aid to recruitment and retention, particularly within the competitive graduate student market. Potential recruits are increasingly likely to ask about a firm's CSR policy during an interview and having a comprehensive policy can give an advantage. CSR can also help to build a "feel good" atmosphere among existing staff, particularly when they can become involved through payroll giving, fundraising activities or community volunteering.

Managing risk is a central part of many corporate strategies. Reputations that take decades to build up can be ruined in hours through incidents such as corruption scandals or environmental accidents. These events can also draw unwanted attention from regulators, courts, governments and media. Building a genuine culture of 'doing the right thing' within a corporation can offset these risks.

Brand Differentiation

In crowded marketplaces companies strive for 'X Factors' which can separate them from the competition in the minds of consumers. Several major brands, such as The Co-operative Group and The Body Shop are built on ethical values. Business service organisations can benefit too from building a reputation for integrity and best practice.

License to Operate

Corporations are keen to avoid interference in their business through taxation or regulations. By taking substantive voluntary steps they can persuade governments and the wider public that they are taking current issues like health and safety, diversity or the environment seriously and so avoid intervention. This also applies to firms seeking to justify eye-catching profits and high levels of boardroom pay. Those operating away from their home country can make sure they stay welcome by being good corporate citizens with respect to labour standards and impacts on the environment.

Critics of CSR will attribute other business motives, which the companies would dispute. For example, some believe that CSR programmes are often undertaken in an effort to distract the public from the ethical questions posed by their core operations. Some that have been accused of this motivation include British American Tobacco (BAT) which produces major CSR reports and the petroleum giant BP which is well known for its high profile advertising campaigns on environmental aspects of their operations. For a comprehensive survey of attitudes of business leaders in the U.S. towards CSR, there are biannual reports at Another view Some critics of CSR, such as the economist Milton Friedman, argue that a corporation's principal purpose is to maximize returns to its shareholders, while obeying the laws of the countries within which it works. Others argue that the only reason corporations put in place social projects is utilitarian; that they see a commercial benefit in raising their reputation with the public or with government. Proponents of CSR, however, would suggest a number of reasons why self-interested corporations, solely seeking to maximise profits are unable to advance the interests of society as a whole.

Key challenges to the idea of CSR include:

- The rule of corporate law that a corporation's directors are prohibited from any activity that would reduce profits
- Other mechanisms established to manage the principal-agent problem, such as accounting oversight, stock options, performance evaluations, deferred compensation and other mechanisms to increase accountability to shareholders.

Because of this, it has been suggested that CSR activity is most effective in achieving social or environmental outcomes when there is a direct link to profits: hence the CSR slogan "Doing Well by Doing Good". Note that this requires that the resources applied to CSR activities must have at least as good a return as that that these resources could generate if applied anywhere else, e.g. capital or productivity investment, lobbying for tax relief, outsourcing, offshoring, fighting against unionization, taking regulatory risks, or taking market risks—all of which are frequently-pursued strategies. This means that the possible scope of CSR activities is drastically narrowed. And corporations, with their constant incentive to maximize profits, often have identified all areas where profits could be increased, including those that have positive external social and environmental outcomes. The scope for CSR is thus narrowed to situations in which:

- Resources are available for investment
- The CSR activity will yield higher profits than any other potential investment or activity
- The corporation has been remiss in identifying this profit opportunity

A conflict can arise when a corporation espouses CSR and its commitment to Sustainable Development on the one hand, whilst damaging revelations about its business practices emerge on the other. For example the McDonald's Corporation has been criticised by CSR campaigners for unethical business practices, and was the subject of a decision by Justice Roger Bell in the McLibel case (which upheld some of these claims, regarding mistreatment of workers, misleading advertising, and unnecessary cruelty to animals). Similarly Shell has a much publicised CSR policy and was a pioneer in triple bottom line reporting, but was involved in 2004 in a scandal over the misreporting of its oil reserves which seriously damaged its reputation and led to charges of hypocrisy.

Universities and business schools, many of them with keen advocates of CSR amongst their teaching staffs, have themselves come in for criticism concerning their dealings with corporations (note the different stances taken by ESADE and Wheeling Jesuit University with regard to Aramark).

Critics of the role of business in society argue that:

- Corporations care little for the welfare of workers, and given the opportunity will move production to sweatshops in less well regulated countries.
- Unchecked, companies will squander scarce resources.
- Companies do not pay the full costs of their impact. For example the costs of cleaning pollution often fall on society in general. As a result profits of corporations are enhanced at the expense of social or ecological welfare.
- Regulation is the best way to ensure that companies remain socially responsible.

Supporters of a more market based approach argue that:

- By and large, free markets and capitalism have been at the centre of economic and social development over the past two hundred years and that improvements in health, longevity or infant mortality (for example) have only been possible because economies - driven by free enterprise - have progressed.
- In order to attract quality workers, it is necessary for companies to offer better pay and conditions which leads to an overall rise in standards and to wealth creation.
- Investment in less developed countries contributes to the welfare of those societies, notwithstanding that these countries have fewer protections in place for workers. Failure to invest in these countries decreases the opportunity to increase social welfare.
- Free markets contribute to the effective management of scarce resources. The prices of many commodities have fallen in recent years. This contradicts the notion of scarcity, and may be attributed to improvements in technology leading to the more efficient use of resources.
- There are indeed occasions when externalities, such as the costs of pollution are not built into normal market prices in a free market. In these circumstances, regulatory intervention is important to redress the balance, to ensure that costs and benefits are correctly aligned.
- Whilst regulation is necessary in certain circumstances, over regulation creates barriers to entry into a market. These barriers increase the opportunities for excess profits, to the delight of the market participants, but do little to serve the interests of society as a whole.

Other Perspectives

Some would argue that it is self-evidently "good" that businesses should seek to minimize any negative social and environmental impact resulting from their economic activity. It can also be beneficial for a company's reputation to publicise (for example) any environmentally beneficial business activities. A company which develops new engine technology to reduce fuel consumption will be able (if it chooses) to promote its CSR credentials as well as increase profits.

Some commentators are cynical about the true level of commitment of corporations to ideas like CSR and Sustainable Development, and their actual motivations for responsible behaviour. (Corporations that create the appearance of acting responsibly just for its public relations value are said to be "greenwashing.")

Such commentators also say, citing Friedman's dictum, that the idea of an "ethical company" is an oxymoron, since the corporation is by its nature compelled to maximize its own interest, whatever the external price. Corporate executives and employees in turn have strong incentives to internalize the corporation's statutory obligations to maximize profits, sometimes to the extent that they abdicate their individual moral and ethical obligations as human beings. This tendency is, of course, encouraged by the desire to keep one's job, and by a system that judges and rewards performance strictly by bottom-line returns. The results of this tendency were clearly seen in the many corporate scandals of the late twentieth and early twenty-first centuries.

So the CSR movement may perhaps be understood as an attempt not so much to regulate the activities of corporations per se, as to remind the people who constitute these corporations that they nonetheless have other responsibilities beyond the corporate ones.

Intangible asset

Intangible assets are defined as assets that are not physical in nature. The most common types of intangible assets are trade secrets (e.g., customer lists and know-how), copyrights, patents, trademarks, and goodwill. The Uniform Commercial Code (Section 9-102(a)(42)) defines "general intangibles" as "any personal property other than accounts, chattel paper, commercial tort claims, deposit accounts, documents, goods, instruments, investment property, letter of credit rights, letters of credit, money, and oil, gas, or other minerals before extraction. The term includes payment intangibles and software."

Research and Development

Millions are spent each year by corporations to research and develop new intangible assets. To protect their research and development (R&D) efforts, corporations generally rely on intellectual property laws and unfair competition laws.

General Standards

The Financial Accounting Standards Board (FASB) offers some guidance as to how intangible assets should be accounted for in financial statements. In general, intangibles that are developed internally are not recognized and intangibles that are purchased from third-parties are recognized.

Expense Recognition

Intangible assets are typically expensed according to their respective life expectancy. Intangible assets have either an identifiable or indefinite useful life. Intangible assets with identifiable useful lives are amortized on a straight-line basis over their economic or legal life, whichever is shorter. Examples of intangible assets with identifiable useful lives include copyrights and patents. Intangible assets with indefinite useful lives are reassessed each year for impairment. If an impairment has occurred, then a loss must be recognized. An impairment loss is determined by subtracting the asset's fair value from the asset's book/carrying value. This impairment loss may only be reversed under certain circumstances. Trademarks and goodwill are examples of intangible assets with indefinite useful lives.

GLOBAL FUND MANAGEMENT INDUSTRY

Assets of the global fund management industry increased for the second year running in 2004 to reach a record $45.9 trillion. This was up 6% on the previous year and 40% on 2002. Growth during the past two years has been due to an increase in capital inflows and strong performance of equity markets. Part of the increase in dollar terms was also a result of a 15% fall in the value of the dollar (USD index) during 2003 and a further 4% fall in its value in 2004. As shown in Chart 8, between 1999 and 2002 the value of assets under management fell as a result of declines in equity markets.

Pension assets accounted for $15.3 trillion of funds in 2004, with a further $16.2 trillion invested in mutual funds and $14.5 trillion in insurance funds. Merrill Lynch also estimates the value of private wealth at $30.8 trillion of which about a third was incorporated in other forms of conventional investment management. The US was by far the largest source of funds under management in 2004 with 43% of the world total. It was followed by Japan with 14% and the UK with 7%. The Asia-Pacific region has shown the strongest growth in recent years. Countries such as China and India offer huge potential and many companies are showing an increased focus in this region.

PHILOSOPHY, PROCESS AND PEOPLE

The 3-P's (Philosophy, Process and People) are often used to describe the reasons why the manager is able to produce above average results.

- Process refers to the way in which the overall philosophy is implemented. For example, which universe of assets is explored before particular assets are chosen as suitable investments; how does the manager decide what to buy and when; how does the manager decide what to sell and when; who takes the decisions and are they taken by committee; what controls are in place to ensure that a rogue fund (one very different from others and from what is intended) cannot arise;

- Philosophy refers to the over-arching beliefs of the investment organisation. For example, does the manager buy growth or value shares (and why), does he believe in market timing (and on what evidence), does he rely on external research or does he employ a team of researchers. It is helpful if any and all of such fundamental beliefs are supported by proof-statements.
- People refers to the staff, especially the fund managers. The question is who are they, how are they selected, how old are they, who reports to whom, how deep is the team (and do all the members understand the philosophy and process they are supposed to be using), and most important of all how long has the team been working together. This last question is vital because whatever performance record was presented at the outset of the relationship with the client may or may not relate to (have been produced by) a team that is still in place. If the team has changed greatly (high staff turnover), then arguably the performance record is completely unrelated to the existing team (of fund managers).

PORTFOLIO STRUCTURES AND INVESTMENT MANAGERS

At the heart of the investment management industry are the managers who invest and divest client investments. A certified company investment advisor should conduct an assessment of each client's individual needs and risk profile. The advisor then recommends appropriate investments.

ASSET ALLOCATION

The different asset classes are stocks, bonds, real-estate, derivatives, and commodities. The exercise of allocating funds among these assets (and among individual securities within each asset class) is for what investment management firms are paid. Asset classes exhibit different market dynamics, and different interaction effects; thus, the allocation of monies among asset classes will have a significant effect on the performance of the fund. Some research suggests that allocation among asset classes has more predictive power than the choice of individual holdings in determining portfolio return. Arguably, the skill of a successful investment manager resides in constructing the asset allocation, and separately the individual holdings, so as to outperform certain benchmarks (e.g., the peer group of competing funds, bond and stock indices).

Long-term Returns

It is important to look at the evidence on the long-term returns to different assets, and to holding period returns (the returns that accrue on average over different lengths of investment). For example, over very long holding periods (eg. 10+ years) in most countries, equities have generated higher returns than bonds, and bonds have generated higher returns than cash. According to financial theory, this is because equities are riskier (more volatile) than bonds which are themselves more risky than cash.

Investment Styles

There are a range of different styles of fund management that the institution can implement. For example, growth, value, market neutral, small capitalisation, indexed, etc. Each of these approaches has its distinctive features, adherents and, in any particular financial environment, distinctive risk characteristics. For example, there is evidence that growth styles (buying rapidly growing earnings) are especially effective when the companies able to generate such growth are scarce; conversely, when such growth is plentiful, then there is evidence that value styles tend to outperform the indices particularly successfully.

Diversification

Against the background of the asset allocation, fund managers consider the degree of diversification that makes sense for a given client (given its risk preferences) and construct a list of planned holdings accordingly. The list will indicate what percentage of the fund should be invested in each particular stock or bond. The theory of portfolio diversification was originated by Markowitz and effective diversification requires management of the correlation between the asset returns and the liability returns, issues internal to the portfolio (individual holdings volatility), and cross-correlations between the returns.

Performance Measurement

Fund performance is the acid test of fund management, and in the institutional context accurate measurement is a necessity. For that purpose, institutions measure the performance of each fund (and usually for internal purposes components of each fund) under their management, and performance is also measured by external firms that specialise in performance measurement. The leading performance measurement firms (e.g. Frank Russell in the USA) compile aggregate industry data e.g showing how funds in general performed against given indices and peer groups over various time periods.

In a typical case (let us say an equity fund), then the calculation would be made (as far as the client is concerned) every quarter and would show a percentage change compared with the prior quarter (e.g. +4.6% total return in US dollars). This figure would be compared with other similar funds managed within the institution (for purposes of monitoring internal controls), with performance data for peer group funds, and with relevant indices (where available) or tailor-made performance benchmarks where appropriate. The specialist performance measurement firms calculate quartile and decile data and close attention would be paid to the (percentile) ranking of any fund.

Generally speaking it is probably appropriate for an investment firm to persuade its clients to assess performance over a longer periods (e.g. 3 to 5 years) to smooth out very short term fluctuations in performance and the influence of the business cycle. This can be difficult however and, industrywide, there is a serious pre-occupation with short-term numbers and the effect on the relationship with clients (and resultant business risks for the institutions).

Absolute Versus relative Performance

In the USA and the UK, two of the world's most sophisticated fund management markets, the tradition is for institutions to manage client money relative to benchmarks. For example, an institution believes it has done well if it has generated a return of 5% when the average manager has achieved 4%. In other markets however, e.g. Switzerland, the mentality is different and clients and fund managers focus on absolute return management, i.e. returns relative to cash (e.g. Swiss franc or Yen cash) where (performance) fees are payable only if the return exceeds some absolute figure (e.g. 10% per annum).

Education or Certification

Increasingly, international business schools are incorporating the subject into their course outlines and some have formulated the title of 'Investment Management' conferred as specialist bachelors degrees. (i.e. Cass Business School, London). Due to global cross-recognition agreements with the 2 major accrediting agencies AACSB and ACBSP which accredit over 560 of the best business school programs, the Certification of MFP Master Financial Planner Professional from the American Academy of Financial Management is available to AACSB and ACBSP business school graduates with finance or financial services related concentrations.

LONG-TERM CAPITAL MANAGEMENT

Long-Term Capital Management (LTCM) was a hedge fund founded in 1994 by John Meriwether (the former vice-chairman and head of bond trading at Salomon Brothers). On its board of directors were Myron Scholes and Robert C. Merton, who shared the 1997 Nobel Memorial Prize in Economics. Initially successful, in 1998 it lost $4.6 billion in less than four months. The fund folded in early 2000.

FOUNDING MEMBERS

In addition to Meriwether, Scholes, Chincarrini and Merton, also joining the company as principals were Eric Rosenfeld, Greg Hawkins, Larry Hilibrand, Dick Leahy, Victor Haghani and James McEntee. On 24 February 1994, LTCM began trading with $1,011,060,243 of investor capital.

Strategy

The company had developed complex mathematical models to take advantage of fixed income arbitrage deals (termed convergence trades) usually with U.S., Japanese, and European government bonds. The basic idea was that over time the value of long-dated bonds issued a short time apart would tend to become identical. However the rate at which these bonds approached this price would be different, and that more heavily traded bonds such as US Treasury bonds would approach the long term price more quickly than less heavily traded and less liquid bonds.

Thus by a series of financial transactions (essentially amounting to buying the cheaper 'off-the-run' bond and short selling the more expensive, but more liquid, 'on-the-run' bond) it would be possible to make a profit as the difference in the value of the bonds narrowed when a new bond came on the run.

As LTCM's capital base grew the need for additional returns on that expanded capital led it to undertake other trading strategies. Although these trading strategies were non-market directional, i.e. they were not dependent on overall interest rates or stock prices going up (or down), they were not convergence trades as such. By 1998 LTCM had extremely large positions in areas such as merger arbitrage and S&P 500 options (net short long-term S&P volatility). In fact some market participants believed that LTCM had been the primary supplier of S&P 500 gamma which had been in demand by US insurance companies selling equity indexed annuities products for the prior two years.

Because these differences in value were minute — especially for the convergence trades — the fund needed to take highly-leveraged positions in order to make a significant profit. At the beginning of 1998, the firm had equity of $4.72 billion and had borrowed over $124.5 billion with assets of around $129 billion. It had off-balance sheet derivative positions amounting to $1.25 trillion, most of which were in interest rate derivatives such as interest rate swaps. The fund also invested in other derivatives such as equity options.

1998 Downturn

The downfall of the fund started in May and June 1998 when net returns fell 6.42% and 10.14% respectively, reducing LTCM's capital by $461 million. This was further aggravated by the exit of Salomon Brothers from the arbitrage business in July 1998.

The scheme finally unraveled in August and September 1998 when the Russian government defaulted on their government bonds (GKOs). Panicked investors sold Japanese and European bonds to buy U.S. treasury bonds. The profits that were supposed to occur as the value of these bonds converged became huge losses as the value of the bonds diverged. By the end of August the fund had lost $1.85 billion in capital.

The company, which was providing annual returns of almost 40% up to this point, experienced a Flight-to-Liquidity. This prompted a bail-out of $3.625 bn by the banks, organized by the Federal Reserve Bank of New York, ostensibly in order to avoid a wider collapse in the financial markets. The fear was that there would be a chain reaction as the company liquidated its securities to cover its debt, leading to a drop in prices which would force other companies to liquidate their own debt creating a vicious cycle.

The total losses were found to be $4.6 billion. The losses in the major investment categories were (ordered by magnitude):

- $1.6 bn in swaps
- $1.3 bn in equity volatility
- $430 mn in Russian and other emerging markets
- $371 mn in directional trades in developed countries
- $215 mn in yield curve arbitrage
- $203 mn in S&P 500 stocks
- $100 mn in junk bond arbitrage
- No substantial losses in merger arbitrage

Long Term Capital was audited by Pricewaterhouse LLP. The lead partner on the engagement was John Reville (Pricewaterhouse LLP - Manhattan office).

A DEEPER UNDERSTANDING OF THE RISKS TAKEN BY LTCM

The profits from LTCM's trading strategies were generally not correlated with each other and thus normally LTCM's highly leveraged portfolio benefited from diversification. However, the general flight to liquidity in the late summer of 1998 led to a marketwide repricing of all risk leading these positions to all move in the same direction. As the correlation of LTCM's positions increased, the diversified aspect of LTCM's portfolio vanished and large losses to its equity value occurred. Thus the primary lesson of 1998 and the collapse of LTCM for Value at Risk (VaR) users is not a liquidity one, but more fundamentally that the underlying Covariance matrix used in VaR analysis is not static but changes over time.

In the end, LTCM's basic idea was correct, in that the values of government bonds did eventually converge, but only after the firm was wiped out. Nonetheless, the incident confirms an insight often (though perhaps apocryphally) attributed to the economist John Maynard Keynes, who is said to have warned investors that although markets do tend toward rational positions in the long run, "the market can stay irrational longer than you can stay solvent."

Many of LTCM's strategies had payouts similar to those from selling an out-of-the-money option; a likely small gain balanced against a small chance of a large loss. Their basic idea was "correct" in that these large losses would not, if the positions were held to maturity, have come to pass. However, the events of 1998 increased the perceived probability of large losses, to the point where LTCM's portfolio had negative value.

ALTERNATIVES TO DIRECT PAY FOR PERFORMANCE

Much of the discussion here has been in terms of individual pay-for-performance contracts; but many large firms use internal labour markets as a solution to some of the problems outlined. Here, there is "pay-for-performance" in looser sense over a longer time period. There is little variation in pay within grades, and pay increases come with changes in job or job title. The incentive effects of this structure are dealt with in what is known as "tournament theory", for multi-stage tournaments in hierarchies where it is explained why CEOs are paid many times more than other workers in the firm). Workers are motivated to supply effort by the wage increase they would earn if they win a promotion. Some of the extended tournament models predict that relatively weaker agents, be they competing in a sports tournaments or in the broiler chicken industry, would take risky actions instead of increasing their effort supply as a cheap way to improve the prospects of winning. These actions are inefficient as they increase risk taking without increasing the average effort supplied.

A major problem with tournaments is that individuals' are rewarded based on how well they do relative to others, co-workers might become reluctant to help out others and might even sabotage others' effort instead of increasing one's own effort. This is supported empirically by Drago and Garvey. Why then are tournaments so popular?

Firstly, because – especially given compression rating problems – it is difficult to determine absolutely differences in worker performance. Tournaments merely require rank order evaluation.

Secondly, it reduces the danger of rent-seeking, because bonuses paid to favourite workers are tied to increased responsibilities in new jobs, and supervisors will suffer if they do not promote the most qualified person.

Thirdly, where prize structures are (relatively) fixed, it reduces the possibility of the firm reneging on paying wages. As Carmichael notes, a prize structure represents a degree of commitment, both to absolute and to relative wage levels. Lastly when the measurement of workers' productivity is difficult, e.g. say monitoring is costly, or when the tasks the workers have to perform for the job is varied in nature, making it hard to measure effort and/or performance, then running tournaments in a firm would encourage the workers to supply effort whereas workers would have shirked if there are no promotions.

Deferred Compensation

Tournaments represent one way of implementing the general principle of "deferred compensation", which is essentially an agreement between worker and firm to commit to each other. Under schemes of deferred compensation, workers are overpaid when old, at the cost of being underpaid when young. Salop and Salop argue that this derives from the need to attract workers more likely to stay at the firm for longer periods, since turnover is costly. Alternatively, delays in evaluating the performance of workers may lead to compensation being weighted to later periods, when better and poorer workers have to a greater extent been distinguished. (Workers may even prefer to have wages increasing over time, perhaps as a method of forced saving, or as an indicator of personal development. eg Loewenstein and Sicherman 1991, Frank and Hutchens 1993.)

For example Akerlof and Katz 1989: if older workers receive efficiency wages, younger workers may be prepared to work for less in order to receive those later. Overall, the evidence suggests the use of deferred compensation (eg Freeman and Medoff 1984, and Spilerman 1986 – seniority provisions are often included in pay, promotion and retention decisions, irrespective of productivity.)

The reason that employees are often paid according to hours of work rather than by direct measurement of results is that it is often more efficient to use indirect systems of controlling the quantity and quality of effort, due to a variety of informational and other issues (eg turnover costs, which determine the optimal minimum length of relationship between firm and employee). This means that methods such as deferred compensation and structures such as tournaments are often more suitable to create the incentives for employees to contribute what they can to output over longer periods (years rather than hours). These represent "pay-for-performance" systems in a looser, more extended sense, as workers who consistently work harder and better are more likely to be promoted (and usually paid more), compared to the narrow definition of "pay-for-performance", such as piece rates.

This discussion has been conducted almost entirely for self-interested rational individuals. In practice, however, the incentive mechanisms which successful firms use take account of the socio-cultural context they are embedded in, in order not to destroy the social capital they might more constructively mobilise towards building an organic, social organization, with the attendant benefits from such things as "worker loyalty and pride can be critical to a firm's success..."

FOREIGN INVESTMENT CODE AND DECREE

In about only twenty lines of text, the Code announces its prohibition on nationalization, the areas in which it permits investment, and the privileges it will extend to investors in enumerated areas. Investments are to be in the form of contractual business cooperations, joint ventures, or private ventures. Although sparse in text, the declaration is one which international investors interested in the Southeast Asian trade arena have impatiently awaited. The Code declares that investment is now allowed in the areas of agriculture, forestry, industry, communications, transport, service, and tourism.

This provision is so all-encompassing that the rhetoric of "allowing" investors seems one last vestige of the socialist government's eternally close supervision. In reality, the 1986 reforms gave provinces unprecedented autonomy to pursue foreign trade with neighboring Thailand. Not only is foreign trade encouraged, but the reforms have also vested factory managers with capitalist-like powers as they switch to "socialist business accounting." This new management policy gives managers more freedom to run their factories by allowing them to pursue raw materials, resources, and trade ties with other South-east Asian nations, such as Vietnam and neighboring Thailand. Technical knowledge imported to Laos must be "appropriate," not yet in use in Laos, advanced, and have high socio-technical efficiency.

In addition, the Decree lists other requirements to which imported technology must "answer to." The language implies that this is a list of desired standards and not of actual requirements. Imported technology should be capable of improving the quantity and quality of products for domestic consumption or international exportation using less labor, power, and natural resources while ensuring worker safety and environmental protection. The Decree requires importers to be in possession of documents and legal certificates to the technology or technical know-how imported.

When machinery is granted entrance, it must be accompanied by the "means of production" (i.e., directions for use thereof). Additionally, support services, which include technical advisors, installation, experimentation, worker training, and distribution of information concerning the imported technology, must also be provided. Moreover, technology grantees must be given authorization to use an industrial model or other technical knowledge that may be contained in the industrial patent. Granted technical know-how may include designs, formulas, or other items with "technical characteristics."

The Lao Peoples' Democratic Republic (LPDR) guarantees protection of the industrial patents of technology donors. However, to make use of this protection, grantors must first enter an agreement with grantees, and then apply to the Foreign Investment Management Committee (FIMC) for a license. The agreement must contain:

1. The name of the donor and the recipient, as well as the content and analysis of "technological characteristics";

2. A schedule of the grant;
3. The price;
4. The terms of the grant;
5. The donor's restrictions on the recipient;
6. Conditions on the industrial patent;
7. The donor's guarantee of the technology;
8. Detailed conditions for worker training for subsequent technology transfer; and
9. Dispute resolution procedures.

A potential problem is that the Decree does not define "technological characteristics," a phrase that might be interpreted in at least three different ways. The most extreme reading of this requirement renders an industrial patent guarantee ineffectual because "technological characteristics" must be divulged to grantees. The FIMC could require that grantors reveal technological characteristics that amount to trade secrets. In the American common law, the protection that guarantees which industrial patents will be recognized does not extend to trade secret protection.

The Decree does not address trade secrets; consequently, trade secret violations that do not rise to the level of an infringement on industrial patents would remain unprotected. A less extreme reading of this provision would require that grantors simply list the superficial "characteristics" of imported technology. Yet a third reading, reductio ad absurdum, would require only a description of imported technology (e.g., "word processing unit"). It is unlikely that this provision would be construed so as to limit the LPDR's control of imported technology. Therefore, until clarification, the broader reading of this requirement appears to be the most likely interpretation, a possibility that may frighten potential investors.

Another definitional problem having to do with liability for damage gives rise to the possibility that contributions of machinery may be subject to further regulation. The Decree requires that such contributions be necessary to the joint venture's commercial production, not yet made in Laos, or too expensive to import based on the world market price. Also, the machinery's quality must be ensured. Anyone responsible for damaging imported machinery before the term of the joint venture ends must "assume the responsibility." The Code states that losses or "damage ... due to the machines, parts of equipment, technical expertise and technologies, contributed by one side to the joint venture ..." must be the responsibility of the contributing side.

Responsibility for losses is a problematic concept. Would a properly trained employee who injures himself be liable for contributory negligence or would his employer be liable under strict liability? The Code declares that whoever provides the machinery, components, technical know-how, or technology will be held responsible. At first blush, this provision inheres fault in the foreign investor, since the investor is the party most likely to contribute technology. The Code's analysis appears to be that "but for" the contribution of the machinery, the injury would not have happened. This looks like a strict liability standard.

The protection afforded by this provision seems to anticipate unscrupulous, exploitative investors who, while taking advantage of the abundant, low-cost labor pool, may also abandon their responsibilities to create safe workplaces for their Laotian employees. However, since Laos remains fairly underdeveloped, most contributions made by foreign investors are likely to be in the form of technology, machinery, and components. It is unlikely that the Lao government would attempt to attract investors with promises of privileged status, only to impose strict liability once their capital is invested in the country. Investors, however, may be hard-pressed to reach this optimistic conclusion, since there are no legal assurances as to a structure of fault allocation. Thus, further regulation is necessary here.

The new laws permit investment in agriculture; forestry; industries using indigenous raw materials and natural resources of Laos; industries that use "modern techniques" to produce goods for export or to produce domestically consumed goods; and the building of major infrastructure. Neither the Code nor the Decree enumerates the privileges that the LPDR may confer upon investors in these areas.

The Decree details the permitted sectors of foreign investment that were outlined within the Code. The Decree appears to delimit permitted areas of planting and processing within the field of agro-forestry by naming various indigenously cultivated crops. However, clauses such as "planting, processing of different varieties of vegetables," "integrated forestry business (planting, exploitation, finished processing)," and "seeds and livestock producing centers," appear to be all-encompassing, allowing almost any conceivable commercial pursuit within the field of agro-forestry.

The Decree delineates other permitted areas in the field of industry, such as electricity, mining and, oddly enough, toys. Unlike the provision for agro-forestry, this provision does not pretend to limit or restrict industry in any way. To the contrary, the provision reveals that Laos intends to open itself up to massive development of its infrastructure and exploitation of its rich store of natural resources.

Another provision encourages construction of hotels, tourist sites, and various other entertainment centers. The Decree's only restriction regarding construction is that it must be in conformity with the programs outlined by the LPDR government. The concern relates to uniformity of quality and scale because the permitted areas of construction are designated specifically to improve the country's infrastructure.

The LPDR clearly articulates that it will not authorize foreign investment in areas that affect the sovereignty, order, and security of society, or which do not conform to requirements for the economic and social development of Laos. The Decree, for instance, prohibits environmentally damaging investment. Recent ecological problems beset Laos' plans for a $500 million dam, the Xeset Dam in southern Laos, which was scheduled to become operational in 1991.

Investors with overwhelming debt are also prohibited from investing in Laos. However, the Decree does not indicate the level of unacceptable debt or point at which leveraging would make a foreign investor unattractive. The government desires to attract capital investors in a world where leveraging is perfectly acceptable as a means of expanding businesses. Thus, the LPDR may have to accept a certain amount of high debt load among its investors.

The Decree also forbids long-term projects that make great use of imported materials, the products of which are locally consumed, but which cannot qualify as import substitutes. Not only does the spectre of socialist austerity rear its head in this provision, but free and rigorous competition is also discouraged.

The provision protects against runaway consumerism by inhibiting the production of goods that otherwise would have been imported as "necessary" items. Practically, however, this provision indicates that the LPDR discourages enterprises that would compete with local entrepreneurs who already meet the local demand. The Decree provides no guidelines to aid in the determination of what qualifies as such a product. Without guidelines, the worst-case scenario becomes possible, one in which a foreign project, after its inception, closes down for violating this provision.

The LPDR also reserves the right to forbid certain projects. Again, this presents problems because it gives the LPDR arbitrary power. Given the developmental circumstances of Laos, however, the LPDR would most likely temper any urge to act arbitrarily. Such action would surely toll the death knell for a country still struggling in the birth of economic reforms. Nevertheless, investors balk at such broad unilateral reservations, and the LPDR would be wise to reevaluate this provision and specify all types of prohibited projects.

The investment managing organ of the Council of Ministers alluded to in the Code is named in the Decree as the Foreign Investment Management Committee (FIMC) and is headed by the Chair of the Council of Ministers. The Ministry of Commerce and the Office of Foreign Economic Relations constitute its standing members. The Decree grants to FIMC the power to interpret the Code and to authorize and approve investment, although implementation of the Decree is shared with ministers, heads of state organs, and chairs of provincial and municipal administrative bodies.

The Decree specifies certain ministers--such as the Minister of Commerce and Foreign Economic Relations, the Minister of Economy, Planning and Finance, the Minister of Science and Technology, the Minister of Foreign Affairs, the Minister of the Interior, the State Bank and other concerned ministries that are responsible--to issue and recommend detailed implementation of this Decree within the limits of their roles and rights.

Ultimately, however, the FIMC appears to be the only governmental body actually empowered to interpret and amend the Code and Decree.

Furthermore, although the Decree explicitly invests the FIMC with power to interpret the Code, it only implicitly vests the Board with power to amend the Decree, declaring that only sectors and localities authorizing foreign investments "in the Lao PDR are to control and amend their authorization to conform with this present Decree." Because only the FIMC authorizes foreign investments, by default it becomes the ultimate arbiter of the Code and Decree, unless it delegates its powers to administrative agencies that it, or the government, might create.

The Council of Ministers may override the FIMC by virtue of the Code's elastic clause allowing the Council to "issue the detailed provisions for the implementation of [the Code]." However, a literal reading would indicate that the Council's power is to "enforce" detailed regulations and not to promulgate them. Hence, the FIMC appears to remain the final arbiter of both the Code and Decree.

The FIMC's supervisory powers over business ventures, be they contractual business with Lao investors, joint ventures, or foreign enterprises, are extremely broad. Thus, the Decree declares that the FIMC shall follow and control the business operations of foreign investors. For instance, the FIMC is required to create a professional auditing organ to control the accounting reports filed by enterprises with foreign shares. In its report to the FIMC, the auditor must assess its own system of auditing enterprises, the system of regulations on general accounting, the state of implementation of an enterprise's accounting system, and the precision of figures and data used in the accounting reports of audited enterprises. The FIMC is also given authority to initiate legal action against persons who deviate from their investment licenses.

Although these provisions seem to indicate a suspicion of foreign investors, the FIMC will not function oppressively because, along with its function as a protectorate of Laotian interests, it acts as a public relations organ with respect to foreign investors. For instance, FIMC advises and holds discussions with foreign investors willing to establish wholly foreign-owned enterprises in Laos.

Further, the Decree requires FIMC to provide facilities so that foreign investors can "discuss and sign agreements on the establishment of joint ventures ...." Additionally, the FIMC must consider and solve issues "as requested by foreign investors," and advise them about investment areas promoted by the LPDR. It would be unwise for the FIMC to provide a strong disincentive to investment by applying overly rigorous standards in scrutinizing company charters and joint venture regulations.

Under the Code, foreign investors must submit four documents to the FIMC: an application for a wholly foreign-owned enterprise or joint venture, a draft contract, draft rules and regulations for the enterprise, and an economic and technical analysis statement. The FIMC may require more documentation, and it has the power to designate fees for business authorization requests. The FIMC will consider the application and notify the parties no later than ninety days after submission. Once approved by the FIMC, investors must report the progress of their investment implementation activities within ninety days.

"Projects for which investment will be promoted ..." must meet five additional standards. First, projects must import advanced technology capable of processing products in a large quantity and of such quality as to possibly compete in the world market, but with the least resource depletion possible. Secondly, projects must develop infrastructure; and third, produce export merchandise or establish services earning mainly hard currencies and using domestic raw materials. Fourth, they should offer training of managers and technicians. Finally, projects must be those deemed especially important by the LPDR.

Contractual business consists of cooperation between foreign investors and either the state collective, state-private economic organizations, individuals, or private sector companies. The Decree defines contractual business as a mutual sharing of responsibilities for business purposes that results in commercial production without the creation of a joint venture bearing the juridical person status. To be valid, all contracts for business in Laos must obtain approval and licensing from the FIMC. Upon receiving a request for contractual business authorization, the FIMC must respond within thirty days.

Contracts must include: (1) the names of the parties to the agreement; (2) nationality; (3) address; (4) objectives of commercial production; (5) rights, interests, and obligations of the parties; (6) conditions for the transfer of interests and obligations; (7) terms of the agreement; (8) dispute resolution regulations; and (9) necessary "main programs," which include a listing of resources, products, and markets, as well as projected earnings in foreign currency and kip, the currency of Laos. A potential problem here is that although the Decree specifies that these necessary "main programs" be included in a contractual business arrangement, it does not issue complementary sanctions for non-adherence to them.

There is some evidence that contractual business can succeed under current conditions in Laos, due to the fact that many state collective enterprises that were operating at a loss have either been privatized, hence the term "state-private," or their managers have been given more autonomy in making business decisions. For instance, in Pakse, Laos' third largest city, a recently converted state enterprise, the Champassak Wood Processing Co., has increased its turnover from kip 95 million in 1985 to kip 266 million in 1988. The manager of Champassak attributes this increase to the company's conversion into an "autonomous enterprise" that allows him to find his own resources and pursue his own trade ties with Thailand.

Partners to a contractual agreement can either transfer their interests and obligations to or invest a third party. The provision allowing partners to invest for third parties is not clear, but it appears to allow partners to contractual agreements to act as an investment liaison. Such a provision could be viewed as meaningless since there are no prohibitions in the Code or Decree that would prevent someone from acting as an investment liaison in the first place.

However, upon closer inspection, this provision might allow third parties using partners to contractual agreements as investment conduits to bypass the FIMC's business authorization requirement, for there are no business authorization regulations governing such third party investors. It is highly unlikely that the LPDR intended this result, but the possibility indicates a need for a clarifying provision.

For transfers to succeed under the Code and Decree, transferrers must reach an agreement with their partners. The Decree mandates that transferees send the enterprise's regulations and the certificate of juridical and financial status to the FIMC. Here, again, the FIMC must approve the transfer in writing. Transfers are not valid unless so approved.

No requirement exists that parties seek FIMC approval for termination of a successfully completed contract before its stipulated termination date. However, if a contract's time term has expired and its terms have not been fully realized, and if the parties desire an extension, they must make a request to the FIMC. The parties must make the request at least one month before the agreement terminates, and the FIMC must then notify the investors of its decision within fifteen days from the receipt of such request.

However, parties might breach a contract by allowing it to expire with outstanding obligations remaining. The Decree anticipates this scenario, declaring that any claims "as mentioned in a lawsuit" are valid even after contract termination and that rights to pursue these claims also continue. The clause "as mentioned in a lawsuit" is vague. The context of the provision implies that claims from the contractual agreement remain valid.

Another reading of the clause requires that one look to Laotian law to ascertain the validity of any ensuing claims or liabilities arising out of contract termination. The better reading is the former. The LPDR provides that purely contractual agreements will be regulated by mutual agreement between the parties, whether they are foreign investors and the Lao business community or Laotians themselves. In light of this, the first reading reflects the full reign granted to contractual agreements by the Code and Decree.

In its request to the FIMC for authorization to conduct business in Laos, a joint venture must provide: 1) a request, signed by both partners; 2) a joint business agreement; 3) a financial, economic, and technical analysis; 4) information on each partner, company regulations, the juridical status of persons to the agreement, and the financial status of each partner; and 5) any other documents that the FIMC deems necessary.

The Decree requires that joint venture business agreements contain the name, nationality and address of parties; location; office; "sector" of commercial production; size of the venture as well as total capital to be invested; licensed capital; and capital as defined in the joint venture agreement. Additionally, agreements must include the percentage of shares, forms of shares, beginning and ending dates for capital contributions, conditions and regulations for the transfer of capital, and profit and loss sharing between partners to the joint venture.

Regarding "organic structure,"the agreement must comprise the number of members appointed by each partner to the management council, duties and rights of the management council, the chairman, the director, and the deputy director. Agreements must state principles of management regarding the venture's financing, accounting, statistics, control of its own accounting, and the percentage of shares attributed to the different funds within the enterprise.

An insurance license should also appear in a joint venture agreement, showing that the assets and property are insured with a reputable insurance company. There is no mention here of any requirement that a wholly foreign-owned enterprise also be duly insured. This suggests the government's emphasis is on protection of the Lao partner to the joint venture. The agreement must also delineate principles of labor management, salaries, and welfare and labor insurance. In addition, the life term of the joint venture, conditions to prolong and terminate it, and methods of paying accounts after the venture's termination must be included.

With respect to methods of resolving disagreements, the Decree states that agreements should contain dispute resolution regulations, which must indicate the language of choice if it is other than Lao. Within the agreement establishing the joint venture, the partners may consent to arbitration or submission of the dispute to any law enforcement body, or they may submit their dispute to the Council of Ministers, which is the economic arbitration body of the Lao government.

Lastly, agreements must declare their own validity as well as the validity of any ensuing addenda. After receipt of the required documentation requesting authorization for the establishment of a joint venture, the FIMC must respond within ninety days.

The Decree requires that joint venture produce documents to show that an agreement was reached as to technical and technological supplies for the venture. This requirement fails to specify which parties are required to come to an agreement on technological supplies. Since the requirement is one of "agreement" and not of "approval," it is possible to read the provision as exclusive of the FIMC.

FOREIGN INVESTMENT LEGISLATION

To a large extent, Mexico's regulations on foreign investment are the result of administrative policy rather than the legislative process. In many cases, these policies have been adopted or changed with little or no publicity, and they frequently have been enforced under laws designed for unrelated purposes. Consequently, the policies are often difficult to define and must be deduced by their application to specific cases.

A prospective foreign investor must examine not only Mexico's foreign investment laws, but also the policies and practices of the executive branch of the federal Government to ascertain if, and to what extent, a business may be established in the country, the conditions under which the business will be received and whether the regulations to which the business will be subject are consistent with its interests.

Throughout the past century, foreign investment in Mexico was affected by divergent trends. During the period spanned by the regime of Porfirio Díaz (1876-1911), it was believed that substantial investments in mining, utilities and basic industries would bring Mexico into a position commensurate with that of industrialized countries. As a result, foreign investment was allowed to such an extent that it dominated the economy. In fact, much of the nationalistic sentiment evoked today in Mexico over foreign investment derives from the prominence attained by foreign enterprises during the lengthy Díaz regime.

In the absence of domestic investment sufficient to build a foundation for further development, extensive infusions of foreign capital were necessary, but they inspired a growing fear of increasing foreign influence. Moreover, Mexico's natural resources and labor were being exploited in the process. By the early 20th century, "the economic penetration of the country by foreign enterprises resulted in almost complete loss of control of the country's destiny to foreigners and foreign interests."

Recovery of Mexico's "economic destiny" was one of the primary ideals to emerge during the country's Revolution of 1910-1920 and has remained an essential tenet of every subsequent administration. The Mexican Constitution, promulgated in 1917, placed restraints on foreign economic activities and foreign ownership of land, which indicated the direction that limitations on the role of foreign capital would take in the future.

The Legislative Process

Although Mexico is a federal republic with both federal and state levels of legislative jurisdiction, the overwhelming majority of the statutes affecting its foreign investors are either federal or modeled after federal laws. Federal legislation is enacted by Congress; however, Congress rarely does more than give approval to statutory drafts submitted by the Executive. To become effective, the legislation must be promulgated by the President and published in the *Diario Oficial de la Federación*.

In addition to indirect control over the legislative process, the President has authority to enact general rules in the form of regulations, which explain and supply detailed precepts for the application of specific laws; to legislate directly in foreign trade; and to exercise other legislative powers pursuant to congressional statutory delegation. Indeed, a significant amount of existing legislation was enacted under the President's "extraordinary legislative power."

In 1938, however, the Constitution was amended to provide that such "authority to legislate could be granted only in connection with a suspension of individual guarantees in times of grave national emergency under article 29." Constitutional guarantees have been suspended only once since that time, in 1944, and, although most of the presidential decrees issued during that period were later repealed, the decree establishing the basis for quantitative restrictions on direct foreign investment remained intact.

Restrictions on Foreign Investment

The Emergency Decree of 1944 granted extensive discretionary control over foreign capital to the Ministry of Foreign Relations and was intended to avert disruption of the economy by temporary investments of flight capital. The decree introduced restraints on the "creation, modification, liquidation and transfer of stock" of Mexican companies that might have foreign shareholders and were organized subsequent to its enactment. While it originally affected few and relatively insignificant activities, the Emergency Decree was nonetheless the precursor of present legal restraints on foreign investment in Mexico.

Two years later, the Interministerial Committee was created to coordinate national and foreign investment. Composed of representatives of the President and several ministries, it was established to make "a systematic and continuing study" of foreign investment in Mexico so that "a proper balance" between foreign and domestic capital could be maintained. The committee, however, "largely ratified the practices already adopted by the Ministry of Foreign Relations under its discretionary powers." Since 1953, the committee has functioned haphazardly, and its significance has depended upon the conduct of the incumbent administration.

Nevertheless, the committee's inaction did not deter enforcement of the Emergency Decree, which the Ministry of Foreign Relations in fact expanded beyond its literal provisions. Even though the Emergency Decree applied only to specifically delineated activities, the Ministry instructed notaries and public registry officials that licenses were required for the incorporation or amendment of the articles of any company, regardless of the purpose or nature of the business.

At the same time, beginning in the early part of World War II, Mexico's attitude toward foreign capital shifted in an effort to improve the economy. Between 1940 and 1965, direct foreign investment almost quadrupled, and by 1969, it exceeded two billion dollars. This increase, however, was accompanied by pressure from Mexican industrialists to limit the inflow of foreign capital.

Extensive foreign investment was noted to result in decapitalization and to increase the country's balance-of-payments problems. Government economists also were concerned and recommended that "the pattern of investment in assembly and processing operations, characteristic of the 1940's . . . be broken and greater use of domestically produced intermediate materials encouraged to stimulate import substitution."

Efforts were increasingly made to displace foreign investment. Joint ventures of Mexican and foreign capital were promoted, as were industrial integration programs, and foreign participation was excluded from certain industries and severely limited in others. In 1966 the Ministry adopted another significant policy: to deny licenses for the acquisition of majority interests in existing Mexican companies.

The mélange of restricted industries suggests that there was no overall planning or general policy concerning foreign participation in the Mexican economy. Some of the restrictions related to national security and the public welfare, while others seem to have been imposed in response to pressure from ad hoc private groups fearful about foreign competition. Furthermore, although special laws were enacted that expressly limited foreign investment in certain industries, other industries were added to the restricted list "solely on the basis of policy decisions by the Ministry of Foreign Relations, acting either on its own initiative or, more likely, on the initiative of, or at least with the concurrence of, other governmental agencies."

By 1970, the only legal restrictions on the amount of foreign participation in industrial activities were those resulting from the application of the Emergency Decree of 1944 and the exclusion of private participation, both domestic and foreign, in nationalized industries. The Government used other techniques, however, to divest foreigners of control and ownership, including tax incentives and the selective application of import controls. As one author has noted, the administration "seemed to prefer the flexibility in shaping its policies to individual investment projects that was allowed by the absence of a general law on foreign investments," and it adopted "specific statutory restraints in selected industries as it felt the need or desirability [to arise]."

The resultant overall attitude toward foreign investment was "one of cautious acceptance," although many perceived it to be excessively protective and nationalistic. Foreign investment was encouraged as a complement to domestic investment, and the Ministry of Commerce and Industrial Promotion increasingly insisted on Mexicanization and industrial integration.

Businesses dependent upon imports of raw or intermediate products or materials, or of machinery or equipment learned that procurement of the necessary import licenses might depend on whether they had become Mexicanized. The Ministry of Commerce and Industrial Promotion supervised not only the issuance of such licenses, but also industrial integration programs. In return for a guarantee by the Ministry that the necessary licenses would be granted, that imports of competing products would be excluded or that

Mexican competitors would need to meet the same conditions, new and existing companies agreed to increase the Mexican content of their products, limit prices and payments abroad, observe quality control standards and divert 51 percent of their capital stock to Mexicans over a specified period of time. Furthermore, foreign investors learned that the availability of tax concessions depended upon Mexicanization. As a result, an informal process of clearing investment projects with the Ministry of Commerce and Industrial Promotion developed, as prospective foreign investors sounded out the administration for assurances that their projects would be favorably received.

The position of the foreign investor also changed. Tax and other concessions were offered to concerns with majority Mexican ownership under the 1972 Law for the Promotion of New and Necessary Industries, to manufacturing businesses in the border zones and areas outside Mexico City, and to enterprises exporting Mexican manufactured products; but the administration was no longer receptive to the establishment of firms for the final processing or mere assembly of imported parts or intermediate products. Also, enterprises that were heavily dependent on imports were subjected to strong pressure to develop domestic production. The informal process of clearing proposed new investments and important expansions of existing facilities was "virtually institutionalized," and although still not required by law, the Ministry usually insisted that the projects be underwritten with a majority of Mexican capital.

Between 1972 and 1976, Mexico extended the controls over foreign investment. Of utmost importance was the Law for the Promotion of Mexican Investment and for the Regulation of Foreign Investment (the Foreign Investment Law or FIL), enacted in 1973. Its purpose was to codify existing laws, regulations and policies, and it established the National Foreign Investment Commission (FIC) to exercise significant discretionary powers created by law, and the National Registry of Foreign Investment (FIR).

The Foreign Investment law and the Foreign Investment Commission

Since 1973, the FIL has been the principal source of foreign investment restrictions. It applies to capital investments in Mexican businesses, to investments in the acquisition of Mexican real or personal property, and to other specified transactions, including the pledging of Mexican corporate shares to foreigners and foreign participation in a real property trust. It is restrictive, however, only with regard to direct investment; it does not explicitly regulate indirect investment such as loans.

Actually, the FIL set forth only two major changes in the restriction of foreign investment. It limited foreign participation in the management of a corporation to the proportion of foreign capitalization and established the 49-51 percent concept as a general rule. This was the first time legislation required majority Mexican participation in a broad spectrum of activities and not in just a single activity. Although the FIL does not explicitly define either foreign investment or foreign investors, it does provide a list of activities and individuals that will be considered as such.

It stipulates those economic activities exclusively reserved to the Government, those reserved to Mexican individuals or corporations without foreign participation and those in which foreign participation is specifically limited to less than 49 percent. It also contains a general provision limiting foreign participation in new businesses whose activities are otherwise not regulated to a maximum of 49 percent. Furthermore, the FIL requires governmental authorization for investments acquiring more than 25 percent of the equity or more than 49 percent of the fixed assets of an existing Mexican company, and for any transaction resulting in the transfer of management to a foreign investor.

Unless a foreign investor is interested in establishing a business with more than 49 percent foreign equity, the business may simply be registered with the FIR. However, the final decision on whether a foreign investor may hold a majority of foreign capital and control rests with the FIC.

Since the 1973 law vested the FIC with broad discretionary powers, the commission could increase the "maximum" 49 percent foreign equity whenever it deemed the project beneficial to the Mexican economy. The burden, though, now fell on the foreign investor to show that majority foreign equity and control would "stimulate a balanced and equitable development" and "consolidate the economic independence of the country."

The FIC consists of representatives of the President and seven ministries, and meets on a monthly basis. Pursuant to its statutory powers, it may:

1. Increase or reduce the percentage of foreign participation in geographical areas or economic activities when there are no required definite percentages and establish the terms and conditions under which the investment will be received;
2. Resolve on specific percentages and conditions for those projects which "may justify special treatment";
3. Resolve on projected foreign investment in companies established or to be established in Mexico;
4. Resolve on the participation of existing foreign investors in new areas of economic activities or in new product lines; and
5. Establish "requirements and criteria" for the application of foreign investment laws and regulations. Pursuant to the FIL, the FIC issues General Resolutions setting forth standards and requirements for applying the law, although there are no "regulations" per se.

Applications submitted to the FIC for approval of majority foreign equity are first analyzed by a technical committee and then submitted to the FIC for formal acceptance. Invariably, applications undergo a process of negotiation, ranging from 4 to 16 months in duration.

Investment with majority foreign equity has had several disadvantages: the length of time required to obtain approval for either the formation or expansion of a company, and the restricted sources of tax and other investment incentives. In contrast, an investment of 49 percent or less foreign equity can be organized immediately, may be expanded into different areas or used for new product lines, qualifies automatically for tax and other incentives, and usually will provide easier access to administrative agencies and the various licenses required for imports. Furthermore, Mexican laws protect minority shareholders, whether Mexican or foreign, against decisions by a majority group of shareholders, and additional protection may be secured by provisions inserted into the bylaws or articles of incorporation.

Since the enactment of the 1973 FIL, exceptions to the 49-51 percent concept have been granted rarely and only under special circumstances. Foreign equity in excess of 49 percent has tended to be approved in such sectors as tourism, priority industries, advanced technology, capitalization and investments preserving employment, and for priority activities of Mexican corporations with severe economic problems. Furthermore, the overwhelming majority of these exceptions have been contingent upon agreement eventually to Mexicanize.

The FIC bases its decisions on the criteria set forth in the National Industrial Development Plan (NIDP) and the FIL. The foreign investment allowed should always be complementary to the Mexican economy; there should not be substitution of fields covered; the company should be ready to export; it should commit itself to a precise plan to train Mexican personnel; a high percentage of the financing should come from abroad; there should be diversification of the sources of investment; the company should have a significant positive effect on local employment; the project should preserve the cultural and social values of Mexico; it should be located in an underdeveloped geographical area; and it should contribute to the technological development of the country.

Two of the most significant criteria considered by the FIC in determining exceptions under the FIL are whether the proposed activity is an industry or is in a geographical area encouraged under the NIDP. Although each presidential administration adopts its own NIDP, the underlying premise remains constant. Accordingly, the 1983-1988 NIDP incorporates criteria set forth in the FIL. Moreover, the 1983 NIDP contains detailed political and economic policies governing "the Mexican State, the diagnosis of the national problems, the purposes and strategies of solutions in a national and international context, and the bases for implementation of those strategies."

Each NIDP, therefore, provides indicators of the attitude and direction to be taken by the incumbent administration toward foreign investment.

In February 1983, the Constitution was amended, enabling "the federal government to adopt measures of great scope in economic matters, and reorienting the principles governing the actions of the state and private individuals." The amendments embody principles consistent with the present administration's philosophy of *la Rectoría del Estado* (the state as sovereign and the sole conductor of the economy). The amendments identify activities reserved exclusively to the Government, but they also provide for the development of the private sector.

In view of the increasing restrictions on the amount of allowable foreign equity in various activities, the formidable effort required to obtain an exception to the 49-51 percent "rule" and the few exceptions granted, the FIC's announcement in February 1984 that it would consider up to 100 percent foreign capital investment in a significant number of activities ran completely counter to the expectations of the investment community.

Mexico's present policy on foreign investment is in the process of evolution and finds support in the FIL, the NIDP, resolutions of the FIC, and declarations by the Executive Secretary of the FIC and the Secretary of Commerce and Industrial Promotion. It focuses primarily on the selective promotion of new or necessary industries. No longer amenable to the acceptance of foreign investment in an indiscriminate manner, it does, however, encourage activities that will further the economic development of the country.

The primary objective of the 1984 Guidelines for Foreign Investment is the active, systematic and selective promotion of foreign investment in specific activities considered the most important for "a fair and balanced growth of the Mexican economy." That promotion is to focus on those areas which will generate a positive foreign exchange balance, produce competitive exports and import substitution, contribute to national scientific and technological development, advance Mexico's further integration into the international community, involve large investments, and create employment and geographical decentralization of industry.

In analyzing the basis of foreign investment policy, the FIC acknowledges that, "[a]lthough an adequate Law exists for direct foreign investments, a systematic policy has not always been followed for an effective utilization of its potential for the country's development." The FIC has found that, in reality, "the effective use of investments to promote national technological development, to efficiently replace imports or generate exports for a positive trade surplus" has been hindered by multinational corporations that "frequently tend to seek benefits through equipment and technologies already obsolete in their own countries, protectively, and obtain excessive gains at the expense of national consumers."

Similarly, the FIC concedes that, while past practices have quantitatively limited foreign investment, such practices have not induced a "favorable direction." Instead, foreign investment policy "has been limited to a simple check of investment propositions, set forth in accordance with international production strategies, or marketing of foreign companies' products, not always adequate to local, or national priorities or those of certain sectors." The FIC also recognizes that negotiations regarding foreign investments have been "limited to imposing local integration requirements or filling export quotas," with "the latter in many cases hav[ing] been difficult or impossible to follow."

The Guidelines represent the FIC's attempt to correct these deficiencies by adjusting Mexico's policies on foreign investment and its regulation. While foreign investment will remain a "complement" to domestic investment, the "policy will cease to be merely defensive and [will] turn active and systematic, promoting the formation of foreign investment alternatives, according to needs derived from national development priorities."

The Guidelines list priority activities that may receive up to 100 percent direct foreign investment. Priority undertakings, as delineated in the Guidelines, include the production of nonelectric equipment and machinery, electric machinery and appliances, electronic equipment and devices, and equipment and material for transportation; metal mechanics; the chemical industry; other manufacturing industries; advanced technology services; and the hotel industry. The Guidelines state, however, that the enumerated activities are of an "indicative character" and that the list may be expanded by the Ministry of Commerce and Industrial Promotion "as a result of specific proposals or through the various groups of the national productive sectors."

Certainly, one of the most important goals of the Guidelines is to encourage national technological development. As the FIC recognizes, however, preference will need to be given to "coinvestment" in order to "guarantee a *real* transference of technology." Nevertheless, compared to large firms, small and medium-sized foreign companies are to receive "more flexible treatment" since it is presumed that their "investments and transference of technology carry lesser risks of dependency and may be valuable in agricultural and livestock sectors and certain branches of capital equipment and consumers' items."

Increases in the percentage of foreign equity in Mexican companies by capitalization of debt, sale of stock or waiver of stock subscription rights of first refusal by Mexican shareholders may be granted for financially troubled industries on the list of national priorities. Alternative measures, however, must first prove unworkable, and the increase of capital must be indispensable to the survival of the company. Furthermore, provision is made for the expansion of existing foreign companies in priority areas where such expansion will lead to the "modernization of the plants, the commitment of greater volumes of exports and increase the level of national integration in the production process."

Another significant aspect of the Guidelines is the absence of a requirement to Mexicanize within a specified time period. Although the FIL does not deal with this issue, almost every exceptional allowance of majority foreign equity that was granted before the Guidelines were issued required Mexicanization, usually within 10 years. The FIC has acknowledged, however, that "the process of Mexicanizing companies in which foreigners participate has in many cases resulted [in] an illusion with undesirable effects on industrial concentration, pricing policies and available investment resources."

Some reports announcing the Guidelines have viewed them as an open invitation to any and all foreign investment. The Guidelines very clearly state, however, that only certain activities will be promoted. Although other activities are generally welcome, the requirement of minority foreign equity will continue to apply. The activities promoted under the Guidelines are strategic in nature, in conformity with the goals of the NIDP, and even those activities will be analyzed by the FIC in terms of the criteria set forth in both the NIDP and the FIL. On August 30, 1984, the FIC published five new resolutions pursuant to the Guidelines.

Their purposes are twofold: to update the FIC's General Resolutions in accordance with the economic priorities of the NIDP and the Guidelines, and to improve and expedite the application process for majority foreign investments. For example, the resolutions eliminate the need for FIC authorization for certain foreign investment activities in in-bond companies; for the substitution of foreign directors, provided the ratio of domestic and foreign capital is not changed; and, under certain circumstances, for the opening or relocation of specified establishments. Additionally, the resolutions enlarge the powers of the Executive Secretary of the FIC, and he may authorize certain actions without prior FIC approval.

The resolutions also include provisions that are expected to decrease significantly the amount of time required to complete an application for majority foreign capitalization. Pursuant to the resolutions, applications to the FIC are to be negotiated through the Executive Secretary, who is then to submit them to the FIC for its formal acceptance within 30 business days of completion of the file.

Announcement of the Guidelines has resulted in much speculation and misunderstanding. Research for this article included interviews that were graciously extended by bankers, corporations, the FIC and foreign investment legal practitioners. Their perceptions of the Guidelines assisted invaluably in the following analysis of Mexico's changing position on foreign investment.

Mexico's Changing Position

Contrary to past practice, the Guidelines were not published in the *Diario Oficial,* although they were announced in all the major newspapers and distributed in the form of a pamphlet. Because the *Diario Oficial* is the official repository of all federal legislation, the failure to publish the Guidelines in it signified a definite effort to make clear that the change was one of policy. Even though the FIL allows for exceptions and the 49 percent limitation on foreign ownership is in essence only a general principle, the fact that the FIC had strictly enforced that limitation with few exceptions for the past 11 years had prompted the erroneous belief that this policy was the law.

When newspapers misleadingly interpreted the change as a new attitude "welcoming" foreign investment, some investors responded with guarded cynicism. Since they had been led to believe that 49 percent was the legal maximum, some foreign investors would have preferred fixed rules in the form of a legislative revision. Fearful that this policy could just as quickly be replaced by past practices, these investors have been critical and have adopted a wait-and-see attitude. Additionally, foreign investors are concerned that the Government will later issue decrees restricting their future activities. The perception of both the newspapers and the critics is limited and faulty in many aspects.

Businesses incorporated under the 1984 Guidelines would retain their 100 percent foreign equity even if Mexico were to return to the 49-51 percent concept. It is extremely unlikely that a future decree could be applied retroactively. It is generally believed that the 1973 FIL cannot be so construed. Moreover, although corporations could not expand by establishing new plants or adding new product lines without Mexicanizing under the FIL, additional protection has been available through the incorporation of an enterprise as a variable capital company since approval of neither the FIC nor the Ministry of Foreign Relations is required to increase or decrease the variable portion of the capital. Consequently, corporations organized as variable capital companies have been able to expand and avoid pressure to Mexicanize when challenged to do so in the past.

Second, Mexico has always "welcomed" foreign investment. It is the manner in which it has structured its foreign investment policies that has led some to believe otherwise. Even after enactment of the FIL in 1973, the amount of foreign investment increased significantly, particularly in the years 1976 and 1980.

Also, the Guidelines do not signify an open door "welcome mat." The Guidelines explicitly state that certain listed activities are being promoted. Certainly, it is not unreasonable for Mexico to refuse to accept indiscriminate foreign investment. A careful examination of Mexican policies and practices over the past century discloses a process that at times has had its divergences, but always with a purpose. An unrestrained open door policy was extended when foreign investment was viewed as beneficial and necessary for industrial growth. When the resultant foreign dominance of the economy became painfully apparent, however, measures were taken to alleviate the detrimental effects. Nonetheless, the character, rather than the magnitude, of foreign investment was affected by the changing regulations.

As was uniformly noted by the bankers, lawyers and government officials interviewed, except for outright exclusions, laws really do not affect the magnitude of foreign investment in a country; other circumstances do, including political and economic views, labor rates and export possibilities. Regardless of the exclusion of foreign investment from certain activities, Mexico generally has been viewed as offering political stability, financial reliability in meeting its debt payments and a safe climate for investment.

Those interviewed were asked why, in their opinion, Mexico did not revise the FIL, and two responses predominated. First, the FIL already allows the FIC to grant exceptions when deemed beneficial to the national economy; there is therefore no need for a legislative revision. Second, although Mexico is politically stable, there is a nationalistic sentiment remaining from the periods in which foreign investment was allowed to dominate the economy. The enactment of a legislative revision would likely create apprehension that Mexico was once again indiscriminately allowing foreign investment to meet a short-term economic problem, and the political cost of such a reaction would be high. As it stands, the Guidelines have not been seen as a threat to Mexican industrialists, but rather as a progressive step toward increased technology.

Furthermore, not only is such a revision unnecessary, it is also not in keeping with the goals of the FIC. The development of a rational economic plan that selectively promotes those industries deemed beneficial to the national economy requires flexibility sufficient to allow continuous reassessment of the country's needs. To lock the administration into further rigidity would preclude the very growth Mexico is striving to achieve.

Views differed over whether Mexico will press for Mexicanization in the future. One of' the corporate officials interviewed believes that the Government is likely to promote Mexicanization in specific areas in which it has an interest. An attorney with extensive experience in dealing with the FIC, however, disagrees on the basis that the Government has nothing to gain from Mexicanization at this time. In the past, nationalistic political motives prompted the policy, or the Mexicanization or nationalization was directed to strategic areas of the economy such as oil, mining and petrochemicals. Additionally, as was noted in the preceding section, Mexicanization in itself is no longer viewed by the FIC as a desirable goal. In fact, one of the elements of the new policy will be to examine the effectiveness of Mexicanization operations.

Even if Mexico does later restrict the availability of investment incentives or press for Mexicanization, the fact remains that it is still an excellent investment choice. Almost every state offers a variety of investment incentives in addition to those provided by the federal Government, such as land, physical facilities and access to utilities; labor is still less costly than in most developing countries; and Mexico's marine, land and air transportation services and its geographical position as a neighbor of the United States help make it an attractive location. There are, of course, advantages to incorporating with majority Mexican capital.

An investment of 49 percent or less foreign equity may be organized immediately by simply registering with the FIR. Although the new resolutions should significantly decrease the length of time required to obtain approval of majority foreign equity by the FIC, common sense suggests that the process will still take considerably longer than incorporating with 49 percent or less. More important, an investment with majority Mexican capital qualifies automatically for tax and other investment incentives pursuant to the 1972 Law for the Promotion of New and Necessary Industries and other decrees. Although an investor may negotiate for incentives with both the FIC and the government of the state in which it will be operating even if majority foreign capitalization is planned, certain advantageous incentives are available only to companies with majority Mexican equity. Also, a company with majority Mexican equity will probably have easier access to administrative agencies and the various licenses required for imports.

Nonetheless, definite benefits may be gained by an investment of 100 percent foreign equity. One foreign banking official noted that there are both accounting and reporting advantages. In addition, a facility constructed by an investor entirely with foreign capital will have an asset worth more than the original investment after completion. If 51 percent is later sold to Mexican investors, the company would then be eligible for tax incentives.

Majority foreign equity has other positive ramifications. From a lending point of view, the risk may be different. A bank is more likely to extend credit to a subsidiary of a company that is well known or with which the bank has had a prior working relationship. Experience has proven that a parent company is much more likely to stand behind and support a wholly owned subsidiary, and any creditor is more comfortable lending to a party with which it is familiar, in contrast to a company newly formed with unknown management or shareholders.

Last, 100 percent foreign equity is unavoidable in certain industries. A company that has developed expensive, unique technology will not share that asset with anyone else. Such an attitude does not spring from a fear of Mexicanization; the intangibility of technology precludes nationalization, as was aptly noted by the chief legal adviser of an industrial conglomerate.

The particular needs of the enterprise dictate the decision whether to invest with majority foreign equity. For investors in Mexico, the fact that the Guidelines promote specific industries and that the new resolutions should expedite approval by the FIC are obviously factors to be considered. Regulations, however, do not necessarily affect the economic and political situation of a company, which is usually the main factor taken into account in such a decision.

Yet regulations can provide an indication of the governing country's attitude and probable treatment. Mexico has decided that the activities delineated in the Guidelines are the ones that most benefit its economy, and it issued the Guidelines to notify the international community that in these areas it will be most accommodating in meeting the needs of the foreign investor.

It is still too soon to detect the impact of the Guidelines, especially when one remembers that there are many other factors that need to be considered in speculating on Mexico's short-term investment growth. At present, Mexican assets have been frozen as banks wait out the financial crisis and debt restructurings. Even if a company decided to locate in Mexico, the freeze alone could inhibit such a move since most prefer to invest with borrowed money. Also, many plants that had expanded in the early 1980s found themselves idle with the recession and are now trying to orient themselves for exports.

Nonetheless, the overwhelming majority of persons interviewed are optimistic in believing that the Guidelines signify an important change in attitude by the Mexican Government. Since 1973, its attitude had been defensive, shaped by an acute awareness of the detrimental effects of unrestrained foreign investment and dominance. The new attitude of selective promotion of specific industries must be viewed not in terms of the percentage of foreign participation alone but, more importantly, as an identification of the administration's goals for foreign investment, including more sophisticated technology, higher employment, substitution of imports and increased exports.

Mexico appears to have finally taken a macroeconomic approach toward foreign investment. It is an instrument that must be used rationally, for only by selectively promoting those industries beneficial to the nation will Mexico achieve the international standards of competitive technology and exports necessary for continued positive economic growth.

Mexico's approach toward foreign investment is in a process of evolution. After veering from completely unrestrained reception to excessively protective and nationalistic restriction of foreign capital, the country appears to have reached an equilibrium. By announcing that it would actively promote foreign investment in specified industries, Mexico has placed the international community on notice of its intention to progress rationally toward further economic growth.

Because its foreign investment regulations are largely the result of policy established by an administrative body with broad discretionary powers, it has been difficult in the past to predict how favorably a prospective enterprise might be received. According to FIC officials, however, one can now look to the criteria set forth in the NIDP and FIL and to the list of activities to be promoted under the 1984 Guidelines and obtain a clearer indication of the conditions to which a company will be subject and whether they are consistent with its interests.

The Guidelines, together with the resolutions of the FIC, signify a changing attitude. Up to 100 percent direct foreign investment will be considered in specified activities; increases in the percentage of foreign equity in Mexican companies may also be arranged; and foreign companies in priority industries will be permitted to expand under certain circumstances. Although the FIL had allowed for these exceptions, prior to the announcement of the 1984 Guidelines they had rarely been granted.

Foreign investments that are subject to these exceptions, however, will not be approved automatically. They will still need to be analyzed by the FIC in terms of the criteria set forth in the NIDP and FIL.

Whether to invest with 100 percent or 49 percent foreign capital is a decision dictated by the needs of the particular company; but the availability of a choice makes Mexico an even more attractive country in which to invest. Fear of future restrictions, such as requirements to Mexicanize, is unreasonable in view of the overall profit potential and should not be a determining factor in whether to select Mexico as an investment choice.

Although persons involved in the field are optimistic about this change in attitude, they are also aware that regulations do not substantially affect the magnitude of foreign investment in a country.

Other circumstances have much greater significance, and owing to the current recession, it will take time to evaluate with accuracy the impact of these policies on Mexico's shortand long-term economic growth. The development of a rational plan that selectively promotes industries deemed beneficial to the national economy, however, should greatly assist Mexico in achieving competitive international standards.

7

Hotel Planning Management

STRATEGIC PLANNING IN HOTEL MANAGEMENT

Strategic planning involves defining objectives and developing strategies to reach those objectives. It may employ methods like SWOT analysis to help clarify objectives and strategies. Strategic planning uses "the big picture" to pursue large scale, long term objectives. This is in contradistinction to "tactical" planning, which has to focuss on short term, smaller objectives. "Long range" planning typically projects current activities and programs onto a model of the external world, thereby predicting likely results. "Strategic" planning tries to "create" more desirable future results by (a) influencing the outside world or (b) adapting current programs and actions so as to have more favourable outcomes in the external environment.

Within business, strategic planning may provide overall direction strategic management to a company or give specific direction in such areas as:

- Financial strategies
- Human resource/organizational development strategies
- Information technology deployments
- Marketing strategy

We want to do Strategic Planning to:

- Have the capability to obtain the desired objective
- Fit well both with the external environment and with an organization's resources and core competencies - it should appear feasible and appropriate
- Have the capability of providing an organization with a sustainable competitive advantage - ideally through uniqueness and sustainability
- Prove dynamic, flexible, and able to adapt to changing situations
- Suffice on its own - specifically providing favorable outcomes without the need for cross-subsidization

Most strategic planning methodologies depend on a three-step process (sometimes called the STP process):

- Situation - evaluate the current situation and how it came about
- Target - define goals and/or objectives (sometimes called ideal state)
- Path - map a possible route to the goals/objectives

An alternative approach is called Draw-See-Think

- Draw - what is the ideal image or the desired end state?
- See - what is today's situation? What is the gap from ideal and why?
- Think - what specific actions must be taken to close the gap between today's situation and the ideal state?
- Plan - what resources are required to execute the activities?

In general terms, strategic planning can proceed incrementally or revolutionarily.

Strategic planning as a set of logical and creative steps

1. Clarification of objective (end-state) to be pursued. The following terms have been used in the literature: desired end states, plans, policies, goals, objectives, strategies, tactics and actions. Definitions vary, overlap and fail to achieve clarity. The following concept has been found useful. The items listed above may be organized in a hierarchy of means and ends and numbered as follows: Top Rank Objective (TRO), Second Rank Objective, Third Rank Objective, etc. From any rank, the objective in a lower rank answers to the question "How?" and the objective in a higher rank answers to the question "Why?" The exception is the Top Rank Objective (TRO): there is no answer to the "Why?" question. That is how the TRO is defined. An example may help to clarify the concept presented above.
2. Information gathering and analysis. This includes an external assessment (such as environmental scanning), and an internal resource assessment. Morphological analysis may be applied to both internal resource assessments and external assessments. SWOT (Strengths, Weaknesses, Opportunities, Threats) Analysis may be used to assess those aspects of the organization and the environment that are important to achieving the objective of the strategic plan.
3. Evaluation of the feasibility of the objective in view of the SWOTs.
4. Strategy-development. This is a creative step that answers these four questions: How can we use the Strengths, stop the Weaknesses, exploit the Opportunities and defend against the Threats in pursuit of the selected objetive.
5. Developing Action Programs for the more attractive strategies, covering: Name of the strategy, Benefits to be expected from implementing this programme, Actions: What will be done? Responsible persons: Who will be in charge of the programme? Timing: When will the programme start? When will it be completed? Location(s): Where will the programme be implemented? Resources: What will be needed: people, money, information, other resources?

Control System: How will progress be measured and reported? Rewards for performance, if any. Contingency plans: What will be done if results fall short?

Strategy as Revolution

- Identify the unquestioned beliefs in the organization and challenge them - look for opportunities to re-write the rules of the environment
- Look for major discontinuities in technology, and embrace such changes wholeheartedly - do not waste time making small incremental adjustments - stand by to create a completely new business model at any time
  - More a mind-set than a formal technique
  - Not rule or ritual-oriented, not reductionist, not reactive, not autocratic

Theorists frequently make the distinction between strategy and tactics. Strategy involves planning how to get where one wants to go. Tactics can potentially comprise the implementation of such over-arching plans. They deal with specific actions by particular people or by particular groups. Some theorists see it as a mistake to separate strategy and tactics. Constantinos Markides describes strategy formation and implementation (tactics) as an on-going, never-ending, integrated process requiring continuous re-assessment and reformation. He sees strategic planning as both planned and emergent - dynamic and interactive. J. Moncrieff also stresses strategy dynamics - he recognizes strategy as partially deliberate and partially unplanned.

The unplanned element comes from two sources:

1. Emergent strategies - resulting from the emergence of opportunities and threats in the environment
2. Strategies in action - ad hoc actions by many people from all parts of an organization

Strategic plans typically look 5 or more years into the future. They differ in this respect from tactical plans (sometimes referred to as functional plans), which look 2 to 4 years into the future; and from operational plans [such as budgets] which have an annual scope.

PHASES IN PLANNING

Whether the system is an organization, department, business, project, etc., the basic planning process typically includes similar nature of activities carried out in similar sequence. The phases are carried out carefully or — in some cases — intuitively, for example, when planning a very small, straightforward effort. The complexity of the various phases (and their duplication throughout the system) depend on the scope of the system. For example, in a large corporation, the following phases would be carried out in the corporate offices, in each division, in each department, in each group, etc.

During planning, planners have in mind (consciously or unconsciously) some overall purpose or result that the plan is to achieve. For example, during strategic planning, it's critical to reference the mission, or overall purpose, of the organization.

For example, during strategic planning, planners often conduct a "SWOT analysis". (SWOT is an acronym for considering the organization's strengths and weaknesses, and the opportunities and threats faced by the organization.) During this analysis, planners also can use a variety of assessments, or methods to "measure" the health of systems.

Based on the analysis and alignment to the overall mission of the system, planners establish a set of goals that build on strengths to take advantage of opportunities, while building up weaknesses and warding off threats. The particular strategies (or methods to reach the goals) chosen depend on matters of affordability, practicality and efficiency. Objectives are selected to be timely and indicative of progress toward goals. Responsibilities are assigned, including for implementation of the plan, and for achieving various goals and objectives. Ideally, deadlines are set for meeting each responsibility.

The above information is organized and written in a document which is distributed around the system.

This critical step is often ignored — which can eventually undermine the success of many of your future planning efforts. The purpose of a plan is to address a current problem or pursue a development goal. It seems simplistic to assert that you should acknowledge if the problem was solved or the goal met. However, this step in the planning process is often ignored in lieu of moving on the next problem to solve or goal to pursue. Skipping this step can cultivate apathy and skepticism — even cynicism — in your organization. Don't skip this step.

A common failure in many kinds of planning is that the plan is never really implemented. Instead, all focus is on writing a plan document. Too often, the plan sits collecting dust on a shelf. Therefore, most of the following guidelines help to ensure that the planning process is carried out completely and is implemented completely — or, deviations from the intended plan are recognized and managed accordingly.

Going back to the reference to systems, it's critical that all parts of the system continue to exchange feedback in order to function effectively. This is true no matter what type of system. When planning, get input from everyone who will responsible to carry out parts of the plan, along with representative from groups who will be effected by the plan. Of course, people also should be involved in they will be responsible to review and authorize the plan.

New managers, in particular, often forget that others don't know what these managers know. Even if managers do communicate their intentions and plans verbally, chances are great that others won't completely hear or understand what the manager wants done. Also, as plans change, it's extremely difficult to remember who is supposed to be doing what and according to which version of the plan. Key stakeholders (employees, management, board members, funders, investor, customers, clients, etc.) may request copies of various types of plans. Therefore, it's critical to write plans down and communicate them widely.

For example, it's difficult to know what someone should be doing if they are to pursue the goal to "work harder". It's easier to recognize "Write a paper". It's difficult to know what the scope of "Writing a paper" really is. It's easier to appreciate that effort if the goal is "Write a 30-page paper". If I'm to take responsibility for pursuit of a goal, the goal should be acceptable to me. For example, I'm not likely to follow the directions of someone telling me to write a 30-page paper when I also have to five other papers to write. However, if you involve me in setting the goal so I can change my other commitments or modify the goal, I'm much more likely to accept pursuit of the goal as well.

Even if I do accept responsibility to pursue a goal that is specific and measurable, the goal won't be useful to me or others if, for example, the goal is to "Write a 30-page paper in the next 10 seconds". It may mean more to others if I commit to a realistic goal to "Write a 30-page paper in one week". However, it'll mean more to others (particularly if they are planning to help me or guide me to reach the goal) if I specify that I will write one page a day for 30 days, rather than including the possibility that I will write all 30 pages in last day of the 30-day period.

The goal should stretch the performer's capabilities. For example, I might be more interested in writing a 30-page paper if the topic of the paper or the way that I write it will extend my capabilities. I'm more inclined to write the paper if the paper will contribute to an effort in such a way that I might be rewarded for my effort.

Plans should specify who is responsible for achieving each result, including goals and objectives. Dates should be set for completion of each result, as well. Responsible parties should regularly review status of the plan. Be sure to have someone of authority "sign off" on the plan, including putting their signature on the plan to indicate they agree with and support its contents. Include responsibilities in policies, procedures, job descriptions, performance review processes, etc.

During the planning process, regularly collect feedback from participants. Do they agree with the planning process? If not, what don't they like and how could it be done better? In large, ongoing planning processes (such as strategic planning, business planning, project planning, etc.), it's critical to collect this kind of feedback regularly.

During regular reviews of implementation of the plan, assess if goals are being achieved or not. If not, were goals realistic? Do responsible parties have the resources necessary to achieve the goals and objectives? Should goals be changed? Should more priority be placed on achieving the goals? What needs to be done?

Finally, take 10 minutes to write down how the planning process could have been done better. File it away and read it the next time you conduct the planning process.

Far too often, primary emphasis is placed on the plan document. This is extremely unfortunate because the real treasure of planning is the planning process itself. During planning, panners learn a great deal from ongoing analysis, reflection, discussion, debates and dialogue around issues and goals in the system. Perhaps there is no better example of misplaced priorities in planning than in business ethics. Far too often, people put emphasis on written codes of ethics and codes of conduct. While these documents certainly are important, at least as important is conducting ongoing communications around these documents. The ongoing communications are what sensitize people to understanding and following the values and behaviors suggested in the codes.

A prominent example of this type of potential problem is when planners don't prefer the "top down" or "bottom up", "linear" type of planning (for example, going from general to specific along the process of an environmental scan, SWOT analysis, mission/vision/values, issues and goals, strategies, objectives, timelines, etc.) There are other ways to conduct planning.

Systems Thinking

Systems thinking is an approach to analysis that is based on the belief that the component parts of a system will act differently when isolated from its environment or other parts of the system, and argues against Descartes's reductionist view. It includes viewing systems in a holistic manner, rather than through purely reductionist techniques. Systems thinking is about gaining insights into the whole by understanding the linkages and interactions between the elements that comprise the whole "system", consistent with systems philosophy. Systems Thinking recognizes that all human activity systems are open systems; therefore, they are affected by the environment in which they exist. Systems Thinking recognizes that in complex systems, events are separated by distance and time; therefore, small catalytic events can cause large changes in the system. Systems thinking acknowledges that a change in one area of a system can adversely affect another area of the system; thus, it promotes organizational communication at all levels in order to avoid the silo effect.

Systems thinkers consider that:

- A "system" is a dynamic and complex whole, interacting as a structured functional unit
- Information flows between the different elements that compose the system
- A system is a community situated within an environment
- Information flows from and to the surrounding environment via semi-permeable membranes or boundaries

- Systems are often composed of entities seeking equilibrium, but can exhibit oscillating, chaotic, or exponential growth/decay behaviour

Systems thinkers are particularly interested in studying systems because changing a system frequently leads to counterintuitive system responses. For example feedback loops may operate to either keep the organization in check or unbalance it.

Traditional decision making tends to involve linear cause and effect relationships. By taking a systems approach, we can see the whole complex of bidirectional interrelationships. Instead of analysing a problem in terms of an input and an output, for example, we look at the whole system of inputs, processes, outputs, feedback, and controls. This larger picture will typically provide more useful results than traditional methods.

System thinking also helps us integrate the temporal dimension of any decision. Instead of looking at discrete "snapshots" at points in time, a systems methodology will allow us to see change as a continuous process.

Systems Thinking is a world view based on the perspective of the systems sciences, which seeks to understand interconnectedness, complexity and wholeness of components of systems in specific relationship to each other. Systems thinking is not only constructivist, rather systems thinking embraces the values of reductionist science by understanding the parts, and the constructivist perspectives which seek to understand wholes, and more so, the understanding of the complex relationships that enable 'parts' to become 'wholes'.

A system is any set (group) of interdependent or temporally interacting parts. Parts are generally systems themselves and are composed of other parts, just as systems are generally parts or holons of other systems.

Systems thinking techniques may be used to study any kind of system — natural, scientific, human, or conceptual.

Systems thinking often involves considering a "system" in different ways:

Rather than trying to improve the braking system on a car by looking in great detail at the composition of the brake pads (reductionist), the boundary of the braking system may be extended to include not only the components of the car, but the driver, the road and the weather, and considering the interactions between them.

Looking at something as a series of conceptual systems according to multiple viewpoints. A supermarket could be considered as a "profit making system" from the perspective of management, an "employment system" from the perspective of the staff, and a "shopping system" — or perhaps an "entertainment system" — from the perspective of the customers. As a result of such thinking, new insights may be gained into how the supermarket works, why it has problems, or how changes made to one such system may impact on the others.

Systems thinking uses a variety of techniques that may be divided into:

- Hard systems - involving simulations, often using computers and the techniques of operations research. Useful for problems that can justifiably be quantified. However it cannot easily take into account unquantifiable variables (opinions, culture, politics, etc), and may treat people as being passive, rather than having complex motivations.

- Soft systems - Used to tackle systems that cannot easily be quantified, especially those involving people holding multiple and conflicting frames of reference. Useful for understanding motivations, viewpoints, and interactions and addressing qualitative as well as quantitative dimensions of problem situations. Soft systems are a field that utilizes foundation methodological work developed by Peter Checkland, Brian Wilson and their colleagues at Lancaster University. Morphological analysis is a complementary method for structuring and analysing non-quantifiable problem complexes.
- Evolutionary systems - the development of Evolutionary Systems Design by Bela H. Banathy integrates critical systems inquiry and soft systems methodologies to create a meta-methodology applicable to the design of complex social systems. These systems, similar to dynamic systems are understood as open, complex systems, but further accounts for their potential capacity to evolve over time. Banathy uniquely integrated the multidisciplinary perspectives of systems research (including chaos, complexity, cybernetics), cultural anthropology, evolutionary theory, and others.

PLANNING A PROJECT

Before describing the role and creation of a specification, we need to introduce and explain a fairly technical term: a numbty is a person whose brain is totally numb. In this context, numb means "deprived of feeling or the power of unassisted activity"; in general, a numbty needs the stimulation of an electric cattle prod to even get to the right office in the morning. Communication with numbties is severely hampered by the fact that although they think they know what they mean (which they do not), they seldom actually say it, and they never write it down. And the main employment of numbties world-wide is in creating project specifications. You must know this - and protect your team accordingly.

A specification is the definition of your project: a statement of the problem, not the solution. Normally, the specification contains errors, ambiguities, misunderstandings and enough rope to hang you and your entire team. Thus before you embark upon the the next six months of activity working on the wrong project, you must assume that a numbty was the chief author of the specification you received and you must read, worry, revise and ensure that everyone concerned with the project (from originator, through the workers, to the end-customer) is working with the same understanding. The outcome of this deliberation should be a written definition of what is required, by when; and this must be agreed by all involved. There are no short-cuts to this; if you fail to spend the time initially, it will cost you far more later on.

The agreement upon a written specification has several benefits:

- The clarity will reveal misunderstandings
- The completeness will remove contradictory assumptions
- The rigour of the analysis will expose technical and practical details which numbties normally gloss over through ignorance or fear
- The agreement forces all concerned to actually read and think about the details

The work on the specification can seen as the first stage of Quality Assurance since you are looking for and countering problems in the very foundation of the project - from this perspective the creation of the specification clearly merits a large investment of time.

From a purely defensive point of view, the agreed specification also affords you protection against the numbties who have second thoughts, or new ideas, half way through the project. Once the project is underway, changes cost time (and money). The existence of a demonstrably-agreed specification enables you to resist or to charge for (possibly in terms of extra time) such changes. Further, people tend to forget what they originally thought; you may need proof that you have been working as instructed.

The places to look for errors in a specification are:

- The global context: numbties often focus too narrowly on the work of one team and fail to consider how it fits into the larger picture. Some of the work given to you may actually be undone or duplicated by others. Some of the proposed work may be incompatible with that of others; it might be just plain barmy in the larger context.
- The interfaces: between your team and both its customers and suppliers, there are interfaces. At these points something gets transferred. Exactly what, how and when should be discussed and agreed from the very beginning. Never assume a common understanding, because you will be wrong. All it takes for your habitual understandings to evaporate is the arrival of one new member, in either of the teams. Define and agree your interfaces and maintain a friendly contact throughout the project.
- Time-scales: numbties always underestimate the time involved for work. If there are no time-scales in the specification, you can assume that one will be imposed upon you (which will be impossible). You must add realistic dates. The detail should include a precise understanding of the extent of any intermediate stages of the task, particularly those which have to be delivered.
- External dependencies: your work may depend upon that of others. Make this very clear so that these people too will receive warning

of your needs. Highlight the effect that problems with these would have upon your project so that everyone is quite clear about their importance. To be sure, contact these people yourself and ask if they are able to fulfil the assumptions in your specification.

- Resources: the numbty tends to ignore resources. The specification should identify the materials, equipment and manpower which are needed for the project. The agreement should include a commitment by your managers to allocate or to fund them. You should check that the actual numbers are practical and/or correct. If they are omitted, add them - there is bound to be differences in their assumed values.

This seems to make the specification sound like a long document. It should not be. Each of the above could be a simple sub-heading followed by either bullet points or a table - you are not writing a brochure, you are stating the definition of the project in clear, concise and unambiguous glory.

Of course, the specification may change. If circumstances, or simply your knowledge, change then the specification will be out of date. You should not regard it as cast in stone but rather as a display board where everyone involved can see the current, common understanding of the project. If you change the content everyone must know, but do not hesitate to change it as necessary.

Having decide what the specification intends, your next problem is to decide what you and your team actually need to do, and how to do it. As a manager, you have to provide some form of framework both to plan and to communicate what needs doing. Without a structure, the work is a series of unrelated tasks which provides little sense of achievement and no feeling of advancement. If the team has no grasp of how individual tasks fit together towards an understood goal, then the work will seem pointless and they will feel only frustration.

To take the planning forward, therefore, you need to turn the specification into a complete set of tasks with a linking structure. Fortunately, these two requirements are met at the same time since the derivation of such a structure is the simplest method of arriving at a list of tasks.

Work Breakdown Structure

Once you have a clear understanding of the project, and have eliminated the vagaries of the numbties, you then describe it as a set of simpler separate activities. If any of these are still too complex for you to easily organise, you break them down also into another level of simpler descriptions, and so on until you can manage everything. Thus your one complex project is organised as a set of simple tasks which together achieve the desired result.

The reasoning behind this is that the human brain (even yours) can only take in and process so much information at one time. To get a real grasp of the project, you have to think about it in pieces rather than trying to process the complexity of its entire details all at once. Thus each level of the project can be understood as the amalgamation of a few simply described smaller units.

In planning any project, you follow the same simple steps: if an item is too complicated to manage, it becomes a list of simpler items. People call this producing a work breakdown structure to make it sound more formal and impressive. Without following this formal approach you are unlikely to remember all the niggling little details; with this procedure, the details are simply displayed on the final lists.

One common fault is to produce too much detail at the initial planning stage. You should be stop when you have a sufficient description of the activity to provide a clear instruction for the person who will actually do the work, and to have a reasonable estimate for the total time/effort involved. You need the former to allocate (or delegate) the task; you need the latter to finish the planning.

Task Allocation

The next stage is a little complicated. You now have to allocate the tasks to different people in the team and, at the same time, order these tasks so that they are performed in a sensible sequence.

Task allocation is not simply a case of handing out the various tasks on your final lists to the people you have available; it is far more subtle (and powerful) than that. As a manager you have to look far beyond the single project; indeed any individual project can be seen as merely a single step in your team's development. The allocation of tasks should thus be seen as a means of increasing the skills and experience of your team - when the project is done, the team should have gained.

In simple terms, consider what each member of your team is capable of and allocate sufficient complexity of tasks to match that (and to slightly stretch). The tasks you allocate are not the ones on your finals lists, they are adapted to better suit the needs of your team's development; tasks are moulded to fit people, which is far more effective than the other way around. For example, if Arthur is to learn something new, the task may be simplified with responsibility given to another to guide and check the work; if Brenda is to develop, sufficient tasks are combined so that her responsibility increases beyond what she has held before; if Colin lacks confidence, the tasks are broken into smaller units which can be completed (and commended) frequently.

Sometimes tasks can be grouped and allocated together. For instance, some tasks which are seemingly independent may benefit from being done together since they use common ideas, information, talents. One person doing them both removes the start-up time for one of them; two people (one on each) will be able to help each other.

The ordering of the tasks is really quite simple, although you may find that sketching a sequence diagram helps you to think it through (and to communicate the result). Pert charts are the accepted outcome, but sketches will suffice. Getting the details exactly right, however, can be a long and painful process, and often it can be futile. The degree to which you can predict the future is limited, so too should be the detail of your planning. You must have the broad outlines by which to monitor progress, and sufficient detail to assign each task when it needs to be started, but beyond that - stop and do something useful instead.

At the initial planning stage the main objective is to get a realistic estimate of the time involved in the project. You must establish this not only to assist higher management with their planning, but also to protect your team from being expected to do the impossible. The most important technique for achieving this is known as: guesstimation.

Guesstimating schedules is notoriously difficult but it is helped by two approaches:

- Make your guesstimates of the simple tasks at the bottom of the work break down structure and look for the longest path through the sequence diagram
- Use the experience from previous projects to improve your guesstimating skills

The corollary to this is that you should keep records in an easily accessible form of all projects as you do them. Part of your final project review should be to update your personal data base of how long various activities take. Managing this planning phase is vital to your success as a manager.

Some people find guesstimating a difficult concept in that if you have no experience of an activity, how can you make a worthwhile estimate? Let us consider such a problem: how long would it take you to walk all the way to the top of the Eiffel Tower or the Statue of Liberty? Presuming you have never actually tried this (most people take the elevator part of the way), you really have very little to go on. Indeed if you have actually seen one (and only one) of these buildings, think about the other. Your job depends upon this, so think carefully. One idea is to start with the number of steps - guess that if you can. Notice, you do not have to be right, merely reasonable. Next, consider the sort of pace you could maintain while climbing a flight of steps for a long time. Now imagine yourself at the base of a flight of steps you do know, and estimate a) how many steps there are, and b) how long it takes you to climb them (at that steady pace). To complete, apply a little mathematics.

Now examine how confident you are with this estimate. If you won a free flight to Paris or New York and tried it, you would probably (need your head examined) be mildly surprised if you climbed to the top in less than half the estimated time and if it took you more than double you would be mildly annoyed. If it took you less than a tenth the time, or ten times as long, you would extremely surprised/annoyed. In fact, you do not currently believe that that would happen (no really, do you?). The point is that from very little experience of the given problem, you can actually come up with a working estimate - and one which is far better than no estimate at all when it comes to deriving a schedule. Guesstimating does take a little practice, but it is a very useful skill to develop.

There are two practical problems in guesstimation. First, you are simply too optimistic. It is human nature at the beginning of a new project to ignore the difficulties and assume best case scenarii - in producing your estimates (and using those of others) you must inject a little realism. In practice, you should also build-in a little slack to allow yourself some tolerance against mistakes. This is known as defensive scheduling. Also, if you eventually deliver ahead of the agreed schedule, you will be loved.

Second, you will be under pressure from senior management to deliver quickly, especially if the project is being sold competitively. Resist the temptation to rely upon speed as the only selling point. You might, for instance, suggest the criteria of: fewer errors, history of adherence to initial schedules, previous customer satisfaction, "this is how long it takes, so how can you trust the other quotes".

ESTABLISHING CONTROLS

When the planning phase is over (and agreed), the "doing" phase begins. Once it is in motion, a project acquires a direction and momentum which is totally independent of anything you predicted. If you come to terms with that from the start, you can then enjoy the roller-coaster which follows. To gain some hope, however, you need to establish at the start (within the plan) the means to monitor and to influence the project's progress.

There are two key elements to the control of a project

- Milestones (clear, unambiguous targets of what, by when)
- Established means of communication

For you, the milestones are a mechanism to monitor progress; for your team, they are short-term goals which are far more tangible than the foggy, distant completion of the entire project. The milestones maintain the momentum and encourage effort; they allow the team to judge their own progress and to celebrate achievement throughout the project rather than just at its end.

The simplest way to construct milestones is to take the timing information from the work breakdown structure and sequence diagram. When you have guesstimated how long each sub-task will take and have strung them together, you can identify by when each of these tasks will actually be completed. This is simple and effective; however, it lacks creativity.

A second method is to construct more significant milestones. These can be found by identify stages in the development of a project which are recognisable as steps towards the final product. Sometimes these are simply the higher levels of your structure; for instance, the completion of a market-evaluation phase. Sometimes, they cut across many parallel activities; for instance, a prototype of the eventual product or a mock-up of the new brochure format.

If you are running parallel activities, this type of milestone is particularly useful since it provides a means of pulling together the people on disparate activities, and so:

- They all have a shared goal (the common milestone)
- Their responsibility to (and dependence upon) each other is emphasised
- Each can provide a new (but informed) viewpoint on the others' work
- The problems to do with combining the different activities are highlighted and discussed early in the implementation phase
- You have something tangible which senior management (and numbties) can recognise as progress
- You have something tangible which your team can celebrate and which constitutes a short-term goal in a possibly long-term project
- It provides an excellent opportunity for quality checking and for review

Of course, there are milestones and there are mill-stones. You will have to be sensitive to any belief that working for some specific milestone is hindering rather than helping the work forward. If this arises then either you have chosen the wrong milestone, or you have failed to communicate how it fits into the broader structure.

Communication is your everything. To monitor progress, to receive early warning of danger, to promote cooperation, to motivate through team involvement, all of these rely upon communication. Regular reports are invaluable - if you clearly define what information is needed and if teach your team how to provided it in a rapidly accessible form. Often these reports merely say "progressing according to schedule". These you send back, for while the message is desired the evidence is missing: you need to insist that your team monitor their own progress with concrete, tangible, measurements and if this is done, the figures should be included in the report. However, the real value of this practice comes when progress is not according to schedule - then your communication system is worth all the effort you invested in its planning.

At the planning stage, you can deal with far more than the mere project at hand. You can also shape the overall pattern of your team's working using the division and type of activities you assign.

Ask your team. They too must be involved in the planning of projects, especially in the lower levels of the work breakdown structure. Not only will they provide information and ideas, but also they will feel ownership in the final plan.

This does not mean that your projects should be planned by committee - rather that you, as manager, plan the project based upon all the available experience and creative ideas. As an initial approach, you could attempt the first level(s) of the work breakdown structure to help you communicate the project to the team and then ask for comments. Then, using these, the final levels could be refined by the people to whom the tasks will be allocated. However, since the specification is so vital, all the team should vet the penultimate draft.

There are two pitfalls to avoid in project reviews:

- They can be too frequent
- They can be too drastic

The constant trickle of new information can lead to a vicious cycle of planning and revising which shakes the team's confidence in any particular version of the plan and which destroys the very stability which the structure was designed to provide. You must decide the balance. Pick a point on the horizon and walk confidently towards it. Decide objectively, and explain beforehand, when the review phases will occur and make this a scheduled milestone in itself.

Even though the situation may have changed since the last review, it is important to recognise the work which has been accomplished during the interim. Firstly, you do not want to abandon it since the team will be demotivated feeling that they have achieved nothing. Secondly, this work itself is part of the new situation: it has been done, it should provide a foundation for the next step or at least the basis of a lesson well learnt. Always try to build upon the existing achievements of your team.

No plan is complete without explicit provision for testing and quality. As a wise manager, you will know that this should be part of each individual phase of the project. This means that no activity is completed until it has passed the (objectively) defined criteria which establishes its quality, and these are best defined (objectively) at the beginning as part of the planning.

When devising the schedule therefore you must include allocated time for this part of each activity. Thus your question is not only: "how long will it take", but also: "how long will the testing take". By asking both questions together you raise the issue of "how do we know we have done it right" at the very beginning and so the testing is more likely to be done in parallel with the implementation. You establish this philosophy for your team by include testing as a justified (required) cost.

Another reason for stating the testing criteria at the beginning is that you can avoid futile quests for perfection. If you have motivated your team well, they will each take pride in their work and want to do the best job possible. Often this means polishing their work until is shines; often this wastes time. If it clear at the onset exactly what is needed, then they are more likely to stop when that has been achieved. You need to avoid generalities and to stipulate boundaries; not easy, but essential.

The same is also true when choosing the tools or building-blocks of your project. While it might be nice to have use of the most modern versions, or to develop an exact match to your needs; often there is an old/existing version which will serve almost as well (sufficient for the purpose), and the difference is not worth the time you would need to invest in obtaining or developing the new one. Use what is available whenever possible unless the difference in the new version is worth the time, money and the initial, teething pains.

A related idea is that you should discourage too much effort on aspects of the project which are idiosyncratic to that one job. In the specification phase, you might try to eliminate these through negotiation with the customer; in the implementation phase you might leave these parts until last. The reason for this advice is that a general piece of work can be tailored to many specific instances; thus, if the work is in a general form, you will be able to rapidly re-use it for other projects. On the other hand, if you produce something which is cut to fit exactly one specific case, you may have to repeat the work entirely even though the next project is fairly similar. At the planning phase, a manager should bare in mind the future and the long-term development of the team as well as the requirements of the current project.

As a manager, you have to regulate the pressure and work load which is imposed upon your team; you must protect them from the unreasonable demands of the rest of the company. Once you have arrived at what you consider to be a realistic schedule, fight for it. Never let the outside world deflect you from what you know to be practical. If they impose a deadline upon you which is impossible, clearly state this and give your reasons. You will need to give some room for compromise, however, since a flat NO will be seen as obstructive. Since you want to help the company, you should look for alternative positions.

You could offer a prototype service or product at an earlier date. This might, in some cases, be sufficient for the customer to start the next stage of his/her own project on the understanding that your project would be completed at a later date and the final version would then replace the prototype.

The complexity of the product, or the total number of units, might be reduced. This might, in some cases, be sufficient for the customer's immediate needs. Future enhancements or more units would then be the subject of a subsequent negotiation which, you feel, would be likely to succeed since you will have already demonstrate your ability to deliver on time.

You can show on an alternative schedule that the project could be delivered by the deadline if certain (specified) resources are given to you or if other projects are rescheduled. Thus, you provide a clear picture of the situation and a possible solution; it is up to your manager then how he/she proceeds.

The most common error in planning is to assume that there will be no errors in the implementation: in effect, the schedule is derived on the basis of "if nothing goes wrong, this will take...". Of course, recognising that errors will occur is the reason for implementing a monitoring strategy on the project. Thus when the inevitable does happen, you can react and adapt the plan to compensate. However, by carefully considering errors in advance you can make changes to the original plan to enhance its tolerance. Quite simply, your planning should include time where you stand back from the design and ask: "what can go wrong?"; indeed, this is an excellent way of asking your team for their analysis of your plan.

You can try to predict where the errors will occur. By examining the activities' list you can usually pinpoint some activities which are risky (for instance, those involving new equipment) and those which are quite secure (for instance, those your team has done often before). The risky areas might then be given a less stringent time-scale - actually planning-in time for the mistakes. Another possibility is to apply a different strategy, or more resources, to such activities to minimise the disruption. For instance, you could include training or consultancy for new equipment, or you might parallel the work with the foundation of a fall-back position.

At the end of any project, you should allocate time to reviewing the lessons and information on both the work itself and the management of that work: an open meeting, with open discussion, with the whole team and all customers and suppliers. If you think that this might be thought a waste of time by your own manager, think of the effect it will have on future communications with your customers and suppliers.

ORGANISATION PLANNING

Planning is also a management function, concerned with defining goals for future organizational performance and deciding on the tasks and resources to be used in order to attain those goals. To meet the goals, managers will invest significant resources for training and incentives to motivate employees.

Planning is the process of setting objectives and determining how to accomplish them. Simply it is the act of thinking before doing. It accesses us in predicting about the future. So, it serves as the standard for the function of controlling if there is any deviation.

In most organizations 'strategic planning' is an annual process, typically covering just the year ahead. Occasionally, a few organizations may look at a practical plan which stretches three or more years ahead.

To be most effective, the plan has to be formalized, usually in written form, as a formal 'marketing plan'. The essence of the process is that it moves from the general to the specific; from the overall objectives of the organization down to the individual action plan for a part of one marketing programme. It is also an iterative process, so that the draft output of each stage is checked to see what impact it has on the earlier stages - and is amended accordingly.

The Corporate Plan

The starting point for the marketing plan, and the context within which it is set, is the corporate plan. In most marketing-oriented organizations the contents of the corporate plan will closely match those of the marketing plan itself; but it will also include the plans for the disposition of the other internal resources of the organization. Thus, the corporate plan is likely to contain three main components:

The first category is intimately involved with the customers. In marketing terms, although there are many other factors to take into account, the most important definition of where the company 'is' revolves around where it is in the market (and hence where it is with its consumers). The same is largely true of the second stage as well; since, no matter how much its managers may wish otherwise, where the company can realistically expect to go is totally in the hands of its customers. It is only at the third stage that the 4 Ps come into play as vehicles for moving the company to reach its objectives.

Corporate Objectives

The overall objectives of commercial organizations are conventionally supposed to be financial. However, other aims are also possible. Many companies choose long-term growth (which may be quite different to revenue maximization in the short term). Almost all have an implicit, and very powerful, aim of survival.

One of the best known 'alternatives', that of 'satisfying' (rather than profit maximization), came from Herbert Simon: "In one way or another, they incorporate the notions of bounded rationality: the need to search for decision alternatives, the replacement of optimization by targets and satisfying [minimal] goals, and mechanisms of learning and adaptation."

Pfeffer and Salancik said that: "We prefer to view organizations as coalitions altering their purposes and domains to accommodate new interests, sloughing off parts of themselves to avoid some interests, and when necessary, becoming involved in activities far afield from their stated central purposes. Organizations are social instruments of tremendous power and energy, and the critical issue becomes who will control this energy and for what purpose."

If we accept the traditional assumption, as to the financial basis of the objectives behind the corporate plan, these objectives are ideally meant to be quantified in numerical and, in particular, financial terms.

In the most general terms, though, the 'objectives' behind a strategy address two questions: ''Where' do we want to be?' and ''When' do we expect to be there?'

Short Term Forecasting

This is the type of forecasting you will recognise. It is normally based upon a projection of historical trends, usually focused on sales volumes. There are many sophisticated techniques, increasingly using large amounts of computing power, but in essence all of these try to separate out the four main components:

1. Long term trends probably represent the most important information you are trying to extract from the mass of data before you.

2. Medium term cycles are supposed to result from regular economic ups and downs which used to be encapsulated in a 5 year 'business cycle' which, unfortunately, became unpredictable in the 1980s. The much quoted 'Kondratieff Cycles' are much longer, if they exist at all, being of the order of 25 - 50 years; and hence do not normally enter into shorter term forecasts.
3. Seasonal is the pattern within a single year, a pattern which most suppliers who are affected by it know well.
4. Random fluctuations, which do not fit regular patterns, afflict all products and services, and make computer analysis a very difficult proposition.

The end result of all these patterns superimposed may appear very confusing indeed. Despite all the sophistication on offer, therefore, by far the best advice is to keep it as simple as possible. The human eye is much better at resolving the complications shown above than the most powerful computer. Thus, the best approach to forecasting (and certainly the best check on any more sophisticated technique) is 'eyeballing' the sales charts! With some practise you should be able to sort out the main features of what is happening - and that is better than most computer models achieve.

The evidence is that the sophistication adds little or nothing to the accuracy (though it does to the image of the forecasters, and the prices they charge). Worst of all, such unnecessary complexity hinders your understanding of what is going on under the covers of the computer (and hides the fact that most forecasts are really based on human judgement). In any case, even if historical trends are accurately analysed, there is no guarantee that the future will be the same as the past. It is much better that you surface all the assumptions, and make your own judgements in full knowledge of what is involved.

Two very simple techniques to use (if nothing else but as a check on the forecasts others are trying to sell to you);

- Eyeballing - the technique I mentioned above is the first, and best, method. It merely requires you to plot historical results graphically; and then look for the patterns. Trust your own judgement - until you are proved wrong.
- Exponential Smoothing - this is the mathematical technique which reportedly gives the best results; probably because it is so simple, and consequently easily understood. Indeed, it is a very impressive title for a simple, but useful, mathematical technique; which can quite easily be handled manually. It just allows greater weight to be given to recent periods. Instead of, for example, the average trend over the whole of the last year being calculated, the sales data for each of the months is given a weighting, depending on how recent that month was. It simply takes the previous forecast, and adds on the latest 'actual' sales figure; except that it does this in a fixed

proportion, which is chosen to reflect the weighting to be given to the latest period. The general form is; Ft+1 = Ft + aEt where Ft+1 is the new forecast you are calculating, Ft is the previous one and Et is the deviation (or 'error') of the actual performance recorded against that previous period forecast; and 'a' is the weighting to be given to the most recent events. Exponential smoothing will not, in this simple form, allow for seasonality; though more sophisticated (but less easily understood) versions can do this.

Long Term Forecasting

This tends to be qualitative (as compared with the quantitative, numeric, focus of short term forecasts). It is even more dependent on judgement; and most of the more complicated approaches to it (such as Delphi, or Jury methods) aim to reduce the risks implicit in the judgement by spreading the process over panels of experts. It does not, in the final analysis, absolve the manager from backing his or her own judgement (which is probably better informed, in terms of the specific situation, than that of the 'experts').

Of all the techniques the most useful involves developing complementary scenarios, which allow for the uncertainties involved; as well as expanding the viewpoint of all the managers involved in the process. Unfortunately, in the form most often described it can also be the most complex and sophisticated of these techniques - and in this form perhaps only the very large corporate planning team at Shell have used it really effectively. A much simplified approach, based on the version which Shell recommend for their line managers who are not part of their corporate planning group, is more practical for most organisations. In this simplified version of the form originally described by Shell the four steps to this process are:

1. Identify the important variables - what (in the whole of the external environment, not just the marketing environment) are the most important factors which will determine the future of the organisation.
2. Brainstorm to find the possible outcomes - work through the different outcomes which different alternatives for these variables may lead to.
3. Link these together in a series of alternative scenarios - start to build six or seven scenarios ('stories' about the future of the organisation, or more importantly its market) which are able to contain these different alternatives.
4. Refine these scenarios - then work on the scenarios until they are condensed to two or three meaningful alternative (but complementary) descriptions of the future.

COMMERCIAL PLANNING

"In the modern world of business, it is useless to be a creative original thinker unless you can also sell what you create. Management cannot be expected to recognize a good idea unless it is presented to them by a good salesman." David M. Ogilvy

The success of a new product depends not only on the idea behind the product, but also on the marketing of the new product before, during and after the product launch. Commercializing a product is commonly known as Commercial Planning. No concrete methods are currently available for New Product Launching (NPL). However, several articles are published about NPL and the essential activities, to launch a new product. This article describes a set of activities and products, that are essential for launching a new product. New Product Launching is part of the New Product Development method.

Strategic management

An organization's strategy must be appropriate for its resources, environmental circumstances, and core objectives. The process involves matching the company's [internal resources (eg IT) and capabilities (eg quality management)] to the external business environment the organization faces. Strategy formulation involves:

- Doing a situation analysis: both internal and external; both micro-environmental and macro-environmental.
- Concurrent with this assessment, objectives are set. This involves crafting vision statements (long term view of a possible future), mission statements (the role that the organization gives itself in society), overall corporate objectives (both financial and strategic), strategic business unit objectives (both financial and strategic), and tactical objectives.
- These objectives should, in the light of the situation analysis, suggest a strategic plan. The plan provides the details of how to achieve these objectives.

This three-step strategy formulation process is sometimes referred to as determining where you are now, determining where you want to go, and then determining how to get there. These three questions are the essence of strategic planning. SWOT Analysis: I/O Economics for the external factors and RBV for the internal factors.

Strategy implementation involves:

- Allocation of sufficient resources (financial, personnel, time, technology support)
- Establishing a chain of command or some alternative structure (such as cross functional teams)
- Assigning responsibility of specific tasks or processes to specific individuals or groups
- It also involves managing the process. This includes monitoring results, comparing to benchmarks and best practices, evaluating

the efficacy and efficiency of the process, controlling for variances, and making adjustments to the process as necessary.

- When implementing specific programs, this involves acquiring the requisite resources, developing the process, training, process testing, documentation, and integration with (and/or conversion from) legacy processes.

Strategy formulation and implementation is an on-going, never-ending, integrated process requiring continuous reassessment and reformation. Strategic management is dynamic. It involves a complex pattern of actions and reactions. It is partially planned and partially unplanned. Strategy is both planned and emergent, dynamic, and interactive. Some people (such as Andy Grove at Intel) feel that there are critical points at which a strategy must take a new direction in order to be in step with a changing business environment. These critical points of change are called strategic inflection points.

Strategic management operates on several time scales. Short term strategies involve planning and managing for the present. Long term strategies involve preparing for and preempting the future. Marketing strategist Derek Abell (1993), has suggested that understanding this dual nature of strategic management is the least understood part of the process. He claims that balancing the temporal aspects of strategic planning requires the use of dual strategies simultaneously.

Strategic Management is actually a solid foundation or a framework within which all the functionning managerial operations are bundled together. This is the highest level corporate activity that sets the terms and goals for a company that it should follow for prosperity.

Strategic management techniques can be viewed as bottom-up, top-down, or collaborative processes. In the bottom-up approach, employees submit proposals to their managers who, in turn, funnel the best ideas further up the organization. This is often accomplished by a capital budgeting process. Proposals are assessed using financial criteria such as return on investment or cost-benefit analysis. The proposals that are approved form the substance of a new strategy, all of which is done without a grand strategic design or a strategic architect. The top-down approach is the most common by far. In it, the CEO, possibly with the assistance of a strategic planning team, decides on the overall direction the company should take. Some organizations are starting to experiment with collaborative strategic planning techniques that recognize the emergent nature of strategic decisions.

In most (large) corporations there are several levels of strategy. Strategic management is the highest in the sense that it is the broadest, applying to all parts of the firm. It gives direction to corporate values, corporate culture, corporate goals, and corporate missions. Under this broad corporate strategy there are often functional or business unit strategies.

Functional strategies include marketing strategies, new product development strategies, human resource strategies, financial strategies, legal strategies, and information technology management strategies. The emphasis is on short and medium term plans and is limited to the domain of each department's functional responsibility. Each functional department attempts to do its part in meeting overall corporate objectives, and hence to some extent their strategies are derived from broader corporate strategies.

Many companies feel that a functional organizational structure is not an efficient way to organize activities so they have reengineered according to processes or strategic business units (called SBUs). A strategic business unit is a semi-autonomous unit within an organization. It is usually responsible for its own budgeting, new product decisions, hiring decisions, and price setting. An SBU is treated as an internal profit centre by corporate headquarters. Each SBU is responsible for developing its business strategies, strategies that must be in tune with broader corporate strategies.

The "lowest" level of strategy is operational strategy. It is very narrow in focus and deals with day-to-day operational activities such as scheduling criteria. It must operate within a budget but is not at liberty to adjust or create that budget. Operational level strategy was encouraged by Peter Drucker in his theory of management by objectives (MBO). Operational level strategies are informed by business level strategies which, in turn, are informed by corporate level strategies. Business strategy, which refers to the aggregated operational strategies of single business firm or that of an SBU in a diversified corporation refers to the way in which a firm competes in its chosen arenas.

Corporate strategy, then, refers to the overarching strategy of the diversified firm. Such corporate strategy answers the questions of "in which businesses should we compete?" and "how does being in one business add to the competitive advantage of another portfolio firm, as well as the competitive advantage of the corporation as a whole?"

Since the turn of the millennium, there has been a tendency in some firms to revert to a simpler strategic structure. This is being driven by information technology. It is felt that knowledge management systems should be used to share information and create common goals. Strategic divisions are thought to hamper this process. Most recently, this notion of strategy has been captured under the rubric of dynamic strategy, popularized by the strategic management textbook authored by Carpenter and Sanders. This work builds on that of Brown and Eisenhart as well as Christensen and portrays firm strategy, both business and corporate, as necessarily embracing ongoing strategic change, and the seamless integration of strategy formulation and implementation. Such change and implementation are usually built into the strategy through the staging and pacing facets.

Management by Objectives (MBO) is a process of agreeing upon objectives within an organization so that management and employees buy in to the objectives and understand what they are. Management By Objectives term was first popularized by Peter Drucker in 1954 in his book 'The Practice of Management'.

It is all too easy for managers to fail to outline, and agree with their employees, what it is that everyone is trying to achieve. MBO substitutes for good intentions a process that requires rather precise written description of objectives (for the period ahead) and timelines for their monitoring and achievement. The process requires that the manager and the employee agree to what the employee will attempt to achieve in the period ahead, and (very important) that the employee accept and buy into the objectives (otherwise commitment will be lacking).

For example, whatever else a manager and employee may discuss and agree in their regular discussions, let us suppose that they feel that it will be sensible to introduce a key performance indicator to show the development of sales revenue in a part of the firm. Then the manager and the employee need to discuss what is being planned, what the time-schedule is and what the indicator might or might not be. Thereafter the two of them should liaise to ensure that the objective is being attended to and will be delivered on time.

Organizations have scarce resources and so it is incumbent on the managers to consider the level of resourcing but also to consider whether the objectives that are jointly agreed within the firm are the right ones and represent the best allocation of effort. Also, reliable Management information systems are needed to establish relevant objectives and monitor their "reach ratio" in an objective way.

MBO is often achieved using set targets. MBO introduced the SMART criteria: Objectives for MBO must be SMART (Specific, Measurable, Agreed, Realistic, and Time-Specific). However, it has been reported in recent years that this style of management receives criticism in that it triggers employees' unethical behaviour of distorting the system or financial figures to achieve the targets set by their short-term, narrow bottom-line, and completely self-centered thinking.

MARKET PLANNING

A product is nothing without a market. Regardless of how novel a product or service is, there must be a way to turn the need it satisfies into revenues. Each hotel, club, restaurant and casino has different needs for handling common issues such as modeling volume driven relationships, multiple templates for different planning needs (e.g. owned vs. franchised locations), and deployment to disparate and multiple locations. Your operation needs the flexibility to meet these divisional challenges while maintaining consistency across your business. Business Objects Planning for Hospitality delivers on both counts:

- Reduce operating expenses, improve staffing levels, and optimize revenues - all while shortening cycle time
- Track the key business drivers for your diverse operations, food and beverage, room occupancy and operations

Though time-consuming, multi-layered, and complex budgeting is a critical component of planning and controlling your day-to-day hospitality and leisure operations. To ensure more timely and accurate budgets, hotels, restaurants, casinos, and food service operators need to streamline and formalize the budgeting process-and produce detailed, yet flexible budgets that are fully aligned with strategic goals.

Business Objects solutions create budgets, sales forecasts, and payroll plans that automatically incorporate data from your long-range plans, source systems, and end users so you can move into action faster.

Whether you are running a single hotel, restaurant, or casino-or a worldwide chain of properties-you need access to timely and accurate information to make the right decisions. Incomplete or out of- date data can hamstring employees, hamper decision making, and compromise enterprise performance. With a comprehensive reporting solution, hospitality and leisure organizations like yours can ensure that the right information gets to the right people at the right time enabling management teams to make smart decisions that improve performance.

BUSINESS PLANNING

Business planning is often conducted when:

- Starting a new venture (organization, product or service)
- Expanding a current organization, product or service
- Buying a current organization, product or service
- Working to improve the management of a current organization, product or service

There are a wide variety of formats for a business plan. The particular format and amount of content included in a plan depends on the complexity of the organization, product or service and on the demands of those who will use the business plan to make a decision, eg, an investor, funder, management, Board of Directors, etc.

Overall, the contents of a business plan typically aim to:

1. Describe the venture (new or current organization, product or service), often including its primary features, advantages and benefits
2. What the organization wants to do with it (buy it, expand it, etc.)
3. Justification that the plans are credible (eg, results of research that indicate the need for what the organization wants to do)
4. Marketing plans, including research results about how the venture will be marketed (eg, who the customers will be, any specific groups (or targets) of customers, why they need the venture (benefits they seek from the venture), how they will use the venture, what they will be willing to pay, how the venture will be advertised and promoted, etc.)

5. Staffing plans, including what expertise will be needed to build (sometimes included in business plans) and provide the venture on an ongoing basis
6. Management plans, including how the expertise will be organized, coordinated and led
7. Financial plans, including costs to build the venture (sometimes included in business plans), costs to operate the venture, expected revenue, budgets for each of the first several years into the future, when the venture might break-even (begin making more money overall than it has cost), etc.

Business planning is usually conducted when starting a new organization or a new major venture, for example, new product, service or programme. Essentially, a business plan is a combination of a marketing plan, strategic plan, operational/management plan and a financial plan. Far more important than the plan document, is the planning process itself.

Business planning usually includes a thorough examination of the idea for a new product/service, if there's really a market for it, who the competitors are, how the idea is uniquely positioned to be competitive and noticeable, how the idea will be produced to a product/service, how much it will cost, how it will be promoted, what overall goals must be accomplished, how the development and ongoing operations will be managed and what resources are needed (including money). As noted above, a business plan is a combination of a marketing plan, financial plan, strategic plan and a operational/management plan. Here are a variety of perspectives.

To start, you need to plan your strategy very well. Your restaurant has to focus on some key elements that'll set it apart from the thousands of other eateries out there. These could be location, cuisine, decoration or even—good luck with this one—price. Maybe it's located where there's a lot of traffic, or across the hall from a gym, or near a bookstore, or outside a theater. Maybe there are no fish tacos in your town, or no good Italian restaurants. Maybe there are no cafes near the river with outside seating. You have to know why you're different. In short, don't try to please everybody generally; find your niche market, and please those people very well.

By differentiating your restaurant, you make marketing it much easier. Marketing is critical to restaurant success, but marketing can be expensive. And in most cases, the most effective restaurant marketing depends on repeat business and word-of-mouth. Think about how you choose a restaurant yourself—do you look through your Entertainment book or other coupon source? Do you research with a Zagat guide or online reviews? Or do you ask for recommendations from friends? Ask yourself how people will describe your restaurant and why they'll recommend it. If you can't put that short conversation into easy words, you're in trouble.

Also, if you have a choice, don't start a low-priced restaurant. Low-priced restaurants are much harder to market than mid- to high-priced restaurants. Fast-food franchises are everywhere, and they have a huge corner on that market. People believe in cheap food when they see strong branding and lots of customers. You don't want to be the dive on the corner that can't attract business.

Unless you're already partnered with an investor, you should assume you won't be. In general, restaurants aren't targets for professional investors because they're so risky. The few exceptions include celebrities who back restaurants that capitalize on their names, and well-known chefs and successful restaurant owners opening new venues.

Not having access to startup financing doesn't mean you shouldn't start the business. It means you should carefully decide whether you're going to start slowly, minding expenses, or borrow enough money to start big. Your borrowing options include commercial bank loans, which require assets you can stake as collateral, and SBA loans, which require less collateral than bank loans but still require you to put up 30 percent of the starting costs to qualify for the guaranteed loan. When in doubt about loans go straight to your favourite bank and ask for advice.

Be sure to count your startup costs well. You don't want to get into a bind where you've spent half of what you thought you needed and you've run out of money. You'll probably have to rent a location and spend a few months fixing it up, and you may need employees some employees to help out during the fix-up period, too. Unless you're moving into an existing restaurant, you'll need to buy kitchen equipment, tables and chairs, cash registers, phone systems and décor to establish ambience. And then you need to budget for what's called "working capital" for the startup period when your spending exceeds your sales. Some say you need at least six months of expenses ready to go; others recommend having 12 months covered.

Your sales forecast is also important. We like to build a sales forecast based on unit sales, meaning meals and drinks, not just gross sales amounts. That helps us break the sales forecast into components I can count. How many tables do you have? How many meals will you serve on Friday night when the place is almost full? What does an average meal cost? How many drinks come with the meals? Then calculate unit sales, average revenue per unit and average cost per unit.

Then comes your expense forecast. With meals and drinks already priced out, your remaining operating expenses are mainly people, rent and other fixed costs. Estimate those per month, and match them to your sales forecast.

When all the costs are tallied, you'll get a good picture of the cash flow and how much money you'll need to keep the restaurant operational. During the early months of startup, your cash flow probably won't cover all your expenses, so you'll want your plan to include how you'll cover the difference.

Finally, as you get started, remember that business plans continually go out of date, and good business plans are never done. You should take an hour or so every month to review the difference between what you planned and what actually happened, and update your plan accordingly.

A business plan is often the entry-level requirement to getting government money, investor capital or bank loans. Although, you may have a complete picture of the business in your head, investors and bankers need to see if you really have an understanding of the business and have thought it through.

Preparing a plan is a long and daunting task but in the end the business owner often sees things from a new perspective and has mitigated any risks. The business plan is not just for banks and investors but also supplies you with a blueprint of succeeding in business. The plan provides you with the direction of your company and is a guidepost for your employees too.

The primary job of a business owner is to manage and run a business. The term manage implies the task of planning and execution. Are you considering bringing in an outside expert to help with your business plan? The idea is appealing to some because planning is daunting and there are experts out there— if you can afford them. However, it's not nearly as simple as you'd like.

Critical fact: your business plan isn't a stand-alone document; it's you, your business and your promise. You have to know every date, every deadline, every last word, and every number in your plan. Investors invest in people, not plans. They buy the jockey more than the horse. Expert help can't change this fundamental principle. It must be your plan, yours down to your bones, and it must not be the consultant's plan.

If you work within the framework that the business plan is yours, then there are some things that outside help can do for your plan and your planning process. If you have the money to spend, and you find the right person or resource, here the benefits of hiring outside help:

- A professional plan review. Does your plan cover the most obvious points? Does it have any obvious logical holes? Is it easy to read and is it easy to find the most important information? Ask an expert to review it.
- Help with the financials. You don't have to be an MBA or accountant to plan your business, but some of the underlying math and financial principles can be daunting. The ideal is doing it yourself with an expert looking on and coaching.
- General planning coaching. An outside expert can facilitate your thinking and planning by guiding discussion towards key issues, drawing out definitions, highlighting and focusing on important points.
- Industry-specific coaching. Don't reinvent wheels when you can leverage off of an expert's experience.
- Contacts and introductions. Be careful with this one, however, because you're swimming in shark-infested waters here (and I'm referring to the consultants as sharks, not just the investors). There are good consultants who deliver on promises, but there are far

more bad consultants who make promises. A consultant can get you an investor no matter how good the plan, because the investor wants (or doesn't want) you, not your plan.

Please be sure to avoid the common problems with outside planning consulting. Some of these come up far too often:

- Misunderstanding the deliverables. Don't pay for vague promises. Business-plan review, coaching and help with the financials are credible deliverables, but getting your plan financed isn't credible because that depends on you, not your plan.
- Wanting a turnkey business plan. That just won't work. If a consultant wants to go away without you and come back with a plan, you go away first.
- Not checking references. Always ask for references of previous clients and talk to those people.
- Paying in advance. Some consultants need to ask a fair payment up front, but not the whole thing.

The worst element of outside consulting is the consultants who let you think that paying their fees will get you investment, when in fact they're just going to give you advice. This happens too frequently and it's the clients' fault too, not just the consultants. You should immediately mistrust somebody who promises open doors and contacts as part of the job. The promise isn't credible unless the consultants very carefully filter their prospective clients and take only those whose background, track record, team and business proposition are likely to succeed. Otherwise, they're making false promises because the investors invest in the people, not the plan.

Writing a business plan is one of the least favourite activities of the majority of small business owners. The traditional rule of credit is if you want to grow and operate your business you will need a business plan to find capital. This is quickly changing as more and more business owners learn about business plan-free financing.

Change has swept through industries, society and careers. Over the last few years, change and its companion, information technology, is altering the face of small business lending.

The relationship-based banking in the small loans and credit market is becoming irrelevant. The decision of loan approval is determined by a computerized credit scoring programme unless a business requires a loan or credit product over $100,000.

BUSINESS CONTINUITY PLANNING

Business Continuity Planning (BCP) is an interdisciplinary peer mentoring methodology used to create and validate an exercised logistical plan for how an organization will recover and restore partially or completely interrupted critical function(s) within a predetermined time after a disaster or extended disruption.

BCP may be a part of an organizational learning effort that helps reduce operational risk associated with lax information management controls. This process may be integrated with improving information security and corporate reputation risk management practices.

British Standards Institute is planning to release a new independent standard for BCP — BS 25999. The draft of standard had been put up for public comments and the final standard is expected in early 2007. This standard would reduce the reliance on Information Security oriented standards which dealt with BCP marginally.

A completed BCP cycle results in a formal printed manual available for reference before, during, and after disruptions have occurred. Its purpose is to reduce adverse stakeholder impacts determined by both the disruption's scope and duration. Measureable Business Impact Analysis (BIA) "zones" include civil, economic, natural, technical, secondary and subsequent.

Business Continuity Planning is not a new concept; plans for disasters, like Noah's Ark, are evidenced from the beginning of human history. Prior to January 1, 2000, governments anticipated computer failures, called the Y2k problem, in important public utility infrastructures like banking, power, telecommunication, health and financial industries. Since 1983, regulatory agencies like the American Bankers Association and Banking Administration Institute (BAI) required their supporting members to exercise operational continuity practices (later supported by more formal BCP manuals) that protect the public interests. Newer regulations were often based on formalized standards defined under ISO/IEC 17799 or BS 7799.

Both regulatory and global business focus on BCP arguably waned after the problem-free Y2K rollover. This lax attitude unequivocally ended September 11th 2001, when simultaneous terrorist attacks devastated downtown New York City and changed the 'worst case scenario' paradigm for business continuity planning.

BCP methodology is scalable for an organization of any size and complexity. Even though the methodology has roots in regulated industries, any type of organization may create a BCP manual, and arguably every organization should have one in order to ensure the organization's longevity. Evidence that firms do not invest enough time and resources into BCP preparations are evident in disaster survival statistics. Fires permanently close 44% of the business affected. In the 1993 World Trade Center bombing, 150 businesses out of 350 affected failed to survive the event. Conversely, the firms affected by the Sept 11 attacks with well-developed and tested BCP manuals were back in business within days.

A BCP manual for a small organization may be simply a printed manual stored safely away from the primary work location, containing the names, addresses, and phone numbers for crisis management staff, general staff members, clients, and vendors along with the location of the offsite data backup storage media, copies of insurance contracts, and other critical materials necessary for organizational survival. At its most complex, a BCP manual may outline a secondary work site, technical requirements and readiness, regulatory reporting requirements, work recovery measures, the means to reestablish physical records, the means to establish a new supply chain, or the means to establish new production centers. Firms should ensure that their BCP manual is realistic and easy to use during a crisis. As such, BCP sits along side crisis management and disaster recovery planning and is a part of an organization's overall risk management.

The development of a BCP manual has five main phases:

1. Analysis
2. Solution design
3. Implementation
4. Testing and organization acceptance
5. Maintenance

Much of the BCP material on the internet is sponsored by consultancies who offer fee-based services for BCP solution development, however basic tutorials are freely available on the internet for properly motivated organizations.

The analysis phase in the development of a BCP manual consists of an impact analysis, threat analysis, and impact scenarios with the resulting BCP plan requirement documentation. An impact analysis results in the differentiation between critical and non-critical organization functions. A function may be considered critical if the implications for stakeholders of damage to the organization resulting are regarded as unacceptable. Perceptions of the acceptability of disruption may be modified by the cost of establishing and maintaining appropriate business or technical recovery solutions. A function may also be considered critical if dictated by law. Next, the impact analysis results in the recovery requirements for each critical function. Recovery requirements consist of the following information:

- The time frame in which the critical function must be resumed after the disaster
- The business requirements for recovery of the critical function, and/or
- The technical requirements for recovery of the critical function

The organizations also banned face-to-face contact between opposing team members during business and non-business hours. With such a split, organizations increased their resiliency against the threat of government-ordered quarantine measures if one person in a team contracted or was exposed to the disease. Damage from flooding also has a unique characteristic. If an office environment is flooded with non-salinated and contamination-free water (e.g.m, in the event of a pipe burst), equipment can be thoroughly dried and may still be functional.

After defining potential threats, documenting the impact scenarios that form the basis of the business recovery plan is recommended. In general, planning for the most wide-reaching disaster or disturbance is preferable to planning for a smaller scale problem, as almost all smaller scale problems are partial elements of larger disasters. A typical impact scenario like 'Building Loss' will most likely encompass all critical business functions, and the worst potential outcome from any potential threat. A business continuity plan may also document additional impact scenarios if an organization has more than one building. Other more specific impact scenarios - for example a scenario for the temporary or permanent loss of a specific floor in a building - may also be documented.

After the completion of the analysis phase, the business and technical plan requirements are documented in order to commence the implementation phase. For an office-based, IT intensive business, the plan requirements may cover the following elements which may be classed as ICE (In Case of Emergency) Data:

- The numbers and types of desks, whether dedicated or shared, required outside of the primary business location in the secondary location
- The individuals involved in the recovery effort along with their contact and technical details
- The applications and application data required from the secondary location desks for critical business functions
- The manual workaround solutions
- The maximum outage allowed for the applications
- The peripheral requirements like printers, copier, fax machine, calculators, paper, pens etc.

Other business environments, such as production, distribution, warehousing etc will need to cover these elements, but are likely to have additional issues to manage following a disruptive event.

The goal of the solution design phase is to identify the most cost effective disaster recovery solution that meets two main requirements from the impact analysis stage. For IT applications, this is commonly expressed as:

1. The minimum application and application data requirements
2. The time frame in which the minimum application and application data must be available

Disaster recovery plans may also be required outside the IT applications domain, for example in preservation of information in hard copy format, or restoration of embedded technology in process plant. This BCP phase overlaps with Disaster recovery planning methodology. The solution phase determines:

- The crisis management command structure
- The location of a secondary work site (where necessary)
- Telecommunication architecture between primary and secondary work sites
- Data replication methodology between primary and secondary work sites

- The application and software required at the secondary work site, and
- The type of physical data requirements at the secondary work site.

The implementation phase, quite simply, is the execution of the design elements identified in the solution design phase. Work package testing may take place during the implementation of the solution, however; work package testing does not take the place of organizational testing.

The purpose of testing is to achieve organizational acceptance that the business continuity solution satisfies the organization's recovery requirements. Plans may fail to meet expectations due to insufficient or inaccurate recovery requirements, solution design flaws, or solution implementation errors. Testing may include:

- Crisis command team call-out testing
- Technical swing test from primary to secondary work locations
- Technical swing test from secondary to primary work locations
- Application test
- Business process test

At minimum, testing is generally conducted on a biannual or annual schedule. Problems identified in the initial testing phase may be rolled up into the maintenance phase and retested during the next test cycle.

Maintenance of a BCP manual is broken down into three periodic activities. The first activity is the confirmation of information in the manual. The second activity is the testing and verification of technical solutions established for recovery operations. The third activity is the testing and verification of documented organization recovery procedures. A biannual or annual maintenance cycle is typical.

All organizations change over time, therefore a BCP manual must change to stay relevant to the organization. Once data accuracy is verified, normally a call tree test is conducted to evaluate the notification plan's efficiency as well as the accuracy of the contact data. Some types of changes that should be identified and updated in the manual include:

- Staffing changes
- Staffing persona
- Changes to important clients and their contact details
- Changes to important vendors/suppliers and their contact details
- Departmental changes like new, closed or fundamentally changed departments.

PLANNING FOR THE FUTURE

With all these considerations in merely the "planning" stage of a project, it is perhaps surprising that projects get done at all. In fact projects do get done, but seldom in the predicted manner and often as much by brute force as by careful planning. The point, however, is that this method is non-optimal. Customers feel let down by late delivery, staff are demotivated by constant pressure for impossible goals, corners get cut which harm your reputation, and each project has to overcome the same problems as the last.

With planning, projects can run on time and interact effectively with both customers and suppliers. Everyone involved understands what is wanted and emerging problems are seen (and dealt with) long before they cause damage. If you want your projects to run this way - then you must invest time in planning.

Significant organizational change occurs, for example, when an organization changes its overall strategy for success, adds or removes a major section or practice, and/or wants to change the very nature by which it operates. It also occurs when an organization evolves through various life cycles, just like people must successfully evolve through life cycles. For organizations to develop, they often must undergo significant change at various points in their development. That's why the topic of organizational change and development has become widespread in communications about business, organizations, leadership and management.

Leaders and managers continually make efforts to accomplish successful and significant change — it's inherent in their jobs. Some are very good at this effort (probably more than we realize), while others continually struggle and fail. That's often the difference between people who thrive in their roles and those that get shuttled around from job to job, ultimately settling into a role where they're frustrated and ineffective. There are many schools with educational programs about organizations, business, leadership and management. Unfortunately, there still are not enough schools with programs about how to analyze organizations, identify critically important priorities to address (such as systemic problems or exciting visions for change) and then undertake successful and significant change to address those priorities.

There are many approaches to guiding change — some planned, structured and explicit, while others are more organic, unfolding and implicit. Some approaches work from the future to the present, for example, involving visioning and then action planning about how to achieve that vision. Other approaches work from the present to the future, for example, identifying current priorities (issues and/or goals) and then action planning about to address those priorities (the action research approach is one example). Different people often have very different — and strong — opinions about how change should be conducted. Thus, it is likely that some will disagree with some of the content in this topic. That's what makes this topic so diverse, robust and vital for us all.

To really understand organizational change and begin guiding successful change efforts, the change agent should have at least a broad understanding of the context of the change effort. This includes understanding the basic systems and structures in organizations, including their typical terms and roles. This requirement applies to the understanding of leadership and management of the organizations, as well. That is why graduate courses in business often initially include a course or some discussion on organizational theory. This topic includes several links to help you gain this broad understanding. Organizational change should not be conducted for the sake of change. Organizational change efforts should be geared to improve the performance of organizations and the people in those organizations. Therefore, it's useful to have some understanding of what is meant by "performance" and the various methods to manage performance in organizations.

The past few decades have seen an explosion in the number of very useful tools to help change agents to effectively explore, understand and communicate about organizations, as well as to guide successful change in those organizations. Tools from systems theory and systems thinking especially are a major breakthrough. Even if the change agent is not an expert about systems theory and thinking, even a basic understanding can cultivate an entire new way of working.

Index

H

I

K

L

M

N

O

P

Q

R

S

T

U

V